PRAISE FOR
EMPLOYEE ENGAGEMENT

'This book is a practical and much-needed guide to improving and developing employee engagement. Featuring a comprehensive range of case studies, tools, templates and tips, it has everything the practitioner needs to ensure that their approach to employee engagement makes a positive difference to their workplace and people.' **Nita Clarke, Director of the Involvement and Participation Association and Co-Chair of the Employee Engagement Task Force**

'*Employee Engagement* is the must-read book for any manager or HR professional who is concerned about raising and maintaining high levels of engagement. Written in an authoritative yet accessible style by one of the UK's leading experts, the book guides the reader step by step through the complex decisions that need to be made in developing and implementing a successful engagement strategy.' **Katie Bailey, Professor of Work and Employment, King's Business School, King's College London**

'Emma Bridger brings a practical and effective approach to the big subjects of employee engagement and organizational culture, which are so vital for any organization's success today. Beneath her warm and friendly style lies considerable expertise, and this book shares the insight she has gained over many years helping organizations like ours to unlock the potential of our people.' **Richard Parry, Chief Executive, Canal & River Trust**

'Emma Bridger's book *Employee Engagement* is a concise reference for the practical implementation of staff engagement approaches within organizations. Managers, HR staff and academics can use this book to plan how to introduce a thorough staff engagement programme and research how it all works in practice. Employee engagement design, measurement, implementation and future action planning are all investigated within this comprehensive book and Emma also provides an easily digestible literature overview within the field.' **Dr Julian A Edwards, Research Fellow, The Open University**

'Utterly practical, totally helpful and beautifully written. Emma brings us the ultimate "how to" that we've all been waiting for. Anyone who understands the importance of people in their organization should give this a read. You won't regret it.' **Ruth Dance, Managing Director, The Employee Engagement Alliance**

'This is essential reading for everyone working in employee engagement and, beyond that, an invaluable source of learning for all individuals working in teams as critical components within organizations striving to deliver better results.' **Rob Neil OBE, Head of Project Race, Ministry of Justice**

Second Edition

EMPLOYEE ENGAGEMENT

A practical introduction

Emma Bridger

CIPD

ACQUISITION

First published in Great Britain and the United States in 2014 by Kogan Page Limited
Second edition published in 2018

2nd Floor, 45 Gee Street	c/o Martin P Hill Consulting	4737/23 Ansari Road
London EC1V 3RS	122 W 27th St, 10th Floor	Daryaganj
United Kingdom	New York NY 10001	New Delhi 110002
www.koganpage.com	USA	India

© Emma Bridger, 2014, 2018

ISBN   978 0 7494 8351 7
E-ISBN   978 0 7494 8352 4

British Library Cataloguing-in-Publication Data

A CIP record for this book is available from the British Library.

Library of Congress Cataloging-in-Publication Data

Names: Bridger, Emma, author.
Title: Employee engagement : a practical introduction / Emma Bridger.
Description: Second edition. | London ; New York : Kogan Page Limited, 2018.
  | Includes bibliographical references and index.
Identifiers: LCCN 2018013912 (print) | LCCN 2018014957 (ebook) | ISBN
  9780749483524 (ebook) | ISBN 9780749483517 (pbk.)
Subjects: LCSH: Employee motivation. | Organizational behavior.
Classification: LCC HF5549.5.M63 (ebook) | LCC HF5549.5.M63 B735 2018 (print)
  | DDC 658.3/14—dc23

Typeset by Integra Software Services, Pondicherry
Print production managed by Jellyfish
Printed and bound by CPI Group (UK) Ltd, Croydon, CR0 4YY

CONTENTS

*Downloadable resources are available at **www.koganpage.com/
engagement***

LIST OF FIGURES

LIST OF TABLES

ACKNOWLEDGEMENTS

My greatest thanks and appreciation go to David MacLeod and Nita Clarke and all the Engage for Success team. Firstly for giving me permission to reproduce some of the wonderful case studies, research and stories originally submitted as part of the Engage for Success movement. But also for their inspirational leadership in helping to create the Engage for Success movement. I really think we've created something quite special and I'm proud to be a part of it.

When I was first approached to write this book, a misunderstanding meant that I initially thought I was just contributing a chapter. On finding out it was actually an entire book, I couldn't say no to such an amazing opportunity. However, when the romance of writing a book had faded, and the hard work really kicked in, there were a whole gang of friends and family behind the scenes, supporting me every step of the way. I'd like to dedicate this book to all of them and say a specific thank-you to those people who maybe had to come second to the book-writing for a while.

For Ted, Harry, Eadie and Teddy.

Introduction

Since the term 'engagement' was first coined by William Kahn in 1990, it has steadily moved up the business agenda. Year on year there has been increasing interest in, and focus on, employee engagement from businesses. The term is now everyday parlance within the workplace. However, despite this increased attention and focus, we are still not seeing the improvements in employee engagement that we would expect. I refer to this paradox as the 'employee engagement gap'. Back in 2016, People Lab launched their first 'Spotlight on the Employee Engagement Profession' research programme to better understand the 'employee engagement gap' – why it occurs and, more importantly, what we can do about it. The first of its kind, the study gathered insight directly from experts in the field – the people championing engagement every day, in a variety of job roles and industries.

There's no doubt employee engagement continues to be a significant area of focus for companies. Deloitte's 2017 Global Human Capital Trends include 'employee experience' in their top 10 global trends, with 79 per cent rating this as important or very important. They define employee experience as '*employee engagement, culture and beyond*'. And yet despite this focus, companies are struggling to develop and improve employee engagement. In their annual 'Global Trends in Employee Engagement' publication, Aon report that employee engagement around the world has retracted in the last year. Just 24 per cent of employees fall into the 'Highly Engaged' category, and another 39 per cent can be categorized as 'Moderately Engaged', with a global engagement score of 63 per cent for 2017, compared to 65 per cent in 2016. There are many benchmarking reports that detail engagement levels, and they tend to differ greatly from report to report. Gallup, for example, state that just 15 per cent of employees worldwide are engaged, with 85 per cent either not engaged or actively disengaged (State of the Global Workplace Report, 2017). Despite these differences in levels of employee engagement reported, what is clear is that very little improvements are being made.

So what is going on? People Lab ran their research for a second time in 2017 to provide some answers and found broadly similar results to the original study. The insights from both studies begin to help us understand the employee engagement gap. For example:

- Just 14 per cent of companies have a company-wide definition of employee engagement (compared to 25 per cent in 2016).

- Only 42 per cent have an employee engagement strategy (compared to 45 per cent in 2016).

- Just 28 per cent said they thought employee engagement was well measured in their organization (compared to 44 per cent in 2016).

- Managers being rated as good or excellent has declined by 25 per cent, from 38 per cent in 2016 to 13 per cent in 2017.

The research clearly demonstrates why we are still seeing an employee engagement gap. The results show a lack of understanding of what we mean by employee engagement, coupled with little investment and development in this area. Less than half of companies have an employee engagement strategy, and believe the impact of employee engagement is well measured. In addition, the study also found that resourcing engagement is an issue for many companies, with shrinking budgets and less time to focus on engagement. What we have seen from the research is that there is still a lot of work to do if we are to unleash the potential of engagement on improving business performance. The findings do however provide some very clear recommendations on how we can close the engagement gap.

When considering the engagement gap it is also worth pointing out that the employee engagement profession has emerged alongside this increased focus on engagement itself; however, currently, there is no established 'best-practice' approach. More often than not, a company's employee engagement approach, subsequent strategy and dedicated team arise from a need to resource and manage the annual survey. The time has come to treat the employee engagement profession and practice seriously. We need to focus on defining and developing skills and expertise within this area. We need companies to set practitioners up for success rather than working against them. We need organizations to put their money where their mouth is when it comes to engagement.

The following chapters of this book will help to close the employee engagement gap. The advice, tools, and case studies are all practical, simple, and based on what is proven to work. By following the guidance contained here practitioners will be able to demonstrably improve and develop employee engagement within their organizations and unleash the power of an engaged workforce.

What is employee engagement? 01

Introduction

Finding an answer to the question, 'What is employee engagement?' is much easier said than done. Currently there is no single, universally accepted definition of employee engagement, although huge amounts of time and energy have been spent trying to agree upon one! Research shows that just 14 per cent of companies have a definition of employee engagement, and where companies do have a definition they report that it is not well understood (Spotlight on Employee Engagement, 2017a, People Lab).

In their groundbreaking report to the UK government, David MacLeod and Nita Clarke (2009) identified over 50 different definitions of employee engagement. No doubt there have been many more definitions added to the list since then. The *Engaging for Success* report (2009) is a good place to start when reviewing the different definitions that exist. The report sparked a country-wide movement focused on improving employee engagement within the UK. There is now a website in place, with a whole range of information, case studies, resources and special interest groups. It's well worth a visit for anyone with even a passing interest in this topic: **www.engageforsuccess.org**.

The lack of a single, universally agreed definition of employee engagement presents a great opportunity to figure out what engagement means for your organization. Over the years, I have run training courses for hundreds of people on employee engagement. The discussion usually begins with, 'What is employee engagement?' Typically the conversation, and then the realization that there is not a straightforward answer, splits the room: those who feel uncomfortable with the lack of an agreed definition and those who are excited about the prospect of coming up with their own answer. However, despite the absence of a single definition, when talking about what engagement means, some key themes emerge pretty quickly. Words such as involvement, commitment, discretionary effort, collaboration, motivation and performance are common. How practitioners then choose to convert these themes into an actual definition is up to them.

There are also those who believe an exact definition is not needed: you know it when you see it; it is something that you feel and is beyond a single definition. In fact, some organizations I work with choose not to define employee engagement at all. Instead they choose to talk about creating a great place to work or similar. The critical success factor is that however you choose to define or talk about engagement within your organization, people understand this. It's vital that, amongst the senior leadership team at the very least, there is a common understanding of what you collectively mean by 'employee engagement'. The term has become so ubiquitous that it is often used freely within organizations to mean different things to different people. Developing a definition, or expressing what you understand by employee engagement within your organization, is a great place to start to improve engagement.

Activity
Engagement brainstorm

You can use this simple activity as a great way to get your stakeholders to begin thinking about what they understand by employee engagement:

- In a team meeting or at an engagement workshop, ask people to take one minute to individually write down as many words as possible that come into their head when they think about employee engagement.
- When the minute is up, ask everyone to circle the one word that resonates most with them.
- Then ask each person to call out their word, and capture the various words on a flip chart.
- Use these outputs to generate a discussion on what engagement means to people.
- Good questions to ask are what employee engagement is and what it isn't. This discussion could form the basis of a definition for your organization.
- What is immediately clear is that it means different things to different people and is very personal.

A brief history of employee engagement

When was the first time you heard the term 'employee engagement'? You might be surprised to learn that engagement was first referred to in an article by William Kahn in 1990, although he talks about personal engagement and disengagement, rather than employee engagement. Kahn's research looked specifically at the psychological conditions of personal engagement and disengagement at work. Within the article Kahn talks about personal engagement as the extent to which people employ and express their personal selves at work, and disengagement as the extent to which people withdraw and defend their personal selves at work. Interestingly Kahn identified meaningfulness, safety and availability as psychological conditions that impact personal engagement at work: these are themes that come up time and again when looking at what employee engagement means.

When looking at the academic literature, engagement is a term used in the following ways:

- to refer to a psychological state (eg involvement, commitment, attachment, mood);
- to refer to a performance construct (eg either effort or observable behaviour, including pro-social and organizational citizenship behaviour);
- to refer to a disposition (eg positive affect);
- or for some a combination of the above.

The hugely influential work of Gallup, as reported by Harter *et al* (2012), played no small part in the rise in interest in employee engagement. Gallup began by looking at what was unique to high-performing businesses and business units. Their extensive work resulted in the development of the Q12® tool, which is essentially a 12-question survey designed to measure engagement. Their substantial credibility and expertise, coupled with a tool allowing measurement of employee engagement, appealed to a number of chief or senior executives (commonly known as the 'c-suite') and an industry of employee engagement surveys was born.

Employee engagement is now everyday language within organizations, and yet there is still a huge amount of discussion as to what it actually means. Let's take a look at some of the definitions of employee engagement that currently exist.

Activity

Engagement timeline

What is the history of employee engagement within your organization? Have a go at mapping the evolution of employee engagement within your company as a timeline:

- When did you first start talking about it or looking at it?
- What sort of activities did you start doing?
- Capture your engagement timeline and track how engagement has improved or declined over time if you have the data.
- Map the different types of activity your engagement programme has involved against your timeline.
- Critically evaluate the activity you have mapped against your timeline: what has worked, what has not worked and are you making any progress in improving employee engagement?

Definitions of employee engagement

Different definitions of employee engagement make reference to a range of human resource management (HRM) and organizational behaviour concepts such as work effort, commitment to the organization, job satisfaction, motivation and optimal functioning. However, what they tend to have in common is that they view engagement as an internal state of being. Engagement is something that the employee has to offer and cannot be 'required' as part of the employment contract or objective-setting process. The following definitions provide a flavour of the many definitions that exist.

The Engage for Success website defines engagement as: a workplace approach resulting in the right conditions for all members of an organization to give their best each day, be committed to their organization's goals and values, be motivated to contribute to organizational success, and with an enhanced sense of their own well-being. The Chartered Institute of Personnel and Development (CIPD), in their work with the Kingston Employee Engagement Consortium, define employee engagement as: 'being positively present during the performance of work by willingly contributing intellectual effort, experiencing positive emotions and meaningful connections to others' (Alfes *et al*, 2010).

This definition provides three dimensions to employee engagement:

1 *Intellectual engagement*, ie thinking hard about the job and how to do it better.

2 *Affective engagement*, ie feeling positively about doing a good job.

3 *Social engagement*, ie actively taking opportunities to discuss work-related improvements with others at work.

Interestingly, academics tend to talk about 'work engagement' as opposed to employee engagement. Schaufeli and Bakker (2004), two well-known and highly regarded academics who have made a significant contribution to the world of engagement, define work engagement as: 'a positive, fulfilling, work-related state of mind that is characterized by vigour, dedication, and absorption. Rather than a momentary and specific state, engagement refers to a more persistent and pervasive affective-cognitive state that is not focused on any particular object, event, individual, or behaviour.'

Vigour is characterized by high levels of energy and mental resilience while working, the willingness to invest effort in one's work, and persistence even in the face of difficulties. Dedication refers to being strongly involved in one's work and experiencing a sense of significance, enthusiasm, inspiration, pride and challenge. Absorption is characterized by being fully concentrated and happily engrossed in one's work, whereby time passes quickly and one has difficulties with detaching oneself from work. It is easy to see that there are overlaps between this academic definition of work engagement and the CIPD's definition of employee engagement.

Professor Katie Truss, who was instrumental in setting up the Kingston Engagement Consortium, defines employee engagement (in Alfes *et al*, 2010) as:

> about creating opportunities for employees to connect with their colleagues, managers and wider organization. It is also about creating an environment where employees are motivated to want to connect with their work and really care about doing a good job... It is a concept that places flexibility, change and continuous improvement at the heart of what it means to be an employee and an employer in a 21st century workplace.

The Institute of Employment Studies (IES) defines (Robinson *et al*, 2004) engagement as:

> [a] positive attitude held by the employee towards the organization and its values. An engaged employee is aware of the business context, and works with colleagues to improve performance within the job for the benefit of the organization. The organization must work to develop and nurture engagement, which requires a two-way relationship between employee and employer.

It is clear to see from these definitions alone that there are common themes that run through them. When asking people to define employee engagement, though, one of the big questions asks whether engagement is an attitude, a behaviour or an outcome.

Some would argue engagement is all about *attitudes* towards the organization, or people we work with. For example, we may feel proud to work at a particular company, we might like the people we work with or our boss. For others engagement is all about *behaviours*, for example, would we recommend our company to others? Or do we go the extra mile to finish a piece of work? Finally for others, engagement is all about the business *outcomes*, for example, are people staying with the company rather than leaving? Are employees less absent, or is there more innovation?

Most engagement surveys seek to measure all three of these components and they are difficult to separate. For example, employees choosing to stay with the company is both a behaviour and a business outcome and quite likely the result of the beliefs and attitudes the employee holds about the organization. However, these attitudes could be, 'I want to keep working here because I love my job and the people I work with,' or they could be, 'I don't really want to be here any more but it's tough out there and I'm not sure I could find another job like this, so I'll stay put.' With this example, you begin to see the danger of simply focusing on one aspect of engagement. People may be staying because they are highly engaged, or they may be staying because there are few jobs in the current marketplace. It's my belief that they are all related and important for engagement. It is less important which comes first, what the preconditions of engagement are; what we tend to observe is that they all reinforce each other to contribute to employees' overall engagement.

The definition I use, which is adapted from the work of John Smythe (2007), author of *The Chief Engagement Officer*, describes employee engagement as: 'the extent to which people are personally involved in the success of the business'. When explaining this definition I use the model in Figure 1.1 below.

I use this definition and model for a number of reasons:

- It's simple and differentiates between simply being happy or satisfied at work and engaged.

- It views engagement as an attitude. I believe I am personally involved in the success of the business, which is related to attitudes such as pride and loyalty.

FIGURE 1.1   What is employee engagement?

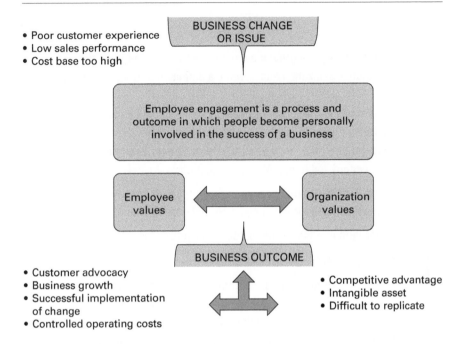

- It views engagement as a behaviour. If I am personally involved in the success of the business then I am more likely to go the extra mile because I care.

- It views engagement as an outcome. The model acknowledges that there is a reason we focus on engagement in the first place, such as reducing employee attrition, and that by engaging our employees we will facilitate the desired business outcome.

Finally, this model also highlights the importance of alignment between an individual's values and the organization's values. Engagement must be a two-way process: the organization has to work hard to ensure it is set up and hard-wired to develop engagement but also the employee has to choose to volunteer themselves to be engaged. In addition, if the values of the organization are incongruent with the employee's personal values, it is unlikely they will feel engaged, at least for any length of time.

Activity

Peak experience

The following activity is a great way to uncover what engagement means within your own organization and develop a definition that works for you.

Ask your team or the group you are working with to think about a time when they were really engaged at work – why they loved what they were doing. Ask them to get into pairs and spend 10 minutes interviewing each other (five minutes each), using the following questions:

- Can you tell me about the most valued or engaging experience you have had in your work life? A time when you really loved your job?
- What were the conditions that made it possible?
- How did these experiences make you feel?

Ask pairs to capture an overview of their partner's story, what made it possible, and how it felt, and to also capture any key themes they observe emerging. Each pair will then feed back their partner's story to the rest of the group. When they do this capture the key themes on a flip chart.

TABLE 1.1   Peak-experience capture template

	The story	**What made it possible**	**How it felt**
ME			
MY PARTNER			

Outputs

As pairs are recounting their stories, capture the key words that they feed back. Typically this will include themes such as:

- valued;
- pride;
- confidence;
- autonomy;

- trusted;
- teamworking;
- great manager;
- challenging work;
- success.

This exercise allows people to reconnect with the emotional side of engagement – by telling their stories people remember what it feels like to be engaged in their work. This is also a great exercise to get a group in a positive state of mind to talk about engagement.

Discuss and explain

When everyone has fed back their stories take a look at the words you have captured:

- What are the group's observations of the words you have captured?
- Using the words you have captured, ask the group to develop a definition or description of what engagement means in your organization.

Approaches to employee engagement

What is perhaps more useful when considering what we mean by 'employee engagement' is to evaluate different approaches to improving or developing it.

In their *Engaging for Success* report to government MacLeod and Clarke (2009) differentiate between level 1 engagement, which they term 'transactional engagement' and level 2 engagement which they term 'transformational engagement' (see Figure 1.2). *Transactional engagement* is defined by a reactive set of transactions aimed at improving engagement, often in response to survey results. A transactional approach to engagement often begins with an engagement survey, which highlights a number of areas for action. An action plan is then put in place and actions are ticked off the list until they are complete, at which point engagement is done, and forgotten about until the next survey comes around. A transactional approach is often identified by a project or programme aimed to improve engagement, with an end date. Engagement is not integrated into the business strategy and culture,

FIGURE 1.2   Transactional engagement versus transformational engagement

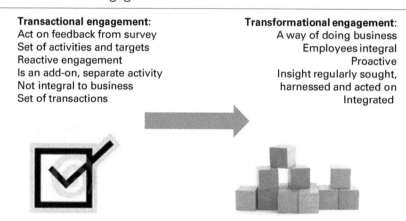

Transactional engagement:
Act on feedback from survey
Set of activities and targets
Reactive engagement
Is an add-on, separate activity
Not integral to business
Set of transactions

Transformational engagement:
A way of doing business
Employees integral
Proactive
Insight regularly sought,
harnessed and acted on
Integrated

but is a separate, add-on activity. *Transformational engagement*, however, is integrated into the business strategy and culture. It is proactive, with employee insight, ideas and opinions regularly sought, harnessed and acted upon. A survey is not necessarily required to understand how employees feel about the organization, or to drive action focused on improving engagement because this already happens as part of the business focus, culture and leadership style. A natural desire to improve engagement exists within the business. In reality, these two types of approach to engagement are not discrete – more often organizations sit somewhere between the two. I have found that discussing where your organization is on this scale is much more beneficial to improving engagement than spending time and energy debating a definition.

Discussion point

- Think about where your organization sits on this scale: are you nearer transactional engagement or transformational engagement or somewhere in the middle?

- How do your leaders view engagement?

- Start thinking about what you could do differently to start to move you towards transformational engagement.

Another way of looking at these different approaches is to consider taking either a *programmatic approach* to employee engagement (similar to transactional approach) or a *philosophical approach* to engagement (similar to transformational engagement). A programmatic approach views engagement as a programme, with a beginning and end, often managed by a project management office. However, a philosophical approach to engagement views engagement as a management mindset, which is common across the whole organization.

TABLE 1.2   What does transformational engagement look like?

Companies with a transactional engagement approach...	Companies with a transformational engagement approach...
• Start with an engagement survey and use the outputs from the survey to take action to improve engagement	• May not even need to do a survey – they have their finger on the pulse and aren't reliant on an annual survey to tell them how their employees feel
• Take a deficit approach – looking only to improve what isn't working	• Ensure engagement is integrated into everything they do: every employee touch-point from recruitment, to on-boarding, to performance management and even exit is designed to ensure it contributes towards employee engagement rather than eroding it
• See engagement as a project or an initiative, owned by HR or worse still a project team	• Employee engagement is a key part of the organization strategy
• Once the actions from the survey have been delivered engagement is not talked about until the next survey	• Managers are developed to ensure they have the skills and capabilities to engage their people
• Don't view engagement as not part of the overall business strategy	• The organization is a listening organization: this listening is ongoing and authentic, not simply a once-a-year survey opportunity
• Have budget for the survey but no budget for what happens after the survey	• Employees genuinely have a voice and can contribute to the success of the organization

(*continued*)

TABLE 1.2 (*Continued*)

Companies with a transactional engagement approach...	Companies with a transformational engagement approach...
• Don't invest in the skills and capabilities of their managers to ensure they can engage their teams	• There is a high level of trust in management
• Don't give employees a voice other than the annual survey	• Take a strengths-based approach to understand the conditions under which employees flourish at work
• Don't listen to employees in an ongoing way	• Engagement is seen as everyone's responsibility

CASE STUDY   What does employee engagement mean for your organization?

Bard are a great example of a company taking the opportunity of the lack of a universal definition of engagement to develop their own. They are part of Napp Pharmaceuticals, founded in 1923 by a chemist called Herman Richard Napp and a UK lawyer called Ernest Alfred Clifford. The current owners acquired the company in the 1960s, and it remains a privately owned company that is part of a worldwide association of independent companies. At the end of 2011 they were ranked 15th largest pharmaceutical company in the UK based on GP prescription sales and were the fastest growing company in the Top 15. They believe this success is driven by the fact that they continue to make the culture and their people a key strategic focus.

Mike Mair, Head of Training and Development at Bard, led a project in 2012 to understand what engagement meant for Bard. Developing effective employee engagement was a key part of their overall business strategy; however, when they further explored this they realized that they did not have a clear understanding of what they meant by employee engagement. Mike recognized that an important first step in developing employee engagement at Bard was to spend time figuring out what engagement meant to Bard, to develop a company-wide understanding. In summary, Mike wanted to demystify engagement. In order to do this he and his colleagues read books and journals, looked at case studies, researched the topic, and spoke to experts, all with a view to answering the following questions:

- What is engagement?
- What does it mean for Bard?

Following their research phase, and to begin to answer these questions, Mike led a session with their leadership team. The team spent time talking about engagement and what it meant to them, building on the knowledge they had acquired over the previous months. On discussing engagement as a team, what was clear was that it meant different things to different people: for some having a company purpose they could connect with was important, for others it was the people they worked with. There was no single definition that could effectively cover the variety of opinions within the room. Thankfully the session did result in a 'light-bulb moment' for Mike and the team. They concluded that for Bard, employee engagement is about the *why*, the *what* and the *who*:

FIGURE 1.3   The 'why, what and who' of employee engagement

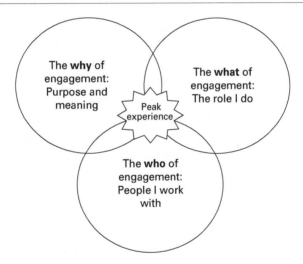

- The *why* relates to the meaning people find within their work, the emotional connection to the company, the overall purpose of the organization. Questions such as 'Why do I come to work?' and 'What does my work mean for me?' helped them to discuss their own personal engagement 'whys'. For some people it is about supplying quality products to patients but for others it might be about making sure employees operate in a safe environment. Whilst the team concluded that the *why* is an important part of engagement for many employees, they also realized the importance of having employees figure this out for themselves, rather than have the company tell them the answer.

- The *what* is essentially about the job people do. For some people the ability to have autonomy was important to their engagement, for others the opportunity for mastery, or structure and process. Again the team observed that the *what* was different for different people; what engages employees in their role is very individual.

- Finally the *who* relates to a sense of belonging. For some employees, engagement and going the extra mile is all about who they work with: their teams, or colleagues, or their manager.

Mike argues that having this model of engagement for Bard has helped to create a common language across the business. The model allows for flexibility, giving employees the opportunity to talk about, and understand, what engages them at work. Mike believes articulating a definition for Bard would have stifled this opportunity to involve employees in thinking about what engagement means for them.

Bard are now using their model to have conversations with their people: asking them which of the three areas are important to their own engagement, and how engaged they currently are with each of the three areas. They have now launched a leadership engagement programme, whereby leaders attend a half-day workshop, which looks at the background and theory of engagement. Leaders are then given a few weeks to assimilate the learning and when they return the model is shared with them. They then share this framework with their teams, having conversations and dialogue about what engagement means to them, but all using the common language that the model offers them.

Bard are also looking at how they can measure the impact of using this approach to improve engagement. The model is of course the starting point for discussions on engagement; leaders are then tasked to take action based on the outputs of their conversations with their teams. Mike believes that they are already seeing better development conversations happening; he states that this approach is enabling the company to get to know its people better. Rather than making assumptions about what engagement means and what will make the difference, they are having company-wide conversations, involving employees in coming up with their own understanding of the term.

Mike is keen to point out that engagement is already good within Bard, as measured by their annual survey; however, he believes that taking this approach will take them from good to great:

We have good engagement but we can make it better – if we can demystify employee engagement and use this model and approach to facilitate good conversations then we believe it will have the impact we need. But of course it's all about what happens as a result of these conversations. Managers will be asked to present back and share what they are going to do as a result of their conversations, this is when we will really see the impact of using this approach.

In summary, Mike believes that using this model enables personalization of employee engagement, to ensure the approach and actions taken are right for individuals, their teams and the company. The model has helped create a flexibility that a wordy definition would not have. This approach has freed Bard from 'ticking the boxes', to move to a more transformational approach.

Should employee experience replace employee engagement?

Airbnb no longer have an HR department, instead choosing to focus on employee experience, with a team headed up by a Chief Employee Experience Officer rather than the traditional HRD. When the company made this move it sparked a great deal of interest from the HR community and beyond. Airbnb's mission is to create a world where you can belong anywhere, and they believe that central to achieving this mission is creating memorable workplace experiences across the entire employee life cycle, which is why they made the move to set up an employee experience function. They argue that this is different to the more traditional HR set up in that the focus is much broader. This wider scope includes the office environment, facilities, food, and CSR. In addition, it includes a group of employees that they call 'ground control', who are tasked to help bring their culture to life via a range of activities such as internal communications, events, celebrations and recognition.

Whilst this certainly sounds like a fantastic approach to creating a great place to work, the more cynical might argue that this is simply a name change. Certainly in my first engagement role back in the late 1990s I worked as part of an organizational development team and the various departments that were part of the wider function included all of the above. We even had an equivalent to the 'ground control' concept who were called the 'smile' team.

There's no doubt that employee experience as a concept is gaining interest and attention, and some commentators are asking if it should replace employee engagement. Unsurprisingly my answer to this question is no! Quite simply, if we get the employee experience right, employees are more likely to be engaged and if employees are more engaged we are more likely to get the customer experience right and achieve a host of other desired business outcomes. In his book *The Employee Experience Advantage*, Jacob

Morgan argues that we need to purposefully design a work experience to create a truly engaged workforce which will unlock business performance.

Many commentators argue the case for a move away from employee engagement to employee experience by citing the lack of improvements seen in employee engagement despite the continued focus, or the 'employee engagement gap' as I call it. However, the reasons we have not seen improvements in employee engagement are because many companies do not have an engagement strategy and plan; they focus on the survey rather than what happens next, and there is little investment in practitioners' development or improving line managers' skills. In fact, much of the rationale I have come across which argues the case for a move away from engagement to experience can be addressed via the chapters and content within this book. For example, some commentators argue that engagement is organization centric, whereas a shift to focus on employee experience is employee centric. I would argue that any decent engagement practitioner knows that we need to understand how employees experience the organization, that we need to involve them in the solutions to create great places to work and that we absolutely cannot make assumptions about what engages our people and teams. These are themes that are further discussed in more detail throughout the following chapters. In addition, in Chapter 5 you'll find an activity that will help you to review your employee life cycle and overall employee experience to design an employee experience which will support employee engagement rather than sabotage it.

Technological advances have also contributed to the rising interest in employee experience. As companies begin to move away from the annual employee survey there are an increasing number of opportunities to gather data and insight on, and from, employees. The Swedish start-up Epicenter even offers implants to employees via microchips that are basically like a swipe card: enabling access to offices, operating printers or buying a latte at the coffee bar, all with a swipe of a hand. It is easy to see how these technologies and other wearables are enabling companies to gather a range of data to help them understand employee experience and behaviours in real time. It is still early days for these technologies and our subsequent understanding of how they might be used to help improve and develop the employee experience in order to positively impact engagement.

In summary, we need to consider both employee experience and engagement if we are to develop workplaces people want to join and contribute their best. Following the principles within this book will help you to develop and improve your employee experience and contribute towards an engaged workforce, which ultimately benefits not only your employees, but your customers and partners too.

Summary

There is no doubt that the debate will continue as to what employee engagement is, how to develop it and the real impact it has. However, what is clear is that this increased focus on engaging employees has been significant not only in improving people's experience of work, but in improving the performance of organizations as well. Companies are increasingly realizing that an engaged workforce is not only good for employees, but good for customers and overall business performance as well.

02 **Does engagement matter?**

Introduction

It seems reasonable to suggest that organizational performance will, to a greater or lesser degree, be dependent upon the people who work in the organization. The way employees feel about working for a company, and the way they subsequently behave will have an impact on the performance of their organization. And yet there are still many sceptics out there who challenge this thinking. All too often a substantial part of developing engagement within your organization involves making the business case and getting buy-in from leaders and stakeholders. In People Lab's 2017 'Spotlight on Employee Engagement' research, they found that 56 per cent of companies are now tasking those with responsibility for engagement to demonstrate ROI on employee engagement activities. This is a jump of 15 percentage points from the 2016 research, demonstrating an increased focus on the business case.

One of the earliest pieces of research to demonstrate a link between engagement and organizational performance was the Sears 'employee-customer-profit chain'. This research was published in the *Harvard Business Review* in 1998, and was the first time a definitive link between how employees feel and how customers then feel, and a subsequent impact on the bottom line had been proven via research (Rucci *et al*, 1998).

The hypothesis that positive changes in employee attitudes leads to positive changes in employee behaviours is at the heart of the substantial amounts of current academic research into organizational behaviour, organizational psychology, human resource management and change management. Academic research continues to provide an evidence base that moves beyond simple cross-sectional correlations and demonstrates longitudinal relationships between engagement and performance.

Much of the evidence within this chapter is taken from the UK's Engage for Success report (D'Analeze *et al*, 2012), simply entitled, *The Evidence*.

The 'evidence' is drawn from three distinct perspectives: academic publications, research by consultancies and organizational case studies. Each of these perspectives has its own strengths and weaknesses, but the combined weight of this evidence indicates that we cannot afford to ignore the links between employee engagement and performance.

Which comes first: engagement or high performance?

Does engagement predict subsequent organizational performance or does working for a high-performing organization result in a more engaged workforce? This is a question that is often discussed when looking at the business case for engagement. The evidence shows that engagement comes first.

Findings published within the Engage for Success report, *The Evidence*, showed that increases in the average level of employee engagement resulted in increases in customer satisfaction, which then resulted in improvements in sales achievement within retail branch networks of one Irish and three UK banking organizations. Specifically one standard deviation increase in engagement was linked to a 6 per cent improvement in branch sales relative to target.

Research on service profit chains in other sectors has also demonstrated a longitudinal linkage between engagement and performance. For example, three years of data gathered from thousands of employees and hundreds of thousands of customers of a large European franchise retail chain in the do-it-yourself (DIY) market has shown that improvements in engagement at the beginning of the three-year period worked through to improvements in customer satisfaction, which then delivered significantly improved operating profit by the end of the period.

The global perspective

A longitudinal study by Towers Watson, with global reach, analysed data gathered from opinion surveys of over 664,000 employees from more than 50 companies representing a range of industries and sizes. The study measured engagement alongside more traditional business performance measures over 12 months. Those companies with a highly engaged workforce improved operating income by 19.2 per cent over the 12-month study period, and those companies with low engagement scores saw operating income decline by 32.7 per cent over the same period. Similarly, those companies with high engagement scores demonstrated a 13.7 per cent improvement in net income growth compared to a decline of 3.8 per cent in low engagement companies (Watson Wyatt, 2009).

CASE STUDY   Marks & Spencer

Marks & Spencer (M&S) completed a longitudinal study (D'Analeze *et al*, 2012) which found that long-term employee engagement trends are directly linked to long-term sales performance. Using data from a study group of 137 high-street stores over four years, the research found that those stores with an improving engagement trend over the four years significantly outperformed the stores where engagement scores were declining (compared to respective sales targets).

Once store size was taken into account, both engagement itself and the changes in engagement from one year to the next were found to correlate to sales performance. Stores with improving engagement had on average delivered £62 million more sales to the business every year than stores with declining engagement.

CASE STUDY   PricewaterhouseCoopers

PricewaterhouseCoopers (PwC) runs a six-monthly survey to measure engagement among staff and partners. These scores are tracked on a firm-wide, line of service and business unit level. Each business unit analyses the results and identifies recommendations for action and how these will be communicated to staff.

PwC's internal data show a clear link between engaged people and better business performance. Voluntary turnover numbers increase 12 months after engagement scores fall, and the top-performing businesses for people engagement have higher average client engagement. Analysis of historical data demonstrates that this link follows through to financial success: top-performing businesses for people engagement also have higher average gross margins.

The evidence clearly supports the view that engagement today drives performance for several years into the future. There is also evidence that good performance in the current period can make improvements in future engagement levels, though this effect appears to be smaller and less enduring.

CASE STUDY Rentokil Initial

Rentokil Initial plc has a 66,000-employee group, £2.5 billion turnover, with services ranging from pest control to parcel delivery. As a people-based service organization, Rentokil Initial's service and business results depend heavily on how engaged their employees feel. The determination and discretionary efforts of employees, particularly sales employees, are crucial to business success, and the cost of replacing employees is approximately 1.5–2 times annual salary plus opportunity costs.

Rentokil used a combination of correlation and gap analysis using 15 months of data and found that those teams who went on to produce the best gross margin began the period with higher engagement levels (+5 per cent) than the initial engagement levels of underperforming teams. The work revealed a key role for engagement in employee retention, especially for sales employees. Rentokil Initial found that a 1 per cent point improvement in engagement improved retention by 0.39 per cent. The teams that improved engagement the most saw retention increase by 6.7 percentage points, providing an estimated saving of £7 million.

Engagement is linked to many types of performance and business outcomes

Engagement can be linked to a variety of performance and business outcomes. Many studies have demonstrated robust links between employee engagement and increases in profits, productivity, innovation, beneficial discretionary effort, customer satisfaction and customer retention. These studies have also demonstrated that employee engagement reduces absence, voluntary turnover, sabotage, and a range of other negative behaviours.

We will explore the links between engagement and these different performance and business outcomes below.

Engagement and profit

There is an abundance of evidence that demonstrates that increased levels of employee engagement can in turn lead to improved revenue growth, profit margins and overall shareholder returns. Academic journals, consultancy reports and individual organizational cases provide compelling evidence of links between employee engagement and profit. These connections doubtlessly work through different channels in different organizations to deliver this improved profitability. For example, the Institute for Employment Studies (IES) demonstrated in a study of 100 retail outlets, 25,000 customers and 65,000 employees that increased employee engagement improved companies' potential to increase sales through three routes: directly on sales; mediated through customer satisfaction; and through reduction in staff absence (Barber *et al*, 1999). They concluded that a 1 per cent increase in their measure of engagement could lead to a monthly increase of 9 per cent in sales. A Towers Watson study in 2004 (cited in D'Analeze *et al*, 2012) across over 2,000 UK retail bank branches found that a 10 per cent improvement in engagement could be expected to drive a 4 per cent increase in sales versus target, which translated into an additional £100 million in personal account revenue for an average-sized UK retail bank.

The Kenexa High Performance Institute (KHPI, 2009) published evidence based on their research in 158 organizations from a wide range of industries illustrating that both diluted earnings per share and three-year total shareholder returns were directly linked to employee engagement. Analysis of work trends survey data from 22,500 employees in 14 countries has also led Kenexa to conclude that organizations with high employee engagement levels outperformed those with low engagement in total shareholder return and annual net income. Those organizations with engagement scores in the top 25 per cent of those surveyed by Kenexa had twice the annual net income ('profit attributable to shareholders' in the UK) of those in the bottom 25 per cent. Those high-engagement organizations also returned a staggering seven times more to shareholders over a five-year period than those in the lowest quartile. The strong link between employee engagement and a company's overall financial performance has been reinforced by several other sources. Kenexa research established the link between engagement and total net income using data from 64 organizations. Organizations with highly engaged employees achieved twice the annual net income (profit) of organizations whose employees lagged behind on engagement, even after controlling for organization size.

Towers Watson's 2012 Global Workforce Study reported that companies with high and sustainable engagement levels had an average one-year operating margin that was close to three times higher than companies with low engagement levels. The Hay Group (2012) reported that organizations in the top quartile of engagement scores demonstrated revenue growth 2.5 times greater than those organizations in the bottom quartile. Gallup data (2006) have also been used to show that the earnings per share growth rates of those units with engagement scores in the top quartile were 2.6 times those of units with below-average engagement scores.

Aon Hewitt research shows a strong correlation between employee engagement and financial performance, even in turbulent financial times (Aon Hewitt, 2011). They analysed their employee engagement database of more than 5,700 employers, representing 5 million employees worldwide, and their work showed that, in 2010, organizations with engagement levels of 65 per cent or greater posted total shareholder returns that were 22 per cent higher than the market average. Conversely, companies with engagement of 45 per cent or less generated returns that were 28 per cent lower than the same market benchmark.

CASE STUDY Belron®

Belron® is the world's largest dedicated vehicle glass repair and replacement service. Ranking 36 regional managers across four countries using 'profit versus budget' as the key performance indicator, Belron® established that those regional managers who created 'high performance and energizing climates' were 4.2 times more likely to deliver above average profit (D'Analeze *et al*, 2012).

CASE STUDY Sainsbury's

Sainsbury's are a prime example of an organization that has continued to increase their employee engagement scores against a challenging economic backdrop with positive business results. Sainsbury's have found a clear link between these higher levels of engagement and sales performance. Engagement had a positive and significant impact on sales growth with the level of engagement contributing up to 15 per cent of a store's year-on-year growth.

CASE STUDY Dorothy Perkins

Dorothy Perkins completed research that found that those environments characterized by high engagement (what they term 'high performing climates') demonstrated better financial performance. Specifically environments with high engagement demonstrated 12 per cent higher growth in sales, delivered

10 per cent improvements in operating savings, and experienced 35 per cent lower stock loss. For a store with an average monthly turnover of £2.3 million, the 12 per cent higher growth could yield an annual financial gain of £445,000 (D'Analeze *et al*, 2012).

Engagement and the customer

Building on the Sears 'employee-customer-profit chain', there is a wealth of evidence that demonstrates just how critical an engaged workforce is for a positive customer experience.

A 2012 Gallup study stated that employees with positive attitudes towards their workplaces carried those attitudes over to customers and engaged in discretionary efforts necessary to deliver high levels of customer service (Harter *et al*, 2012). Customer-facing employees exercised this discretion through their customer interactions while non-customer-facing employees did this through the quality and consistency of the products they produced. An earlier Gallup report that examined over 23,000 business units showed that companies with engagement scores in the top quartile averaged 12 per cent higher customer advocacy than those in the bottom quartile (Gallup, 2008, cited in MacLeod and Clarke, 2009). Towers Watson client-specific research within a high-performance global bank observed that effective teamwork in branches enhanced customer perceptions of courtesy and competence, which in turn improved customer loyalty (share of wallet) (Towers Watson, 2012).

Employees themselves share the view that engagement and customer satisfaction go hand in hand. In particular, 78 per cent of highly engaged employees in the UK public sector in 2007 said they could make an impact on public services delivery or customer service, while just 29 per cent of the disengaged felt the same way. Evidence supplied to the Task Force from the NHS reveals important relationships between engagement, patient satisfaction and patient mortality, and Professor Mike West of the Centre for Performance-Led HR at Lancaster University concludes: 'Employee engagement emerges as the best predictor of NHS trust outcomes. No combination of key scores or single scale is as effective in predicting trust performance on a range of outcomes measures as is the scale measure of employee engagement' (D'Analeze *et al*, 2012).

The Hay Group's 2010 study into the employee engagement strategies of the World's Most Admired Companies® also supports the impact of engagement on customer outcomes (Royal and Stark, 2010). It found that 84 per cent of the admired companies stated that they believed their efforts to engage employees had strengthened customer relationships, as compared with 72 per cent of their peer group. Kenexa compared the employee engagement scores of 16 US retail organizations with the associated American Customer Satisfaction Index (ACSI) scores. The top five organizations in this group ranked by their engagement scores were the same as the top five ranked by their ACSI.

Engagement is also linked to customer service in The Royal Bank of Scotland, with a 7 percentage point difference in customer service scores between the top 10 per cent of business units and the bottom 10 per cent, ranked by employee engagement in 2011. An analysis of 1979 business units in 10 companies showed that those units that scored above the median on both employee and customer engagement were on average 3.4 times more effective financially than units in the bottom half of both measures, judged on total sales and revenue performance and annual gain in sales and revenue.

Understanding customer needs enables employees to exercise discretion in ways that strengthen customer relationships. PwC has shown that there is a strong correlation between highly engaged staff and client satisfaction that is driven by an improved understanding of customer needs and greater advocacy of their own organizations. In particular, PwC found that 70 per cent of engaged employees indicated they have a good understanding of customer needs compared to only 17 per cent for non-engaged employees. Similarly, 67 per cent of engaged employees were happy to advocate their organizations compared to only 3 per cent of the disengaged.

CASE STUDY National Health Service

The customer in the National Health Service (NHS) is the patient, and NHS sector research completed by Aston University (cited in D'Analeze *et al*, 2012) showed that patient satisfaction is significantly higher in trusts with higher levels of employee engagement, as well as revealing some of the key drivers of this relationship. The percentage of staff receiving job-relevant or health and safety training, the prevalence of well-structured appraisal meetings and reports of good support from immediate line managers were all linked to improvements in levels of patient satisfaction.

The research also showed that NHS trusts with high engagement had lower standardized patient mortality rates, even when controlling for prior patient mortality, and these effects were of meaningful size. Patient mortality rates were approximately 2.5 per cent lower in those trusts with high engagement levels than in those with medium engagement levels.

The evidence reveals stark differences between engaged and non-engaged employees with clear implications for an organization's customer experience. Given that customer perceptions can significantly impact financial performance through repeat business and word-of-mouth, there is a clear incentive for companies to consider engagement strategies as a means of improving their customer interactions.

CASE STUDY Serco

Serco is a FTSE 100 international service company with more than 100,000 employees, delivering services to government and private clients in over 30 countries. Serco provided Aon with a Net Promoter Score (NPS) for 264 separate contracts in the UK and Europe in 2011. The net promoter score is a measure of customer loyalty where customers are asked to assess the likelihood that they would recommend the company to others. Those who score the question highly are classed as 'promoters', those who score the question poorly are classed as 'detractors', and those in between classed as 'passives'. The NPS is constructed by subtracting the percentage of detractors from the percentage of promoters. Values above zero indicate more promoters than detractors.

Aon segmented Serco's contracts into groups based on the percentage of engaged employees identified in their 2011 employee survey. Aon matched the survey data with the NPS scores and revealed a strong relationship between engagement and NPS. Contracts delivered by engaged employees showed much better customer loyalty than those with less engaged employees.

Engagement and productivity

Improvements in performance can also arise through increased productivity, and there is a strong evidence base for links from employee engagement to this business outcome. Research sponsored by the CIPD demonstrated that the impact of employee engagement on productivity arose, at least in part, because engaged employees were more involved and socially connected with their work, allowing them to develop better solutions. Further analysis of data from that CIPD project identified a relationship between employee engagement and task performance amongst UK employees. A focus on engagement is also likely to be associated with the positive exercise of discretion in the workplace and a reduction in counterproductive behaviour.

For example, Gallup data from 23,910 business units demonstrated that those units with engagement scores in the top quartile averaged 18 per cent higher productivity than those units in the bottom quartile. The Corporate Leadership Council (CLC) analysed the engagement of 50,000 employees in 59 organizations from 27 countries and found that 71 per cent of companies with above-average employee engagement achieved company performance above their sector average, against only 40 per cent of companies with below-average employee engagement (Gallup, 2008, cited in MacLeod and Clarke, 2009). The CLC concluded that 'by increasing employees' engagement levels, organizations can expect an increase in performance of up to 20 percentile points and an 87 per cent reduction in employees' probability of departure'.

One mechanism for increasing the overall productivity of an organization is the enhancement of the workforce's desire to exceed performance expectations. Instilling a sustained culture of high performance within a workforce is the key aspiration of many leadership teams, and employee engagement can play a central role in achieving this goal. Research from the Hay Group (2012) linking employee survey data to performance ratings showed that highly engaged employees were 10 per cent more likely to exceed performance expectations. Similarly, Towers Watson (2012) reported that the highly engaged were more than twice as likely to be top performers, with almost 60 per cent of them exceeding or far exceeding performance expectations.

Productivity is not just about the amount of output: it is also about quality. Development Dimensions International (DDI) reported that in a *Fortune* 100 manufacturing company, quality errors were significantly higher for poorly engaged teams (Wellins *et al*, 2005). Sila (2006) analyses data from 2,000 manufacturing and service companies randomly selected from the American Society for Quality (ASQ) mailing list and identifies strong links between total quality management (TQM) and productivity/defect rates. Meta-analytic research has also verified the broad importance of employee engagement for productivity, product quality and associated complaints.

Despite the obvious benefits of increasing productivity through enhanced engagement, employee perceptions indicate that many companies are lagging behind. According to research completed by Aon Hewitt in 2011, the largest drop in employee views that year was in employees' perceptions of how companies manage performance. Employees worldwide believed their employers had not provided the appropriate focus or level of management that would lead to increased productivity, nor had they connected individual performance to organizational goals. This indicated a pressing need for organizations to provide a 'strategic narrative' that addressed employee concerns around performance management before they could expect to increase workforce engagement and improve productivity.

CASE STUDY   RSA Insurance Group

RSA Insurance Group plc is a multinational insurance group employing 23,000 people. Research in their MORE TH>N call centres has shown that engaged people have 35 per cent lower average 'wrap' times (time between calls) than disengaged people. Engaged staff are able to talk to, on average, an additional 800 customers per year (based on an average call handling time of 365 seconds). Put another way, for every eight engaged people they employ they get the equivalent of an additional member of staff without any increase in the wage bill.

Engagement and innovation

Innovation is high on the agenda of many organizations as they strive to differentiate themselves from their peers in an increasingly competitive environment, and the link between employee engagement and organizational innovation is compelling. An abundance of research has shown that happier and more content employees are more likely to foster an innovative environment.

Hakanen *et al* (2008) demonstrated using longitudinal data that job resources led to engagement, and that this engagement generated subsequent effects on personal initiative and work-unit innovativeness. Similarly, Alfes *et al* (2013) examined data from over 2,000 employees of a recycling and waste management company and found results indicating that line manager behaviour and perceived organizational practices drove employee engagement, which in turn was strongly linked to innovative work behaviour. Analysis of Gallup data indicated that higher levels of engagement were strongly related to higher levels of innovation: 59 per cent of engaged employees said that their job brings out their most creative ideas against only 3 per cent of disengaged employees (Krueger and Killham, 2007).

CIPD research has also suggested that higher levels of engagement lead to more innovative work behaviour, with engaged employees much more likely to search out new methods, techniques or instruments, and transform innovative ideas into useful applications (Alfes *et al*, 2010). The same report also found that 38 per cent of employees said that they developed innovative ideas only a few times a year, while a mere 15 per cent showed innovative work behaviour on a weekly or daily basis. There would appear to be a substantial zblock of employees (47 per cent) who are almost completely divorced from the generation of innovative ideas.

The Corporate Leadership Council (CLC, 2004) has found that while organizations value innovation and initiative at every level, creating an environment where both thrive is a challenge. Organizations are likely to increase engagement levels and workforce commitment when they actively encourage employees to innovate, improve methods, research solutions, and participate in the decision-making process. The Chartered Management Institute (CMI) found a significant association and influence between employee engagement and innovation in 2012 based on survey returns from the Institute's membership. They concluded that: 'The prevailing management styles in growing businesses are far more likely to be open, empowering, innovative, entrepreneurial and high trust environments' (Hope-Hailey *et al*, 2012).

CASE STUDY   BAE Systems

BAE Systems plc is a global provider of defence and security products. Previous attempts to modernize production processes had stalled within the Military Aircraft and Information (MAI) division, and relations between the recognized trade union and the company were difficult and unproductive. The company introduced a new scheme in November 2009 as part of what both the union and company teams described as a 'conversation' rather than a 'negotiation'. This conversation involved small groups of union negotiators and managers. The union also ensured far more detailed and ongoing communication with members.

By September 2011 the scheme was having a major effect on production levels and producing substantial cost savings. More than £26 million of improvement opportunities were identified by the shop floor in the first year, and during the second year the required reduction in build hours for aircraft had been exceeded. In the case of the Typhoon aircraft, build hours fell by more than 25 per cent.

CASE STUDY UKTV

Formed in 1997 as an independent commercial joint venture between BBC Worldwide and Scripps Networks International, UKTV's 10 distinct channel brands include: Watch, Gold, Dave, Alibi, Yesterday, Blighty, Eden, Home, Really and Good Food.

When Darren Childs arrived at UKTV as the new CEO in September 2010, he found a culture that was the opposite of engaged, and an employee survey backed up his initial impressions. Eighteen months after Darren took over, UKTV had risen 6 per cent in revenues against the same quarter in 2011, while the overall market was 10 per cent down, and UKTV also saw a marked decrease in absenteeism and turnover.

UKTV continues to manage innovation differently than other organizational processes. Hierarchies for idea approval are much flatter, and individuals who suggest programming ideas that are 'green-lighted' for production are financially well rewarded. Darren and his senior team stress the importance of giving high recognition to the individual and the idea by communicating it across UKTV.

SOURCE D'Analeze *et al* (2012)

CASE STUDY Welsh Government

In January 2010 the Welsh Government launched the 'Managing with Less' initiative in response to a substantial reduction in the budgets available to run the organization. Since it began, it has secured the active engagement of most of their 5,500 employees. Ninety-eight per cent of employees were aware of the 'Managing with Less' initiative, 83 per cent of employees participated in discussion sessions to generate cost-saving and efficiency-enhancing ideas, and 86 per cent of employees felt that their colleagues were committed to the 'Managing with Less' approach.

A key part of the initiative involved briefing and training divisional leaders to talk their teams through the financial scenarios and the potential impacts of the reduction in budgets. This led to some very direct conversations about the benefits of cutting 'discretionary' areas of spend in order to save jobs. Team members were typically prepared to be much more radical in their approach to cost-saving than senior leaders.

The Welsh Government believes this style and level of engagement has allowed them to achieve the required spending reductions without the need for compulsory redundancies.

During 2010–11, 'Managing with Less' resulted in reductions in spend of more than £20 million.

SOURCE D'Analeze *et al* (2012)

Engagement and people indicators

1 *Turnover/retention*: The cost of employee turnover has historically been one of the driving forces behind the push to raise employee engagement, and the importance of employee turnover to the performance of Rentokil Initial and PwC was demonstrated earlier in this chapter.

Organizations such as the CIPD report that engaged employees are significantly more likely to want to stay with their organization compared with those who are less engaged. Highly engaged organizations have the potential to reduce staff turnover by 87 per cent, at least in part because disengaged employees are four times more likely to leave the organization than the average employee. Other work has shown that those who are highly engaged are half as likely to leave the organization as the average employee. Gallup has also shown a strong link between lower engagement scores and higher employee turnover, both for organizations with historically high turnover and those with much lower turnover. In looking at those firms with 60 per cent or higher annualized employee turnover, those in the bottom quartile ranked by employee engagement had 31 per cent higher employee turnover than those in the top quartile of engagement scores (Harter *et al*, 2012). For firms with annualized turnover of 40 per cent or lower the results indicated that those in the bottom quartile had 51 per cent higher annualized turnover than top quartile firms. Wellins *et al* (2005) reinforce this view with evidence from a *Fortune* 100 manufacturing company where turnover in low engagement teams averaged 14.5 per cent, compared with only 4.8 per cent in high engagement teams.

The Hay Group (2012) estimate that in an organization with 20,000 employees and an annual voluntary turnover rate of 8 per cent, the cost of turnover is approximately US $56 million, assuming an average salary of US $35,000. They also estimate that companies with high levels of engagement show turnover rates 40 per cent lower than companies with low levels of engagement. Application of this estimate to the projected costs of employee turnover suggests that effecting change from a low engagement to a high-engagement environment could yield annual savings of US $22.4 million. In the Royal Bank of Scotland, business units in the bottom 10 per cent ranked by employee engagement had almost twice the voluntary turnover rate in 2011 of those business units in the top 10 per cent, at a cost of around £650,000.

These examples illustrate the scale of the positive effect that increased employee engagement can have on workforce turnover. This link between turnover and engagement illustrates why many see engagement strategies as an essential method for managing their workforce and the significant costs and risks associated with turnover. Furthermore, these approaches appear to be working, with 94 per cent of *Fortune*'s World's Most Admired Companies stating that they believed their efforts to engage employees had both created a competitive advantage and reduced staff turnover (Royal and Stark, 2010).

2 *Well-being/absence*: The work environment has a potentially large role to play in determining levels of well-being, and it is not surprising to see the strong connections between employee engagement, well-being and absence. Research using data collected from 9,930 employees across 12 UK public- and private-sector organizations, including police forces, utilities, manufacturing, higher education, a local council and the financial services, found a correlation between engagement and psychological well-being of 0.35 (demonstrating a moderate relationship), and that these two variables collectively explained a meaningful proportion of the variance in performance (D'Analeze *et al*, 2012).

Over half of disengaged employees (54 per cent) say that work has a negative effect on their physical health as opposed to only 12 per cent of engaged employees. Analysis carried out within PwC reported a similar correlation between engagement and well-being in their business: the less engaged PwC's staff, the lower their well-being levels. Engaged employees show higher levels of well-being all round, meaning that they are more likely to enjoy their work activities, are able to cope with work-related problems and are less likely to lose sleep over work-related issues. The CIPD found that those who were absorbed in their work were almost three times as likely to have six key positive emotions at work (enthusiasm, cheerfulness, optimism, contentment, calm and feeling relaxed) as negative ones (feeling miserable, worried, depressed, gloomy, tense or uneasy). Aon Hewitt research reported that 28 per cent of employees experienced a high level of job-related stress in 'high engagement' companies (65 per cent engagement and over) versus 39 per cent of employees in low engagement companies.

The level of absenteeism within the workforce is recognized as one of the main indicators of well-being for organizations today (D'Analeze *et al*, 2012). The CIPD (2010) estimates place the cost of absence in the UK alone at between £10 billion and £20 billion per year in 2009. The same CIPD publication reported a median cost of absence per employee per year of £600, and listed minor illnesses, stress and mental health among the five leading causes of absence.

Fortunately, the research suggests that employee engagement can also have a significant impact on absence. High-engagement companies report employees taking seven absence days per year on average, or approximately half of the 14 days per year reported in low-engagement companies (Aon Hewitt, 2012). Similarly, Towers Watson reported that the highly engaged missed 43 per cent fewer days of work due to illness, and evidence from a *Fortune* 100 manufacturing company demonstrated that absenteeism in low-engagement teams hovered around 8 per cent, as compared with only 4.1 per cent in high-engagement teams (Watson Wyatt, 2009; Wellins *et al*, 2005). The Royal Bank of Scotland reported that absence rates were 1.5 per cent higher at a cost of around £250,000 for business units in the bottom 10 per cent relative to those in the top 10 per cent ranked by employee engagement in 2011 (D'Analeze *et al*, 2012).

CASE STUDY Nampak

Following the introduction of a new employee engagement programme, Nampak recorded a 5 per cent increase in the number of strongly engaged employees. During the same period they recorded a 26 per cent reduction in absence levels, which they attributed to their employee engagement. In recognition, Nampak was named the People Management/CIPD Employee Engagement category and overall winner in 2010.

CASE STUDY NHS

NHS employees were absent 10.7 million days in 2009. This equates to a loss of 10.3 million days annually at a cost of around £1.75 billion.

Research from Aston University has demonstrated that an increase of one standard deviation in engagement is associated with reductions in absence sufficient to generate savings equivalent to around £150,000 in salary costs alone for an average acute trust. Given the 164 acute trusts in the UK this represents a potential saving of £24.6 million each year, not including non-salary costs or the prospect of similar savings in other NHS trusts.

SOURCE D'Analeze *et al* (2012)

3 *Health and safety*: Engagement has been shown to improve safety performance in organizations, with the impact of engagement being approximately half as important to safety performance as employee awareness of the occupational health and safety policies in the workplace. Research based on 203 independent samples has demonstrated that increases in employee engagement are associated with reductions in unsafe behaviour in the workplace, adverse events, accidents and injuries: all of which are key contributors to important business outcomes. Analysis of the Gallup Q12® engagement measure found that organizations with engagement in the bottom quartile averaged a staggering 62 per cent more accidents than those in the top quartile (Harter *et al*, 2012).

Engagement and reputation

If, despite all of the evidence cited within this chapter, you are still struggling to convince the sceptics that engagement matters, it might be worth focusing on engagement and reputation. With the rise of the internet the days of being able to contain what it's really like to work in your organization are long gone. Sites like Glassdoor (**www.glassdoor.com**) are ensuring that any-one can take a look inside and rate your workplace, citing pros and cons of working there and even being able to give advice to senior managers and rate the CEO. While sites like these are still in their infancy, it's only a matter of time before they are more widely used for potential employees, current employees and customers. Clearly information like this in the public domain can have a huge impact on corporate and brand reputation: both in a positive and negative way! However, surely the argument for investing now in employee engagement, rather than costs later for crisis management, stack up when making the business case to stakeholders for focusing on engagement within your organization.

Conclusion

The evidence is clear: engaged employees perform better all round. The growing body of evidence shows clearly that engaged employees work harder, better, longer, smarter, are absent less, go the extra mile, overcome barriers and are more resilient. Engaged employees create competitive advantages that are difficult to replicate, which surely places engagement as a key component of a successful business strategy.

More and more organizations are waking up to the advantages that an engaged workforce can create. In fact, active monitoring of employee engagement is rising year on year, with 66 per cent of senior HR professionals saying that they measure engagement, up from 55 per cent only two years previously (D'Analeze et al, 2012).

The case studies included within this chapter highlight some of the many benefits that arise from having an engaged workforce. They also serve as a health warning for companies who continue to choose not to focus on the engagement of their workforce, for the opposite effects are observed within a disengaged workforce: high absenteeism, low productivity, high employee attrition, and so the list goes on. It seems hard to believe that when faced with the evidence, a company would choose to ignore employee engagement and the impact an engaged workforce will have on their overall performance.

03 Developing your employee engagement strategy

Introduction

In Chapters 1 and 2 we looked at what employee engagement is and the business case for engagement. Developing an engagement strategy is still not commonplace though, with just 42 per cent of practitioners saying that they have a strategy in place (Spotlight on Employee Engagement, People Lab, 2017a). Clearly a well-defined strategy and plan are crucial to develop and improve engagement. In this chapter, we will introduce you to the building blocks of an effective employee engagement strategy. In order to help you design your engagement strategy as we move through various sections of this book, we recommend you use the strategy roadmap or similar (see Table 3.1). Using the roadmap will help you to develop a succinct 'strategy-on-a-page' that will enable you to communicate your strategy and plan clearly to key stakeholders.

Introducing the strategy roadmap: developing your definition and vision

In Chapter 1, we explored the various definitions of employee engagement that exist, and recommended an activity to enable you to come up with a definition that works for your organization. Whatever definition you decide upon, it's important that key stakeholders within your business understand and support your definition. Your definition is an important building block of your engagement strategy, underpinning the subsequent plan and activity.

TABLE 3.1   Your strategy roadmap

Employee engagement definition	
Future vision	
Goals	Outcomes
Action plan – drivers	
Measurement	

Activity

What's your definition?

Building on the work from Chapter 1, insert your definition of employee engagement into your strategy roadmap. Use the following points to help you:

- In your organization, do you want to view engagement as an outcome, a behaviour, or an attitude?

- Do you need to define engagement specifically or could you talk about it in terms of 'creating a great place to work' or 'becoming an employer of choice'?

- Solicit and gather opinions from key stakeholders as to what they understand by the term 'engagement'.

- When you come up with a definition, will it be easy to explain to others? If the answer is no, your definition probably needs work.

- How can you ensure your definition will appeal to key stakeholders within your organization and not sound too 'HR-centric'? Remember you need to get them and others involved with this to make it happen.

- Complete the following statement: 'When we talk about employee engagement around here, what we mean is...'.

- Road-test your definition with a variety of employees from your organization: Do they understand what you are talking about? Is it in plain English (no 'management-speak' if possible)?

Getting your definition right is an important step in developing your engagement strategy. In addition, coming up with an aspirational vision for the work you are proposing is also helpful. A good vision will provide inspiration and direction for your employee engagement activity, helping employees to understand where this is going and motivating them to want to get there. Your vision for your employee engagement strategy should align with your organization's vision, and if they can be one and the same, then so much the better! This is an important step in ensuring your engagement strategy aligns with and supports your company strategy.

Activity

Developing your vision

Vision statements are often the result of workshops at executive or senior management level. However, involving your employees in developing the vision for your employee engagement strategy is an effective way to get more 'buy-in' to your work and can be a good way to engage employees at the same time. Asking people to focus on what the future *could* be like is a great way to develop a vision as well as focusing employees on shared goals and common ground. All too often when talking about engagement within organizations, the conversation turns to what is wrong and what isn't working. By involving employees in talking about the desired future culture of the company you can avoid this. Use the following questions to gather feedback from your employees and involve them in defining your engagement vision:

1   Imagine anything is possible: what could it be like to work here in the future?

2   Describe what would be happening: what will it look like and feel like?

3   What will a typical day be like?

4   Why will people want to come and work here?

5   Why will people want to stay?

There are a variety of ways you can choose to have this conversation with your employees:

- Run workshops with representation from across your organization.

- Ask employees to create mood boards to visually describe this desired future state.

- Ask employees to create short films to advertise this future company to prospective employees.

- If you have social media capability within your company, you can host a one-day 'jam', which is a company-wide conversation on the desired future culture.

It doesn't really matter how you involve employees in coming up with ideas and taking part in this dialogue; the important part is to focus on possibilities and an aspirational view of the future rather than getting caught up in all the reasons why this won't work. When you have gathered any inputs from this activity, use the various contributions to craft your vision.

Aligning your engagement strategy to your company strategy: defining your goals and outcomes

In Chapter 1 we introduced the concept of transformational engagement, arguing that it is integrated into the business strategy and culture. The process of defining the goals and outcomes of your engagement strategy will enable you to ensure that it is aligned to your business strategy. Understanding the purpose of engagement within your company, and why and how it will help you achieve your overall business strategy, is the cornerstone of achieving alignment. In addition an engagement strategy that can be clearly linked to the overall business strategy enables practitioners to demonstrate value to the business and get buy-in from key stakeholders.

Very often the focus on employee engagement comes from objectives such as wishing to gain a specific Investors In People (IIP) Award, or perhaps to gain entry into a list such as the UK's *Sunday Times* Best 100 Companies to Work For. Sometimes the objective is to create a great place to work, or become an employer of choice. These are examples of employee engagement goals. The practitioner then needs to link these goals to desired business outcomes that are part of the company strategy. For example, these outcomes could include lowering employee turnover, or increasing customer satisfaction metrics. Table 3.2 below sets out some common employee engagement goals and business outcomes.

TABLE 3.2   Common employee engagement goals and business outcomes

Typical employee engagement goals	Example business outcomes
Achieve Investors in People Gold	Reduce employee turnover
Get on the *Sunday Times* or *Fortune* Top 100 list	Reduce absenteeism
	Increase productivity
Become a great place to work	Increase sales
Become an employer of choice	Improve customer experience
Increase survey response rates	Improve company reputation
Increase employee engagement index on annual survey	

Activity

Defining your goals and outcomes

When designing the goals for your engagement strategy, there are a few questions you might wish to consider:

- What do you need employee engagement to deliver for you?
- What does success look like?
- Where do you want to be in five years' time? For example:
  - IIP Gold Award;
  - *Sunday Times* Best 100 Companies to Work For;
  - Improve scores by x per cent, etc.

You can capture these engagement goals within your strategy roadmap.

When evaluating the business outcomes you are aiming to impact as part of your employee engagement strategy, there are a few questions you might wish to consider:

- What are the outcomes you are hoping to achieve?
- How are they aligned to your organization or business outcomes?
- What is their purpose? For example:
  - to reduce employee attrition;
  - to improve customer experience;
  - to innovate products, etc.

Take a look at some of the information below to help you identify those business outcomes you believe you can impact.

Outcomes of engagement

- Engaged employees in the UK take an average of 2.69 sick days per year; disengaged employees take 6.19.
- Seventy per cent of engaged employees indicate they have a good understanding of how to meet customer needs; only 17 per cent of non-engaged employees say the same.
- Engaged employees are 87 per cent less likely to leave the organization than disengaged employees.

- Engaged employees advocate their company or organization – 67 per cent against only 3 per cent of the disengaged. Seventy-eight per cent would recommend their company's products or services, against 13 per cent of the disengaged.

- Research by Ipsos Mori on Audit Commission data showed that staff in councils rated as 'excellent' had much better results than those in 'weak' or 'poor' councils when asked about factors such as being informed and consulted, having confidence in senior managers and understanding the overall objectives of their organizations; they were also twice as likely to be advocates for their organizations than staff in weak or poor councils.

You can then capture the business outcomes you will impact within your strategy roadmap.

Top tip

Most people are familiar with the acronym SMART when it comes to setting objectives or goals. As a quick reminder:

- *Specific*: Goals must be clear and unambiguous in what they need to achieve.

- *Measurable*: Goals must include concrete criteria to allow progress and delivery to be tracked.

- *Achievable*: Goals must be within the organization's power to reach.

- *Realistic*: Goals must be attainable given the resources available within the organization.

- *Timely*: Goals should have a time frame allocated for delivery.

It is important to ensure our goals and objectives are tangible and concrete, so that you can track performance and ultimately measure our success in achieving them. A good way to assess how concrete your goals and outcomes are is to ask yourself: 'How will I measure that?' and: 'How will I prove that we have been successful in achieving this goal?' Some of the goals listed above are already SMART, such as achieving Investors in People Gold; however, some are less so, such as, 'create a great place to work'. We will come onto measurement in Chapter 8, but we highly recommend that when you set your goals and objectives for your employee engagement strategy you also define your measures and metrics at the same time. If you are struggling to articulate how you will measure the success in achieving one of your goals, it probably isn't concrete enough.

CASE STUDY Marks & Spencer, aligning engagement to the organizational strategy

(This article has been reproduced with kind permission from *Changeboard*, the leading magazine for HR leaders. Its global community of more than 100,000 senior professionals brings together exclusive insights, thought-leadership and knowledge-sharing from around the world, to help HR professionals progress their careers.)

Engaging and connecting with employees is a value steeped in Marks & Spencer's 130-year heritage and continues to be at the heart of the company. Marks & Spencer (M&S), an iconic brand, now graces the streets in 54 territories across Europe, Middle East and Asia with over 455 wholly owned, partly owned and franchised stores. It was in the 1930s that the *Personnel Department* was created at M&S. This was headed up by Flora Solomon, who had met Simon Marks, son of Michael Marks, at a dinner party in 1932. Simon Marks, often described as the architect of the modern Marks & Spencer, built the business on a simple philosophy that 'a happier workforce was a more productive workforce'.

Emotional connection

Plan A was introduced in 2007 and extended in March 2010. Plan A is Marks & Spencer's eco- and ethical programme, which aims to make M&S the world's most sustainable major retailer by 2015. Currently there are around 3,500 Plan A volunteers in stores who really drive this programme. M&S states:

> Plan A takes an holistic approach to sustainability focusing on involving customers, involving all areas of the business and tackling issues such as climate change, waste, raw materials, health and being a fair partner. M&S believe the key driver of employee engagement is creating emotional connection. The CSR function is not an add-on. Plan A is about how M&S do business. It's a strong lever in demonstrating sustainable leadership, where they're doing the right thing for their people, the community and the environment.

However, M&S argue that the HR challenge lies in how to continue to engage with employees even in difficult times, so they feel absolutely aligned with the business plan, are committed and passionate about what they do and so they act in a way that will further the performance of the organization. Today, organizations need to be much closer to their people in communicating the 'what' and 'why' of the company so they can really get behind it to drive the business plan and strategy. The 'M&S way' is to build a strong coalition of people to come together so that individuals look beyond their own specific roles and see themselves as the sum of all parts in totality – one team working together to deliver the end results. M&S are committed to making work meaningful for people. The whole area of discretionary effort in order to drive productivity has become key for organizations. M&S has always invested in its people to make sure they feel energized, motivated and engaged. Everything is linked back to the M&S values of 'quality, service, value, innovation and trust' – starting right at the top. They use language externally and internally around 'doing the right thing'. There's not a 'silver bullet'. There are many small initiatives M&S do to create a constant drum-beat of how this is important around the company.

Each year Marks & Spencer supports over 700 people – those at risk of homelessness, young people, disabled people and single parents, who face real barriers getting into work – by giving them work experience placements of between two and four weeks. M&S works closely with M&S charity partners Gingerbread, Business Action on Homelessness, Remploy and the Prince's Trust. Marks & Start, set up in 2004, is now the biggest company-led work experience programme in the UK and Ireland. Each person is assigned a buddy and a coach, and spends the placement shadowing their buddy who coaches them in three specific areas: products, services and customer service. The scheme is so successful that 90 per cent of participants say it's a life-changing experience as it gives them the confidence to get into the world of work. Around 40 per cent of the people who complete their placements gain meaningful employment with M&S or another employer within three months. There are also annual Marks & Start awards which reward the buddies who have done the most to support individuals where they've had the most significant life-changing experiences.

The payback? The stores that have Marks & Start placements and buddies have some of the lowest sickness absence figures and employee turnover, reducing recruitment costs. The buddies are hugely motivated. Once they've worked with someone through their placement and that person goes on to become successfully and gainfully employed, the buddy feels extremely proud. Plus the placements, who feel they've been given a second chance in life, are incredibly appreciative and therefore very committed to working, especially if they then secure employment within M&S. This creates loyalty.

Community spirit

In addition, M&S bridges the gap between young people and the world of work by working directly with schools and creating 2,500 work experience placements a year for young people aged 16. Every employee has one paid day each year to do local volunteering in the community and often people team up and volunteer together.

Trust has become increasingly challenging, particularly as there are various examples of companies where trust has been eroded. To live the value of trust,

HR ensures it has very clear communication at all levels of the organization, which is continuously reinforced. M&S runs an employee network called BIG (Business Involvement Group). There are around 3,500 members of BIG. They recently introduced a scheme called 'the Big Idea' through the network which runs every couple of months. Employees are asked a specific question and they get back on average 2,000 responses. Employees send through their submissions, which are then filtered down and the people who have submitted the best ideas get them implemented as well as winning a prize. Every three months a retail conference of about 1,000 retail store managers and area managers come together to meet, connect, network and hear from senior people within the team. In addition, regular top 100 meetings are hosted where the CEO and executive directors engage with top teams. It's hardly surprising that following the results of M&S's annual 'Your Say' survey with a 94 per cent response rate, the results around employee engagement levels are high. Seventy-four per cent of employees are really engaged against typical external research, which reveals that the average for the retail sector stands at 33 per cent and on the area of trust, there is a scoring of 93 per cent. No one seeks permission to do the right thing. At M&S they just quietly get on with it, making a small difference, that's really invaluable to their employees.

Conclusion

Aligning your engagement goals and strategy to your organizational goals and strategy is critical to ensure engagement adds value to your business. The more clearly you can do this the more buy-in and commitment you will enjoy from your stakeholders. Within this chapter we have introduced the strategy roadmap to help you to clearly articulate your engagement strategy to the business. The following chapters will enable you to add more detail to your engagement strategy, helping you to build a robust plan to improve engagement within your organization.

How it works

Introduction

Employee engagement has come a long way in the past decade. It has moved from a management buzzword to something that is taken seriously in companies, and seen as a critical element of the HRM approach. However, whilst the business case has been well made and we now have a much greater understanding of what we mean by employee engagement, steps taken to actually improve engagement are falling short, not just in the UK but globally.

In the UK, only a third of employees say that they are actively engaged at work, which means that 20 million workers are not delivering their full capability at work or realizing their full potential (D'Analeze *et al*, 2012). Globally the picture is much the same. In their 2012 Global Workforce Study, Towers Watson (2012) reported that just over a third (35 per cent) of 32,000 full-time workers who took part in their research said that they were highly engaged. It seems that despite acceptance and recognition that employee engagement can help to improve organizational performance and create a competitive advantage, many organizations are struggling to actually engage their people.

In this chapter we will seek to understand how and why engagement works, as well as looking at the psychology of engagement: why is it that engaged employees outperform those who are not engaged, and what implications could this have for improving engagement? It's important to understand how engagement works – if we understand the science of engagement we have a much better chance of actually then improving engagement. Employee engagement is not rocket science, so why does it elude so many organizations, and worse still, how is it that some organizations still get it so wrong? In previous chapters we have talked about the difference between transactional and transformational engagement, and the continued focus on the survey as a panacea for improving engagement. This continued obsession with viewing the survey as the 'magic bullet' to improve engagement is part of the problem, and in some cases actually a barrier to improving engagement. We will explore why this is the case here, and what steps could and should be taken to engage your employees.

The (positive) psychology of engagement

Do you ever stop to ask why it is that engaged employees go the extra mile? Why engaged employees work harder, produce better results, are more innovative, ultimately outperform those employees who are not engaged or actively disengaged? Being engaged is a positive state for an individual – it's a good place to be. Think about those times when you were really engaged at work, how you felt, what was going on, and how you remember the experience: those were good times weren't they?

There is much we can learn about how engagement works, and therefore how to engage people, from the positive psychology movement. Positive psychology is a branch of psychology that has been around for about the past 20 years. Positive psychology as a movement within the academia of psychology was born out of Martin Seligman's research on learned helplessness, which in turn led to a focus on learned optimism. In 1998, Seligman was elected President of the American Psychological Association and positive psychology became the theme of his term. Positive psychology does not claim to have discovered the value of a positive approach and thinking, but it helps to understand under what conditions individuals flourish and thrive. And whilst we can debate exactly how we define employee engagement, it is difficult to argue against the idea that engaged employees flourish and thrive. Evolving from areas such as social psychology and humanistic psychology, it is not entirely new, but takes a strengths-based approach, looking to learn from what works, rather than always focusing on what doesn't work and how problems can be fixed. This is a subtle, but significant, shift in the way we approach and think about human behaviour.

Shawn Achor, an educator, speaker and consultant, spent 12 years at Harvard researching what makes people happy. His book, *The Happiness Advantage* (Achor, 2011), describes how happiness at work fuels success and performance – the research also helps to explain why engaged employees outperform others. In his book Shawn talks about the formula for success that many of us have followed throughout our lives.

This encapsulates the way many of us are educated and parented, and certainly the way many of us approach work: 'If I can get a new job, more money, a promotion I'll be happier in my job, and I'll be engaged.' However, what Shawn Achor argues is that this formula is broken: with each victory our goal posts are pushed over the cognitive horizon, and whilst we may experience an initial high from achieving these goals, pretty soon we're moving onto the next one: we never quite reach the place we're trying to

FIGURE 4.1   Focus on the (positive) psychology of engagement

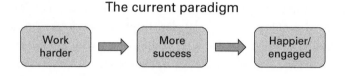

FIGURE 4.2   The happiness advantage

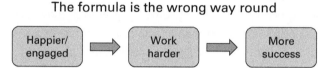

- Being in a positive brain state releases dopamine
- This makes you feel happier
- But it also turns on all your learning centres in your brain

get to. In fact what Shawn argues is that the formula is the wrong way around, and that we need to think about it in the following way (see Figure 4.2).

Advances in positive psychology and neuroscience over the past decade or so have provided a body of evidence to back this up. What we find is that being in a happy or positive state is actually a precursor to success, rather than the result of such success. These findings certainly help to explain why engagement is a lead indicator rather than a lag indicator of performance within organizations. That is if we have an engaged workforce, we see this play out in subsequent business performance and outcomes. In essence, engagement comes first.

And there is a relatively simple, scientific explanation as to why this is the case. When we experience positive emotions, we observe a rise in levels of serotonin and dopamine, which are neurotransmitters: chemicals released by nerve cells to send signals to other nerve cells. These particular chemicals not only make us feel good, but they also enhance the learning centres within our brains. These learning centres help us to organize new information more effectively, retain information for longer, and retrieve information more quickly. They also enable us to make and sustain more neural connections which then allow us to think more quickly and creatively, see things in a different way, improve our problem-solving capability, and analyse complex information more skilfully. To summarize, when we are engaged at work we experience more opportunity for positive emotions, and when we experience these positive emotions the release of associated chemicals enables us to perform at a higher level – engagement leads to better performance.

There is a wealth of evidence to back up these claims. For example, in one study doctors who were primed to be in a positive state before making a diagnosis showed three times more intelligence and creativity than doctors in a neutral, stressed or negative state. They also made accurate diagnoses 19 per cent faster. A team of positive psychologists conducted a meta-analysis to further test this hypothesis, looking at over 200 studies on 275,000 people worldwide. What they found was that in nearly every domain the findings were the same: happiness and positive emotions lead to success.

Obviously, priming employees to be in a positive state before they perform critical tasks each and every time they perform them would be fairly intensive. However, creating a workplace that develops, supports and enhances employee engagement means that there is much higher likelihood of employees experiencing positive states and emotions.

What's interesting is that despite this groundbreaking research, it is still little known or used within the business world. Happiness is often still a dirty word within organizations, with a view that if employees are happy they aren't working hard enough. Despite the business case for engagement, it is still often viewed as 'fluffy' and intangible. This I believe is part of the reason a focus on engagement surveys continues to dominate. The survey provides the illusion of taking engagement from something that is about people and emotions to a place where there are data, numbers and charts, a place where senior leaders within organizations can feel more comfortable and in control. I believe this could be part of the explanation as to why we see such slow progress in engaging people globally, why only a third of employees report that they are actively engaged, and why companies are still not capitalizing on the benefits an engaged workforce can bring about. There are, however, some early adopters, those CEOs who intuitively understand this, one such example being Sir Richard Branson, CEO, Virgin Group, who believes that 'more than any other element, fun is the secret of Virgin's success'.

The implications for improving engagement at work

Within *The Happiness Advantage*, Shawn Achor argues: '[It's] the lens through which your brain views the world that shapes your reality. And if we can change the lens, not only can we change your happiness, we can change every single educational and business outcome at the same time.'

Often when companies go through the survey cycle, they will focus on all of those areas that scored poorly, that is, all of those activities they are not strong in. The lens through which they, and all their employees, are viewing engagement is a *negative* lens, one that points out everything that is currently wrong with the organization. It is little wonder companies are struggling to improve employee engagement when the conversation continually revolves around dissecting the reasons why people *don't* want to work there, or give their best at work. In later chapters we will share a new model and approach to improving employee engagement: a model which focuses on taking a strengths-based approach, one which seeks to define what 'good' looks like, what is happening when people are engaged and then put in place activities to get more of this. This approach is sometimes referred to as an *abundant* approach. It fits well with science and research we have now tapped into from the positive psychology movement, in that we need to seek to understand the conditions under which people flourish at work, the conditions under which they are engaged and build on this knowledge. It is a subtle but significant shift in thinking, backed up by not only academic research but a host of real-life case studies with the kinds of return on investment (ROI) that will make leaders sit up and listen.

Activity
Rewiring your brain

We have more control over our emotional well-being than we realize, and making small changes in our daily lives can have a big impact on how we feel longer term. You can train your brain to be more positive by following the simple steps below for 21 days:

- *Gratitudes*: Each day write down three things you are grateful for. It is easy to get caught up with focusing on everything that has gone wrong, but by consciously focusing on the good parts of our day we are retraining our brains to scan for the positive as well as the negative.

- *Conscious acts of kindness*: Each day do something altruistic. Research shows that people who report carrying out acts of kindness report feeling much happier than a control group and this effect is found to last for days after the exercise has ended.

- *Exercise*: Each day engage in some kind of physical activity, even if it's only popping out for a walk. There is a huge body of evidence that demonstrates exercise not only boosts positive moods, but also reduces stress and anxiety and provides us with mastery experiences – all of which contribute to our well-being.

- *Meditation*: Meditate daily for 10 minutes, or more if you have the time or inclination. Neuroscientists have found that monks that mediate are actually able to grow their left prefrontal cortex, which is the part of the brain associated with feeling happy.

- *Looking forward*: Find something each day to look forward to. Research shows that even just thinking about watching our favourite movie can increase endorphin levels by 27 per cent.

(Achor, 2011)

Have a go at the exercises above for 21 days and keep a journal to record how you feel at the beginning, during and at the end of the exercise. Think about what worked for you and if anything learned from this exercise could be applied to your organization to improve engagement and employee well-being.

Employee engagement: time for a new approach?

When it comes to employee engagement, there seems to be a gap between what science knows and what business does. Often when talking to businesses about engaging their employees, their default position is around the need to pay people more, or reward people more, and a reluctance to do so for a whole host of reasons. The current business paradigm is often built around external, 'carrot-and-stick' motivators; however, the science demonstrates time and again that this often doesn't work. In real life human behaviour is incredibly complex and can be difficult to predict. For every employee that is engaged by winning the company 'star of the month' recognition scheme, there is another that cringes at the thought of public recognition, wishing simply to be thanked personally for a job well done. What engages us as individuals is very personal; what works for one may not work for another, which is part of the reason improvements in engagement can be hard to achieve. Off-the-shelf, set-piece initiatives often miss the mark for many employees, and rely on external, carrot-and-stick-style motivators.

In his book, *Drive*, Dan Pink (2009) argues for a new approach for human capital practices designed to engage and motivate employees. This new approach involves three essential elements:

1 *Autonomy*: The desire to direct our own lives.

2 *Mastery*: The urge to get better and better at something that matters.

3 *Purpose*: The yearning to do what we do in the service of something larger than ourselves.

Pink's persuasive theory on what motivates us – in work, school and in our personal lives – is backed by four decades of solid scientific research on human motivation, and highlights an extreme mismatch between the human capital practices that businesses use and the practices that really work.

Below is a summary of Dan Pink's theory on motivation, from the company Checkside (2012), which looks at how it applies to the business world, and how you can update the human capital practices in your organization so as to have the most motivated and productive employees possible.

Motivation revamped: a summary of Daniel H Pink's new theory of what motivates us

In the early 1900s, the practice of scientific management was born. The brainchild of Frederick Winslow Taylor, scientific management was based on the premise that all work consisted largely of simple, uninteresting tasks, and that the only viable method to get people to undertake these tasks was to incentivize them properly and monitor them carefully.

Put simply, in order to get as much productivity out of your workers as possible, you must reward the behaviour you seek, and punish the behaviour you discourage – otherwise known as the 'carrot-and-stick' approach.

This theory assumes that the main drive that powers human behaviour is the drive to respond to rewards and punishments in our environment. As Pink notes, this suggests 'human beings aren't much different from horses – that the way to get us moving in the right direction is by dangling a crunchier carrot or wielding a sharper stick.'

However, scientists began to encounter situations during their experiments where the reward-punishment drive wasn't producing the expected performance results. This led to the discovery of a possible *third drive* for human behaviour.

The third drive

Scientists have long known that two main drives power human behaviour – the biological drive including hunger, thirst and sex and the reward-punishment drive already discussed. However in 1949, Harry F Harlow, Professor of Psychology at the University of Wisconsin, argued for a third drive – intrinsic motivation – the joy of the task itself.

His theory was based on studies of primate behaviour when solving puzzles. Harlow found that when presented with a puzzle, monkeys seemed to enjoy solving the puzzles without the presence or expectation of rewards. He found these monkeys, driven by intrinsic motivation, solved the puzzles quicker and more accurately than monkeys who received food rewards.

Edward Deci, a university psychology graduate student, went on to replicate these findings with humans in 1969, concluding that human beings have an inherent tendency to seek out novelty and challenges, to extend and exercise their capabilities, to explore, and to learn.

Why the carrot-and-stick approach doesn't always work

Studies such as the ones mentioned previously demonstrated that the carrot-and-stick approach was flawed. It worked well for some tasks, but not others. Why?

The carrot-and-stick approach worked well for typical tasks of the early 20th century – routine, unchallenging and highly controlled. For these tasks, where the process is straightforward and lateral thinking is not required, rewards can provide a small motivational boost without any harmful side effects.

But jobs in the 21st century have changed dramatically. They have become more complex, more interesting and more self-directed, and this is where the carrot-and-stick approach has come unstuck.

Pink demonstrates that with the complex and more creative style of 21st-century jobs, traditional rewards can actually lead to less of what is wanted and more of what is not wanted. He provides ample evidence to support the notion that this traditional approach can result in:

- diminished intrinsic motivation (the third drive);
- lower performance;
- less creativity;

- 'crowding out' of good behaviour;
- unethical behaviour;
- addictions; and
- short-term thinking.

There are a number of studies cited in the book, and it makes for interesting reading if you can spare a few moments to read the book, but let me use one example to illustrate his claim about rewards leading to reduced performance and creativity.

The candle problem

A study was conducted a few decades ago (Pink, 2009), which analysed what happens when people are given conceptual challenges and offered rewards for finding a solution quickly. The exercise presented to the participants was the 'candle problem', as shown in Figure 4.3.

To complete the exercise, participants must attach the candle to the wall so the wax does not drip on the table. The solution to the exercise is demonstrated in Figure 4.4 on page 57.

The key to solving the exercise is to overcome 'functional fixedness'. Participants must see the box as more than a container for the tacks; they must also be able to see its function as a platform for the candle. This task

FIGURE 4.3   The 'candle problem'

FIGURE 4.4   Solution to the 'candle problem'

is neither routine nor algorithmic; it requires a relative amount of creative thinking and problem-solving ability. Participants were split into two groups – one group were told they were being timed in order to collect norms on solution times for the exercise, the other group were offered monetary incentives for completing the exercise quickly.

The results were very interesting. They found that the incentivized group took nearly three and a half minutes *longer* to complete the exercise than the group who were not offered an incentive. Why? Pink suggests, 'rewards, by their very nature, narrow our focus.'

This study further supports the notion that rewards can be effective for routine tasks, but may stifle performance and reduce creativity when tasks demand flexible problem-solving or conceptual thinking.

A new theory of motivation

So, what to do with all this scientific information? Pink proposes that businesses should adopt a revised approach to motivation that fits more closely with modern jobs and businesses, one based on self-determination theory (SDT). SDT proposes that human beings have an innate drive to be autonomous, self-determined and connected to one another, and that when that drive is liberated, people achieve more and live richer lives.

Organizations should focus on these drives when managing their human capital by creating settings which focus on our innate need to direct our own lives (autonomy), to learn and create new things (mastery), and to do better by ourselves and our world (purpose). Here are a few initiatives that fit with Pink's revised motivation theory which will assist your organization to motivate its employees in the correct way:

- *Autonomy*: Provide employees with autonomy over some (or all) of the four main aspects of work:
  - *When they do it (time)*: Consider switching to a ROWE (results-only work environment) that focuses more on the output (result) rather than the time/schedule, allowing employees to have flexibility over when they complete tasks.
  - *How they do it (technique)*: Don't dictate how employees should complete their tasks. Provide initial guidance and then allow them to tackle the project in the way they see fit rather than having to follow a strict procedure.
  - *Whom they do it with (team)*: Although this can be the hardest form of autonomy to embrace, allow employees some choice over whom they work with. If it would be inappropriate to involve them in the recruitment/selection process, instead allow employees to work on open-source projects where they have the ability to assemble their own teams.
  - *What they do (task)*: Allow employees to have regular 'creative' days where they can work on any project/problem they wish – there is empirical evidence which shows that many new initiatives are often generated during this 'creative free time'.
- *Mastery*: Allow employees to become better at something that matters to them:
  - Provide 'Goldilocks tasks': Pink uses the term 'Goldilocks tasks' to describe those tasks which are neither overly difficult nor overly simple – these tasks allow employees to extend themselves and develop their skills further. The risk of providing tasks that fall short of an employee's capabilities is boredom, and the risk of providing tasks that exceed their capabilities is anxiety.
  - Create an environment where mastery is possible: To foster an environment of learning and development, four essentials are required: autonomy, clear goals, immediate feedback and Goldilocks tasks.

- *Purpose*: Take steps to fulfil employees' natural desire to contribute to a cause greater and more enduring than themselves:
  - *Communicate the purpose*: Make sure employees know and understand the organization's purpose goals, not just its profit goals. Employees who understand the purpose and vision of their organization and how their individual roles contribute to this purpose are more likely to be satisfied in their work.
  - *Place equal emphasis on purpose maximization as you do on profit maximization*: Research shows that the attainment of profit goals has no impact on a person's well-being. Organizational and individual goals should focus on purpose as well as profit. Many successful companies are now using profit as the catalyst to pursuing purpose, rather than the objective.
  - *Use purpose-oriented words*: Talk about the organization as a united team by using words such as 'us' and 'we': this will inspire employees to talk about the organization in the same way and feel a part of the greater cause.

Over the last few years we have seen an increased focus on the notion of purpose within organizations. Chris Crofts, Global Employee Engagement Director at Diageo, talks about why we need a purpose uprising and shares her practical tips to develop a compelling purpose.

Why we need a 'purpose uprising'
By Chris Crofts

Chris is currently the Global Employee Engagement Director at Diageo, the beverage company that owns brands such as Guinness, Johnnie Walker, Smirnoff and Baileys.

Chris has a personal and professional passion for 'Purpose' and has published and spoken about the topic and the important role Internal Communications can play in creating purpose-driven organizations. She shares her views and top tips to create 'Purpose' below.

Talk about purposeful companies is everywhere. A Google search of 'purposeful companies' reveals more than 96 million results (that's more than Harry Potter and Donald Trump combined!). In January 2018, Larry Fink, CEO of Blackrock, one of the largest investment companies in the world, wrote to every CEO in the FTSE 100 and S&P 500 saying:

> Without a sense of purpose, no company, either public or private, can achieve its full potential. ...To prosper over time, every company must not only deliver financial performance, but also show how it makes a positive contribution to society. Companies must benefit all of their stakeholders, including shareholders, employees, customers, and the communities in which they operate.
>
> (Blackrock, 2018)

Never before has there been so much talk of purpose amongst world leaders, business leaders and broader society. But why now? Purpose is not a new concept and certainly the marketing community has been talking about purposeful brands for decades.

What is emerging now is a multidimensional sense of purpose. It's not just about what a company does for customers anymore. It's about the difference the company makes in the world, in society, for its employees, customers and shareholders. Today's concept of purpose is much more humanistic and broader than it's ever been.

Academics, consultants and business schools have discussed many reasons for this. First, society is changing. As more and more countries reach higher levels of development, so they move through Maslow's hierarchy of needs, approaching the pinnacle of Maslow's pyramid – 'self-actualization' and we see a shift from 'material want' to 'meaning want'. This is also a result of the ageing population, and reflects that the older you get, the more meaning you seek in life, and you become less interested in material wealth. For the first time ever there are now more adults over the age of 45 than under. Think of the impact that is having on our global society.

But it's not just about the older generation's shifting expectations. The younger generations, certainly in mature markets, mostly get whatever they want, instantly. Obtaining material things no longer gives them the same satisfaction. As they begin to join the workforce, they are demanding greater meaning from their work and lives. They want a strong sense of purpose.

> A transition from 'material want' to 'meaning want' is in progress on a historically unprecedented scale – involving hundreds of millions of people – and may be eventually recognised as the principle cultural development of our age.
>
> (Gregg Easterbrook, 2003)

Lastly, the business world is on the brink of another revolution. We've heard how VUCA (volatile, uncertain, complex and ambiguous) is disrupting every industry and the pressure to address the productivity gap is immense. Only the agile, innovative, customer-centric and highly productive will survive. And this is where a greater sense of purpose comes in. Organizations – and their boards in particular – are beginning to realize that a strong sense of purpose can actually build greater resilience, innovation and super charge engagement and productivity. Study after study confirms it and if you're interested in finding out more, visit EY's Beacon Institute (http://www.ey.com/gl/en/issues/ey-beacon-institute).

What makes a compelling purpose these days?

I've briefly mentioned that the modern concept of organizational purpose is multidimensional and humanistic. But what does that really mean? It means that your purpose should:

- aspire to make something about the world or society better;
- inspire a call to action;
- create value for employees;
- maximize shareholder value;
- bring value to customers.

A compelling articulation of the above should evoke an emotional connection to your brand.

An example of such a purpose is Whole Foods, recently bought by Amazon for US $13.7 billion:

> With great courage, integrity and love – we embrace our responsibility to co-create a world where each of us, our communities and our planet can flourish. All the while, celebrating the sheer love and joy of food.
>
> (Whole Foods, 2018)

Much is written about this successful organization but if you read their annual report and accounts or visit their website, you will get a strong sense that it is indeed driven by a strong sense of purpose. In their 2012 annual report, Whole Foods Co CEO John Mackey, said:

> We believe that much of our success to date is because we remain a uniquely mission-driven company.
>
> (Whole Foods, 2012)

If purpose is so great, why isn't everybody using it?

In a *Harvard Business Review* paper entitled 'The Business Case for Purpose', a great question is raised. If almost all the CEOs and executives HBR interviewed said that purpose would improve employee satisfaction and success of transformation efforts, what is stopping them? The research found one key differentiator between those who had embedded purpose and those who hadn't: poor leadership communication was preventing them from 'activating' purpose in their organizations.

Top tips to develop purpose

So you now know that most CEOs are thinking about this, and maybe you already know this because you're already working on the purpose of your organization. At a recent conference I asked the question, 'How many of you are currently working on refreshing or creating a new purpose for your company?' and over 50 per cent of the audience put their hands up.

How? Here are my five top tips:

1 Step up and *own the 'purpose opportunity'* in your organization. Initiate the conversation with your CEO. Spend time thinking about your own purpose and values and then work on your teams'.

2 Help *articulate the company's purpose* – make it compelling, positive and customer-focused.

3 *Communicate it* awesomely. And keep doing it.

4 Develop ways to help leaders inspire through purpose. Provide them with *tools and opportunities to talk to their teams* about their own purpose and values and how they connect to their organization's values. And continue this by proving regular hooks for them to keep the conversation alive (this shouldn't feel like a campaign).

5 Work closely with marketing and PR to *align purposeful messages externally and internally.* Employees feel the organization's purpose everywhere, in their dealing with managers, in the advertising they see, and in how the media talks about the company.

In summary, I'd say that purpose is not going to go away, it is only going to be amplified – by our employees, by our customers, by society and increasingly by mainstream investors. Like it or not, your organization will at some point in the future, if it isn't already, be thinking about how it can be more purposeful. And if it isn't, then perhaps you should start the conversation!

The notion of increasing employee satisfaction through the intrinsic motivational methods of autonomy, mastery and purpose has obvious implications for remuneration models and incentive schemes traditionally used by organizations.

I highly recommend reading Pink's book to get a more thorough understanding of his theory of motivation. If you're more visually inclined, there is a 10-minute visual depiction of Pink's theory (also entitled *Drive*) on YouTube.

The enablers of employee engagement

In the original Engage for Success report, David MacLeod and Nita Clarke (2009) detailed what they believe to be the four enablers of employee engagement. Although there is no 'one-size-fits-all' approach and no master model for successful employee engagement, there were four common themes that emerged from the extensive research captured in the Engaging for Success report to government. Taken together, they include many of the key elements that go to make successful employee engagement. These four enablers of engagement provide a useful framework, which helps organizations assess the effectiveness of their approach to engagement:

1 Visible, empowering leadership that provides a *strong strategic narrative* about the organization – where it's come from and where it's going.

2 *Engaging managers*, who focus their people and give them scope, treat their people as individuals and coach and stretch their people.

3 There is *employee voice* throughout the organizations, for reinforcing and challenging views, between functions and externally; employees are seen as central to the solution.

4 There is organizational *integrity*: The values on the wall are reflected in day-to-day behaviours. There is no 'say–do' gap.

There is a further enabler of engagement, which I would recommend adding to this list:

5 *Employee involvement*, that is, the extent to which employees are personally involved in the success of the business, and the opportunities the organization creates for employees to get involved with their company.

In the next chapter, we will explore these enablers and others, to understand how to improve and drive engagement. However, it is useful to consider them within the context of the evidence discussed within this chapter, looking at why engagement works. Many of the enablers link directly to the psychological evidence discussed here.

Dan Pink's work talks about the importance of purpose, which clearly links to the strategic narrative enabler mentioned above. In the blog below, from Julian Burton of Delta 7 Consulting (2013), it is easy to see how a strong purpose, or strategic narrative, is capable of contributing towards engaging employees in the work of an organization.

What makes a strategic narrative compelling?

'I'm putting a man on the moon!'

We all know this Kennedy anecdote: JFK was touring NASA in the 1960s and stopped to ask a guy sweeping the floor what he was doing. His answer? I'm helping to put a man on the moon. But what was it that made these employees proud of their contribution and inspired to play their part?

In 1961 Kennedy told the world that the USA would put a man on the moon and bring him home back safely by the end of the decade. Somehow this compelling story inspired people to act to overcome the impossible by giving them a clear vision and a sense of their role achieving it.

A compelling strategic story is an opportunity for the leader to show that they understand what their people really care about and how they can play their part shaping a future that they want.

We've found that for a story to be compelling it needs to be:

- meaningful to those hearing it;

- about something people care about;

- exciting, dramatic and inspiring;

- believable (no matter how audacious it is!).

How compelling is your company's strategic narrative?

A strong purpose motive also links to the integrity of an organization. Dan Pink argues that when the purpose motive of the organization becomes detached from reality bad things happen; there is a lack of integrity. This then negatively impacts the way employees feel about working for a company: they become disengaged. Mats Lederhausen, investor and former McDonald's executive, puts it succinctly: 'I believe whole-heartedly that a new form of capitalism is emerging... more stakeholders, customers, employees, shareholders and the larger communities want their businesses to have a purpose bigger than their product.'

When we consider autonomy and mastery experiences, it is easy to see that they are more likely to happen in an organization that fosters employee involvement and gives people a voice. In addition, organizations with good leadership are much more likely to provide opportunities for autonomy and mastery. If autonomy is about being more self-directed, not having things done to you, and having the opportunity to co-create, then clearly a manager who supports this mode of working, gets out of your way and actively provides opportunities for you to get involved, is going to facilitate this. There are a number of ways employees can have autonomy over elements of their work, such as task, time, team and technique. Even in highly regimented and structured organizations, I have observed positive changes to a team's engagement simply by passing the job of organizing the rota and shifts to the team: that is, involving them in this activity, giving them a voice, providing greater autonomy and contributing positively to the way they felt about working for the company. Being involved means having the opportunity to contribute, to have your say, to co-create solutions; it means not having things done *to* you. When you are involved, whether at a micro-level, within your day-to-day role, or with your team, or at a macro-level contributing to the bigger picture, you have the opportunity to exercise more autonomy.

Mastery relates to the desire to get better and better at something. For over 10 years I have been capturing stories of peak experiences, literally hundreds. Whilst there are always differences in the stories people tell about what engages them, there are also a number of themes which come out time and again. One such theme is *mastery*: people nearly always report that they felt really engaged when the situation required some type of mastery, when it was challenging and difficult and there was effort required to get better at something, and overcome problems. Again a good manager provides opportunities for employees to have mastery experiences. Involving employees also contributes towards mastery experiences, allowing employees to get involved in bigger projects, areas that are new to them or maybe outside of their comfort zone: they will all contribute towards increased engagement.

CASE STUDY   Taking a strengths-based approach to improving employee engagement

This insurance company had been in a period of immense change aimed at turning the business around. The performance of the company had been steadily improving, with the share price rising and the focus moving to achieving sustainable growth. However, the company suffered from many of the same issues prevalent in customer contact centres across the UK: high levels of employee attrition, above-average absenteeism, problems recruiting the right people and low morale. The company recognized that to achieve their growth ambitions they needed to transform their contact centres into great places to work. The challenge was to increase employee engagement, which would be measured via lower attrition and absenteeism and increased engagement scores and essentially create a great place to work.

The solution

Previous attempts to address these issues had been unsuccessful. It was recognized that a different approach was needed, one which had not been created by senior leaders in an 'ivory tower'. Employees needed to volunteer themselves in the changes, and the way to achieve this was via an approach that would involve employees to help ensure changes were sustainable.

The significant difference this time, however, was the decision to take a strengths-based approach to improving employee engagement. Previous attempts had failed and the company knew it needed to try something else. The starting point this time was to begin by having conversations with employees about what good engagement looked like. The project team wanted to understand the conditions under which employees felt really engaged, and understand how to create more of these experiences. Using an activity similar to the 'peak experience' activity detailed in Chapter 1, these conversations began to take place across the company.

It began with a two-day mobilization workshop, which involved 25 represent-atives who would become 'Great Place to Work' (GPTW) ambassadors. These reps were carefully recruited to ensure they had the right attitude and potential to lead this piece of work. The workshop set out the rationale of the programme. Over two days attendees were involved in designing a programme of activity that would contribute towards creating a great place to work. The workshop took a strengths-based approach and involved reps in having peak experience conversations. The reps felt the workshop process itself was a very engaging experience and that others within the company should have the opportunity to go through a similar experience. They therefore designed the ongoing programme around a series of face-to-face workshops.

Then followed a series of workshops aimed at leaders, which were facilitated by the representatives. These workshops asked participants what makes a great place to work and what values were important, using an innovative card-sorting exercise. Leaders were also asked what role they could play in making the changes happen. Leaders then delivered workshops to their teams, whereby they were also asked what makes a great place to work, what values were important to them and the role that they could play. This face-to-face dialogue was a vital part of the process of engaging employees. Time was spent really listening to their thoughts and ideas, giving them an opportunity to be involved in the change and contribute to the solutions. The process was not outsourced to HR or internal communications but was owned and delivered by leaders themselves, which ensured dialogue was established. Support functions, for the first time, played a genuinely supporting role, behind the scenes partnering with leaders to ensure the workshops were a success. They were not the face of change – as had happened previously. The outputs from all of the workshops were collated and fed back to staff through a variety of channels.

A second workshop was then held for all staff, delivered by leaders, communicating the findings from the first workshops, and participants were asked to get involved with action planning, to come up with ideas to tackle the issues raised. A full communication plan was designed to ensure dialogue was established throughout the programme. This included a dedicated intranet site, a local newsletter written by site representatives to update employees on progress, and a DVD to communicate progress and showcase the initiatives each area was undertaking. Different areas were also asked to nominate colleagues from their sites as their 'Face of Great Place To Work'. The winning entries then enjoyed a makeover and photo session in London. Following this their photos were used to relaunch the look and feel of Great Place To Work, and included posters, intranet sites and other materials.

To ensure ongoing involvement and sustainability of the programme, frontline staff were identified to act as 'champions'. They facilitated local action groups and a two-day course was delivered to empower them to drive change at their centres. In addition a fun and thought-provoking session with leaders challenged them to look at how they recognize people in their teams. During the session, case studies of real employees were looked at to see if they really knew how to hit the right note when saying 'well done'.

The outcomes

Results demonstrated the success of the overall programme. Ninety-five per cent rated the workshops as good or very good, with 100 per cent understanding why the programme was happening and 99 per cent understanding the contribution they could make. However, the most compelling evidence for the success of the programme was the sheer volume of activity that took place at local sites. For the first time, employees were driving changes to make this company a great place to work.

Increases in engagement survey scores were seen across the board and crucially attrition decreased by 19 per cent within a year of the programme commencing.

Conclusion

This chapter has attempted to share some of the psychology of employee engagement, to explain why it is that engaged employees should outperform disengaged employees. Understanding the science helps practitioners in a number of ways. First, the science moves employee engagement from a 'fluffy' intangible, nice-to-have discipline, into a scientifically proven 'must-have' for any organization that wants to create a difficult-to-replicate competitive advantage. The science is helpful when talking to stakeholders who deal in hard facts and figures and are more likely to listen to this type of argument. Second, understanding the science behind engagement enables us to more effectively impact and improve employee engagement. If we understand why it is that engaged employees outperform others, and what we need to focus on, we are better prepared to make a difference. For example, we know that giving employees a voice and involving them helps to facilitate autonomy and mastery experiences. Finally, we have a duty as practitioners to share the research and the science to help reduce the engagement deficit that exists globally. Many current people management practices are based on outdated science or even unproven theories. If we can champion these new ways of working, focus on taking a strengths-based approach, move past the carrot-and-the-stick approach, then we can start to make a real step change in the engagement of our people worldwide.

05 **Employee engagement**

How do you do it?

Introduction

In the previous chapter we looked at why engaged employees can create a competitive advantage, understanding why it is that engaged employees outperform others. In this chapter we will take a look at how to improve engagement. We'll examine how the science of engagement translates into practical application, outlining the ways in which engagement can be improved within the workplace. In order to do this we will focus on the enablers of engagement:

- leadership;
- strategic narrative;
- employee voice;
- integrity;
- involvement.

The enablers are not separate and distinct from each other, they don't operate in isolation from one another; they are interrelated and co-dependent to some degree. For example, a compelling strategic narrative is needed to give employees purpose and meaning, but equally managers then need to live and breathe that narrative, role-model and communicate it, which links to the leadership and integrity enablers. In addition, providing opportunities for employees to craft their roles to align with their strengths, values and interests not only contributes to them finding meaning at work, but also gives employees a voice and involves them in the organization.

Throughout this chapter we'll share case studies which show how organizations have successfully focused on these enablers to demonstrably improve employee engagement, as well as providing ideas, tips and activities to help you improve engagement within your own organization.

Activity

The employee engagement health check

The following questions have been put together to stimulate your thoughts on employee engagement within your organization. This is a simple diagnostic to help you evaluate your current employee engagement activity against each of the enablers: leadership; strategic narrative; employee voice; integrity; and involvement. It's not science but hopefully it will help you to think about where you currently focus your attention and identify any gaps to inform your future plans.

Thinking about your own organization, please review the following statements and score them in the following ways:

Strongly disagree – 1;

Disagree – 2;

Agree – 3;

Strongly agree – 4.

For each of the enablers add up your scores to understand those areas of high performance and those areas which need focus to develop. You can add in further questions if required and change questions to better suit your organization. For each enabler, score as follows:

 5–10 = low score: area for immediate action;

10–15 = average score: monitor progress;

15–20 = high score: best practice area.

Leadership:

- Managers here really listen to you.
- My manager knows me as a person.
- I feel supported by my manager.
- My manager makes sure I know what is going on within the company.
- My manager has a good relationship with our team.

Strategic narrative:

- I understand the direction of the company.
- I know how my work contributes towards the company goals.

- I am inspired by our company vision.
- There is clear communication about where we are heading as a company.
- I believe in the direction of the company.

Employee voice:

- It's easy to make my voice heard here.
- My thoughts and opinions are actively sought.
- We get feedback when asked for our opinions.
- There are lots of opportunities here to make my voice heard.
- My thoughts and opinions are valued.

Integrity:

- I trust managers here to do the right thing.
- Decisions are made in line with our values.
- I see behaviours in our management community that are in line with our values.
- Employees are trusted to do the right thing.
- I believe that managers and leaders will follow through on promises made.

Involvement:

- I have the opportunity to contribute towards projects or initiatives that impact me.
- Employee ideas are acted upon.
- I am actively encouraged to get involved with different aspects of our business.
- Employees are given credit for their ideas and involvement with the organization.
- I have an input, where relevant, into decisions affecting me within the organization.

Leadership and line managers

There is no doubt that the capability of leaders and managers to engage their teams is critical to employee engagement. It's often said that people join companies but leave managers. Managers can make or break the employee experience within the workplace. The CIPD *Managing for Sustainable Employee Engagement* report (Lewis *et al*, 2012) highlighted line managers as one of the most important influences on employee engagement. Whilst practitioner reports have cited line managers as critical for an engaged workforce, until recently, the academic literature supporting this assertion has lagged behind in providing evidence.

One recent study, which is worth a mention, looks at the effects of a transformational leadership style on employee engagement. Tims *et al* (2011) researched the ways in which line managers' leadership style influences engagement. They analysed the diaries of 42 employees over five days to test their hypothesis. The findings from their research indicated that daily transformational leadership related positively to employees' daily engagement, and further investigation highlighted that it was in fact the optimism of leaders that mediated this relationship. So an optimistic leadership style, in this case, had an impact on the engagement of employees.

In other studies the impact of authentic leadership has been found to impact employee engagement. Authentic leadership was defined by Walumbwa *et al* (2010) as:

> a pattern of leader behavior that draws upon and promotes both positive psychological capacities and a positive ethical climate, to foster greater self-awareness, an internalized moral perspective, balanced processing of information, and relational transparency on the part of leaders working with followers, fostering positive self-development.

In their 2011 study, Walumbwa *et al* (2010) found that authentic leadership behaviours were positively related to employee engagement.

One further study conducted by Xu *et al* (2011) looked at how leaders can achieve high employee engagement with their teams. In their study they set out to investigate the link between leader behaviours and subsequent employees' engagement levels. Using a 360-degree feedback instrument, they uncovered three specific leadership behaviours that predicted employee engagement:

- supports the team;
- performs effectively;
- displays integrity.

Further analysis revealed that 'supports the team' was the strongest predictor of subsequent engagement. The evidence that supports the link between line manager behaviours and employee engagement is growing, but what are the practical implications? How can we effectively support line managers to foster engagement with their teams?

In 2011 the CIPD conducted research to identify specific management behaviours that are important for sustainable employee engagement (CIPD 2011). This research identified competencies, which are detailed below.

TABLE 5.1   Summary of the 'Managing for sustainable employee engagement' framework

Competency	Brief description
Open, fair and consistent	Managing with integrity and consistency, managing emotions/personal issues and taking a positive approach in interpersonal interactions
Handling conflict and problems	Dealing with employee conflicts (including bullying and abuse) and using appropriate organizational resources
Knowledge, clarity and guidance	Clear communication, advice and guidance, demonstrating understanding of roles and responsible decision-making
Building and sustaining relationships	Personal interaction with employees involving empathy and consideration
Supporting development	Supporting and arranging employee career progression and development

When considering how to support line managers and leaders in driving engagement within your workplace the 'managing for sustainable employee engagement' framework is a good place to start. Competencies such as these can be used in a number of ways to facilitate the behaviour changes required for managers to develop and improve engagement within their teams. The framework could be integrated into your management development offering, or used as part of a 360-degree feedback process if you have one. In addition the framework and associated competencies could be used within your performance management and appraisal systems, helping not only to communicate the desired behaviours, but also to reinforce the value of demonstrating them. Selection and promotion are further areas within which the competency framework could be used. Managers who are seen to role-model these behaviours could be promoted. Also, competency-based questions could be developed in line with the framework to assist recruiting managers who either have these skills already or have the potential to develop them.

Perhaps the most useful element of the framework, though, is the ability to articulate clearly to managers what 'good' looks like. As discussed in Chapter 1, the definitions of engagement are varied and wide. Therefore, to task a manager to engage their teams can feel somewhat abstract and intangible. By communicating the competency framework, managers are able to understand the behaviours and competencies they need to in order to help to engage their teams, thus making engagement much more concrete and tangible.

Activity

Evaluating managers' engagement competencies

The *Managing for Sustainable Employee Engagement* framework identifies which behaviours are helpful for a manager to engage their teams (Lewis *et al*, 2012). You can use the questionnaire below to assess the engagement competencies of your managers, helping them to understand what they already do well, what they need to do more of and what they need to do less of or stop doing altogether. The questionnaire can be used in a variety of ways:

- as a stand-alone 360-degree review;
- as part of your current 360-degree review process;
- self-assessment;
- as part of your selection process;
- pre-work for management development training.

Questionnaire

1 *Open, fair and consistent:*
  - is not overly critical of me or other team members;
  - does not blame me or other team members for decisions taken;
  - does not focus on mistakes;
  - demonstrates faith in my capability;
  - consults with me rather than tells me what to do;
  - allows decisions to be challenged;

- uses humour and sarcasm appropriately;
- does not show favouritism; never talks about team members behind their backs;
- does not criticize me and other team members in front of others;
- treats me with respect;
- is predictable in mood;
- acts calmly in pressured situations;
- does not pass on his/her stress to me;
- is consistent in his/her approach to managing;
- is calm about deadlines;
- seems to give more positive feedback than negative feedback.

2 Handling conflict and problems:
- acts as a mediator in conflict situations;
- deals with squabbles before they turn into arguments;
- deals objectively with employee conflicts;
- deals with employee conflicts head on;
- uses HR as a resource to help deal with problems;
- seeks help from occupational health when necessary;
- follows up conflicts after resolution;
- supports employees through incidents of abuse;
- addresses bullying;
- makes it clear he/she will take ultimate responsibility if things go wrong.

3 Knowledge, clarity and guidance:
- gives advice when required;
- takes responsibility for problem-solving to senior management;
- gives specific rather than vague advice;
- clarifies role requirements and expectations;
- is clear of their own role requirements;
- demonstrates a good understanding of the role I do;
- communicates whether I am on track or not;
- gives adequate time for planning;
- demonstrates understanding of processes and procedures;

– follows up on action points;

– always has time for me;

– is decisive.

4 **Building and sustaining relationships:**

– shows interest in my personal life;

– checks I am feeling okay;

– shows understanding of the pressures I am under;

– provides regular opportunities to speak one-to-one;

– brings in treats;

– socializes with the team;

– is willing to have a laugh at work;

– takes an interest in my life outside of work;

– regularly asks, 'How are you?'.

5 **Supporting development:**

– takes time to discuss my career development;

– actively supports my career development;

– offers opportunities for career development;

– plans or arranges time off/out for career development opportunities;

– arranges development activities.

Activity

How to become a more engaging manager

The Engage for Success movement has published this helpful guide on how to become a more engaging manager. You can use these 20 hints and tips with your own managers in a variety of ways:

- on-boarding;
- leadership development;
- online toolkits for managers;
- self-assessment.

1   *Welcome new employees*: Send new employees a welcome pack containing a letter from you welcoming them, and introductory information about the business, including brochure or other marketing materials, your strategic narrative, any sports or social clubs or any other workplace benefits. Include specific information about their role, including their job description, an organization chart, any material about the team they will join and logistical information, for example location maps, canteen information.

2   *Get to know individual employees*: If a manager knows and understands an employee as an individual, they will be better able to motivate them. This could be done through making time for informal discussions outside work discussions, for example catch-ups over coffee or at social events, and regularly visiting or holding conference calls with any employees based in different locations or satellite sites. By making sure you are in contact they will know they are involved and supported.

3   *Communicate with employees*: Managers need to communicate with employees and give them the chance to share their views and to contribute to defining the business's goals. You could consider holding regular business update meetings with a set date, time, location and agenda to brief employees on business developments, answer their questions and discuss team objectives and activities. Hold regular team Q&A sessions during which employees can come and talk to you about any issues or ideas, for example at lunchtime discussions or surgery sessions.

4   *Focus and support employees*: The way managers shape the roles of employees and oversee their work has a huge effect on individual well-being, commitment and performance. To help support employees you could consider discussing job design and responsibilities with employees. Employees who have input into shaping their work are far more engaged than those who are simply given tasks to get on with. Create compelling objectives linked to business goals so employees understand how their work and performance directly contribute to the strategy.

5   *Coach and develop employees*: Managers need to help employees identify solutions to issues they encounter so they keep developing their skills and confidence and have clear development paths. Create personal development plans for each team member. Make sure these

plans have clear links with individual roles, team activities and corporate goals. Give employees the opportunity to try new areas of work and develop new skills in line with this plan. Open discussions about goals and encourage team members to be open about their ambitions. By doing so you can help them feel their ambitions are compatible with the business.

6   *Handle feedback from employees*: Respond to feedback received by acknowledging suggestions or concerns, explaining your view (whether you agree or not) and involving employees in developing actions to address emerging issues. Talk to individual employees on a regular basis to check their understanding of objectives or key issues and invite them to raise any questions or concerns they haven't discussed. Respond regularly and honestly to employee feedback, taking action on issues identified and sharing the steps you are taking so that employees know that their voices are being heard.

7   *Recognize employee performance*: To help motivate employees you need to show genuine appreciation for good work and recognize the improvements they make. Here are some steps you could take:

   – Say thank you – It is a powerful way of recognizing someone's contribution.

   – Use internal publications, a note round the team or a poster to celebrate an individual's success and to show employees their commitment and effort are appreciated.

   – If you have an intranet, create a bulletin board or forum so employees can thank colleagues for their efforts and help with key issues.

   – Give spot rewards for specific contributions or tasks where employees have exceeded all expectations.

   – Establish an award scheme so employees can nominate colleagues for their work.

   – Host social events when you achieve key milestones or targets to thank your team for their work.

   – Hold celebrations for employees' personal milestones or significant life events.

8   *Improve your performance as a manager*: Engaging managers keep improving their own performance by seeking views and feedback from the people they work with. Ask your team members for their views on your management style and effectiveness. For example, ensure

evaluation forms or cards are always available after any briefings or presentations you have given. Approach your own manager. Managers should proactively ask their manager for feedback against their objectives. You could also use a 360-degree feedback approach so that formal reviews include feedback from team members.

9 *Engage employees more fully – joint problem solving*: Regularly ask team members, 'What do you think?' to draw solutions out of them rather than solving problems for them; engaging people's brains, not doing their thinking for them. This activity will create a greater feeling of involvement in deciding what should be done, first in the employee's own job and second with respect to larger strategic issues facing the manager. The aim of asking employees for input is to foster greater shared ownership rather than simply directing them.

10 *Engage employees more fully – participative planning*: Involve team members in operational, strategic and change planning. Fostering shared ownership rather than doing their own planning and viewing team members as just implementers. Once again, this activity promotes employee involvement which results in greater shared ownership.

11 *Engage employees more fully – managing people*: Show that they value team member contributions; celebrating success, providing regular feedback, inspiring and empowering team members. Managers must reach out to employees to foster a sense of belongingness and a feeling that there is a future for them in the organization. These actions create a culture where employees feel valued.

12 *Communication*: Communicate openly, fully and regularly to keep team members informed so they have a sense of purpose and show initiative with confidence. Managers must reach out to employees to foster a sense of belonging and a feeling that there is a future for them in the organization. These actions create a culture where employees feel valued.

13 *Developing people*: Proactively develop, encourage and coach team members to make them feel valued and important to the team's success.

14 *Engage employees more fully – approachability and fairness*: Be approachable, open to challenges, putting team members at ease and treating them fairly to help them feel confident and valued. Providing a safe environment where employees feel free to express themselves in the knowledge that managers are not going to jump on them, treat them unfairly or over-react emotionally when their views are challenged.

15 *Engage employees more fully – relationship-building*: Foster teamwork and supportive relationships, helping team members get to know each other and connecting them with valuable colleagues; cultivating a sense of belonging and self-worth. As before, managers must reach out to employees to foster a sense of belonging and a feeling that there is a future for them in the organization, thereby creating a culture where employees feel valued.

16 *Engage employees more fully – morale and resilience*: Maintain morale and resilience under pressure, helping to relieve stress in their teams while maintaining a positive outlook despite setbacks and obstacles, so team members feel positive about coming to work and doing their best. Again, the provision of a safe environment is key, so that employees feel free to express themselves without fear of negative repercussions from management.

17 *Make yourself accessible to the front line*: Make sure you have the support to be able to reply promptly and authoritatively.

18 *Engaging managers' employee survey*: There is no set format for an employee survey. This guidance sets out best practice examples for creating an employee survey that you can tailor to suit your business needs.

19 *Everyday coaching and informal opportunities*: Encourage team members to discuss challenges they encounter so you can help them understand the issues and decide on a course of action. Create on-the-job development opportunities, for example shadowing employees in different roles or working alongside colleagues in other teams. This can help people understand more about those roles and improve their interaction.

20 *Mentors or personal managers*: Give employees career mentors to help share experiences and encourage their development. This could be someone who joined in the same position a few years ago. You could also consider introducing a personal management system to provide care and support.

TABLE 5.2   Engaging managers employee survey

	Strongly agree	Agree	Disagree	Strongly disagree
I have clear objectives				
I understand what is expected of me				
I have the information I need to do my job				
My manager treats me as an individual				
My manager cares about me as a person				
I find my work motivating and challenging				
I have a clear role within my team				
I tend to do work that plays to my strengths				
I have the guidance and support I need to do my job				
I am trusted to do a good job				
I am encouraged to learn from mistakes				
My manager gives me opportunities to grow/ develop				
I receive regular praise for good work				
I receive direct/timely feedback on my performance				

CASE STUDY Lancashire County Council

Engaging Managers at Lancashire County Council: published with kind permission from Engage for Success

Background

Like many public sector organizations in early 2010, Lancashire County Council (LCC) found itself at the mercy of the forthcoming critical spending review (CSR). The financial crisis inevitably made this likely to be the most challenging budgetary reduction the public sector had ever faced. LCC knew it could be looking at cuts of up to 25 per cent over a three-year period.

Given the magnitude of these changes, the director of resources at LCC, Phil Halsall, became acutely concerned at the impact they could have on morale and future effectiveness of the authority. He argued that the traditional approach of top-down dictated actions (the so-called slash and burn approach) on such a scale would alienate the workforce so acutely that the council would struggle way beyond the timetable of simply taking the necessary cost out of the business.

Accordingly a plan was drawn up to address the challenges of the CSR through a process of employee engagement, which became known as *The Lancashire Way*. Here, instead of presenting the workforce with a detailed description of what was going to happen over the three-year period, the council simply outlined the financial challenge and sought to involve each area in finding their own solutions. All employees were invited to contribute.

Designing a means to tackle these huge reductions was never going to be easy. The council, like most big organizations, already had a track record of continuous change programmes over many years and had not been too successful. Employees, and many in management alike, were acutely cynical of new initiatives and not likely to respond favourably to yet another one in such a difficult situation. Morale was already compromised by a massive equal pay review. Despite there being many more winners than losers, the reaction was generally negative as pay reviews are wont to be.

Two decisions were made which characterized Lancashire's approach to employee engagement:

- Firstly it was recognized that the prime movers in any culture change programme had to be management themselves. In any organization, management past and present are the major contributors to the prevailing culture. In a large public authority this was certainly likely to be true. There seemed therefore to be major dangers in going to the workforce and promising change without fully understanding how to get the full management team, from the CEO to the most junior supervisor, to deliver it.

The first decision was therefore to focus immediately on changing the general managerial paradigm in the authority to one that put people management at the heart of what they did, 24/7. The traditional technocratic approach had to migrate to one based on a chain of activities from simple motivational skills at one end to a suite of increasingly sophisticated continuous improvement techniques at the other.

This sounds simple but in practice this had to be done reasonably quickly across an organization of some 20,000 employees, excluding those employed in the delivery of education. The range and complexity of the services delivered by the council were also unhelpfully huge.

The intention was, without formally announcing the change to the workforce at large, to progressively introduce a more people-centric philosophy across all in management. Employees would hopefully gradually experience a more positive improvement in the working ambience around them. This would be far healthier and less risky than banging a big drum about the brave new world coming towards them, and then in all probability losing credibility as the change emerged too slowly to match expectations.

- The second major decision was to consciously avoid presenting The Lancashire Way to the management group as any form of structured initiative. It had to be seen as a basic shift in philosophy where the general mindset of management had to change. This was simply 'the way we do business around here now', placing employee motivation and personal accountability at the heart of the LCC manager, irrespective of seniority or status.

Whilst it was intended to provide an extensive support infrastructure to managers so that they understood the requirements of the new way, the principal driver of behavioural change was to be self-development through self-realization.

Process

There have been six discrete elements to The Lancashire Way:

- educating and convincing management;
- self-realization through management style questionnaires and peer reviews;
- simple values/behavioural sets;
- extensive recognition processes;
- improved communication channels;
- continuous improvement.

Educating and convincing management

A comprehensive series of workshops was organized to introduce the top 500 managers to the concept of employee engagement and The Lancashire Way. Some 400 copies of *Growing Your Own Heroes* (Oliver and Memmott, 2012) were issued to ensure a consistent understanding and implementation. Extensive use was made of the MacLeod report (MacLeod and Clarke, 2009) with all managers encouraged to access the report electronically. Summaries of the report were also widely circulated to ensure that the evidence to support employee engagement was fully appreciated. This was important as the risks of it being seen as another 'flavour of the month' had to be minimized. Time here was really of the essence.

Initial training at senior level was conducted by Professor John Oliver, who cross-referenced the successful work undertaken nearby at Leyland Trucks, Runshaw College and Blackpool NHS Trust (all case studies in the MacLeod report: MacLeod and Clarke, 2009). Thereafter senior directors, including the new Chief Executive Phil Halsall and Environment Director Jo Turton, undertook keynote roles to reinforce commitment and ownership.

The task of educating all people managers in the authority is now underway, using a core package modified to suit the audience. Leadership programmes have been revised to major on the fundamentals of employee engagement. LCC already had an excellent provision in both programme content and in a supportive and professional HR and training department. They were quickly able to adapt their offerings to suit the approach.

Management self-awareness

As indicated earlier, the emphasis is placed very much on managers taking on the responsibility for self-development. In addition to the myriad of training opportunities noted above, subordinate and peer appraisal have been introduced through the simple management style questionnaire/peer review processes used at Leyland and elsewhere. Managers are encouraged to seek to understand their 'shadows', the way they influence people around them through their conscious and unconscious behaviours. The processes have been successfully trialled with the top 500 and are now being rolled out to all people managers in the authority.

Behavioural sets

The successful approach to establishing an accessible and memorable value/behavioural set, pioneered by Runshaw and used successfully at Blackpool NHS trust, has been replicated at LCC. Using a limited number of one-word values agreed by a facilitated focus group of junior staff, the behaviours of the Lancashire person and the Lancashire manager have been developed. By gently cascading the concepts into the organization, it is hoped to generate a positive peer pressure to encourage employees to engage in new opportunities for continuous improvement.

Recognition

Repeated staff surveys at LCC exposed a real need for employees to feel more valued. Again using a facilitated staff focus group, procedures for individual and team recognition were developed. Each directorate has implemented this energetically resulting in real positive feedback. This is now being actively linked into the continuous improvement (CI) process (see below). Recognition in its purest form (ie not confused with reward systems) is seen to be a powerful enabler of encouraging engagement.

Communication

LCC has always taken internal communication seriously and has had some impressive vehicles for keeping the workforce informed. Nevertheless the whole approach to communicating has been reassessed in line with the demands of the economic situation and those of The Lancashire Way. Alongside an extensive and highly impressive web-based system geared to promoting communication in general and employee engagement in particular, a host of other initiatives have been introduced with no little success. Regular face-to-face sessions are always well attended. The chief executive's weekly e-mail is well received for its simplicity and honesty.

Continuous improvement

The concept of continuous improvement (CI) allied to employee engagement may be increasingly familiar to manufacturing operations in the UK but is rarely practised in public sector companies like LCC. Great care has been taken to develop practices that suit both the culture of the organization and the relative newness of the philosophy. The emphasis has been placed on simplicity, avoiding at this stage broader techniques such as total quality management (TQM) or European Foundation for Quality Management (EFQM). Following training from Leyland Trucks, recent Shingo prize-winners, in-house programmes have been delivered to good effect. Each directorate now has a range of CI activity going on throughout their activities. Big-ticket CI projects are obviously essential given the challenges on the council. However, getting employees involved in more modest, bite-sized exercises is also a priority and lots of good practice has been reported.

Building up to an embedded CI culture, where it is seen as routine and integral to day-to-day working, is key to real employee engagement. It satisfies underlying desires for interest, intellectual satisfaction, self-esteem, ownership, personal accountability and a lot more beyond.

Measurement

There are two absolute measures of the success or otherwise of the Lancashire Way:

- staff morale as measured by routine staff surveys;
- achievement of corporate goals, particularly those stemming from the CSR.

On both accounts LCC appears to be on course. Despite the fragile climate within the public sector in the UK, the executive team decided to survey staff attitudes in June 2011. The technique they used was to take the previous survey and realign it to a more cultural audit looking at the key factors identified in the MacLeod report (MacLeod and Clarke, 2009). Not satisfied with a simple statistical output, the council added directorate-level focus groups to distinguish between symptoms and underlying causality. This process has been well received at all levels and has served to underline the executive team's determination to move to a more people-centric organization.

The outcome of the survey was perhaps, given the general unpleasantness in the public sector, on balance surprisingly positive. Employees generally expressed a great affiliation for the organization and enjoy working there. The relationship between individuals and their immediate supervisors was remarkably good.

Progress here will be monitored by interim sample surveys. Soft measures, such as frequency of recognition, will be restricted in number but used vigorously to maintain progress.

Initial progress was unsurprisingly slow as managers grappled with the practical implications of employee engagement against a backcloth of unfamiliar and often unpleasant change. However, the pace has accelerated since the turn of the year with all directorates showing progress and some generating their own momentum.

There are many reasons to now be optimistic about the success of employee engagement at Lancashire County Council. Despite some initial scepticism, there are few concerns that this is the right way to go. The project management activity, from the board through to the leads, has been first-class with little in the way of disagreement and a total absence of the politicking or inter-departmental rivalry which can be the norm in big companies. The basic elements for success are now all in place. LCC will be a place to visit this time next year.

Reproduced with kind permission from *Engage with Success*.

Strategic narrative

Visible, empowering leadership providing a strong, strategic narrative about the organization, where it's come from and where it's going is a key enabler of employee engagement. In Chapter 4, we explored this from the perspective of providing purpose and meaning to employees within the workplace. It is not enough for employees to be motivated simply because the organization provides them with a job. Providing a compelling purpose at work, or strategic narrative, can help create meaning for employees, which contributes towards employee engagement. There are a number of ways we can find meaning at work. Pratt and Ashworth (2003) talk about this as both meaning 'in working', which is a belief that their job contributes to the greater good, and meaning 'at work', which is a belief that one is helping others to contribute and/or achieve satisfaction; or indeed a combination of the two. There should be congruence between an employee's personal values or goals and those of the organization to enable this to happen. For example, just because someone works for a charity with a strong sense of purpose, this alone may not be enough to engage them at work, if this purpose does not resonate with their own personal values.

Dr Amy Wrzesniewski, an Associate Professor of Organizational Behavior at Yale, has worked within this field for many years. Her research looks at how people find meaning at work. In summary, work is seen as either:

- a job – often motivated extrinsically by things such as financial rewards; a necessity rather than a choice; not a major positive or priority of life;

- a career – where there is an investment in work and a focus on advancement and achievement, more intrinsically motivated;

- a calling – whereby work gives life meaning and purpose, contributes to the greater good and draws on an employee's own strengths and values; the focus is rewarding work and an end in itself or a means of self-expression.

Wrzesniewski has found that you can't always predict a particular type of job, job title or salary with the categories above. In fact in most professions orientation is fairly evenly divided – with about a third of workers falling into each category. There are a couple of interesting implications arising from research. First, by enabling employees to get involved with crafting their roles to align with their personal values, strengths and interests there is a greater chance of finding meaning at work. And second, the responsibility of providing a compelling strategic narrative does not sit entirely with the leadership and managers within an organization. Employees should also play a role in figuring out their own personal work narrative, how they contribute to the bigger picture and how they can craft their roles to align with not only their personal interests and strengths but the company direction and purpose too.

Indeed, we have all heard the story about a janitor at NASA who, when asked what he did, replied that he was 'helping to put a man on the moon'. This is the nub of the strategic narrative: a workforce that is helping to put a man on the moon. And having a compelling story, mission, vision, direction, brand and values, that employees understand, feel part of, buy into, believe and can contribute to, is one of the building blocks of an engaged workforce.

CASE STUDY West Kent Housing

Employee engagement at West Kent is underpinned by a strong, coherent and well-understood strategic narrative. West Kent sets out to be 'more than just a landlord.' Their vision is to be the leading community provider of affordable homes in Kent and they aim to provide affordable homes to those who struggle and to nurture the community around their homes. They also aim to 'put residents at the centre' of everything they do.

The workforce at West Kent demonstrates a high degree of identification with the organization's strategic narrative. This was emphasized by the Investors in People assessor who found that 'all members of staff fully embrace the mission and values of the organization and endorse the principle of West Kent being "more than just a landlord".' This was brought out in some stakeholder perception research conducted by an independent organization. One partner said: 'West Kent puts residents at the heart of everything they do – this is a reality and embedded in the way the organization works, it's not just corporate jargon.'

As staff explained, the targets set out in their annual personal development reviews and monitored in meetings with their line manager, are aligned with the organization's goals, allowing them to 'put our aims and achievements alongside those of the organization.' As was acknowledged in the Investors in People report, the effect of this is that individual employees 'have a very clear line of sight between their own objectives and key performance measures and those of their department and West Kent.'

There is a strong sense of social purpose that is key to the strategic narrative at West Kent. All the staff recognize how their individual work and that of the organization as a whole aims to provide local residents with affordable and decent accommodation. As Sue Ludbrook, Office Services Manager said, 'There's a reason for us being here. It's not just a job at the end of the day. You can make a real difference to a tenant's life, to a person's life.'

Part of the success in achieving such a strong and well-understood strategic narrative has been the way in which it is communicated. Everything West Kent does is explained with reference to their residents. The narrative is communicated regularly and clearly. As Frank Czarnowski explained, 'Our narrative has been quite consistent across the years. It all comes back to a focus on our residents, and a sense of place.' What's more, given the nature of the organization and the fact that most roles are resident-facing, it is easier for staff 'to see what they're doing' and understand the part they play.

The degree of confidence in the strategic narrative is evident. The latest staff survey found that 77 per cent of the staff believe that the senior management team have a clear vision for the future of the organization, a massive 23 per cent above the average figure for housing associations nationally.

SOURCE West Kent Housing Strategic Narrative, reproduced with kind permission from Engage for Success

Top tips: creating your strategic narrative

1.0 How do you develop a strategic narrative? Contribution from the storytellers

The storytellers are world leaders in the use of narrative and storytelling techniques that help business leaders realize the potential of their people. They help leaders to execute strategy, build cultures, improve performance and make change happen, so who better to ask how you go about developing one than them? Here are their top tips:

1.1 *Through co-creation.* Leaders are far more likely to co-own the narrative if they have had an opportunity to contribute to its creation. Identify the key leaders that need to own the narrative and involve them from the start – ideally through individual interviews. Then at draft stage bring them together as a plenary group to interrogate the narrative and agree on the key themes and ideas. The strength of the narrative is often determined by the quality of the conversation used to create it.

1.2 *Using a narrative framework.* A good strategic narrative should answer the key questions about the journey the business is on. It is useful therefore to start with these questions (see Section 2). Storytelling is an art, but like all art forms it has an underlying structure. A good example is the 'hero's journey' developed by Carl Jung and Joseph

Campbell (Campbell, 2013). If this framework is too complicated try starting with the simple questions: 'Where are we now?'; 'Where do we want to get to?' and, 'How will we get there?'

1.3 *With brevity*: Blaise Pascal (in a quotation often misattributed to Mark Twain) wrote: 'I have made this letter longer than usual, only because I have not had time to make it shorter'. A good strategic narrative needs to be clear and simple in order to focus the business on the key messages and the core strategic argument. The challenge is often not what you put into the narrative, but what you leave out. Set yourself a limit for the number and length of messages within the narrative; it will make for a sharper story.

1.4 *By enabling leaders to personalize the narrative*: A strategic narrative will contain some non-negotiable elements. However, leaders and managers are more likely to adopt it if they are able to bring the narrative to life in a way that they feel is authentic to them and will resonate with their teams. Using the narrative framework, share the story with leaders and managers and then facilitate a conversation that enables them to personalize the messages. Encourage them to use their own illustrative stories (see below).

1.5 *By keeping the narrative alive*: Employees are more likely to focus their energy on the narrative if they believe it has longevity and is not just another short-term initiative. Reinforce key messages from the narrative via ongoing internal communications. Encourage leaders to reference the narrative in their interactions with employees, connecting business decisions and initiatives back to the story. Challenge leaders to plan how they will 'live' the story through their own actions and decisions. Recognize employees' contributions to the narrative, showing how their actions are contributing to its success. After 12 to 18 months, update the narrative, highlighting the parts that remain the same, and the parts that have now moved on.

2.0 What should a strategic narrative include?

2.1 *A purpose and vision*: In their book *Built to Last*, Collins and Porras (2005) identified that companies that enjoy enduring success have a clear purpose and envisioned future. The purpose helps employees to reaffirm why they should be part of this organization. The envisioned future should inspire them with what they can achieve together, and the benefits that this behaviour will create for the business, its shareholders, customers, employees and communities.

2.2 *An authentic current reality.* Almost all strategic narratives will demand some kind of change from the organization. John Kotter, in his book *Leading Change* (1996) identifies the need to establish a sense of urgency for the change required, by authentically setting out the current reality of where the business is and the challenges it faces. This current reality also provides the dramatic tension the narrative needs in order to capture its audience's attention. Don't restrict the narrative to just good news.

2.3 *A clear strategic argument.* A good strategic narrative should link together why the business is – or needs to go – on a journey, what the direction and destination of that journey is, and how it is going to get there. This link should make logical sense. In fact human beings are hard-wired to think in narrative structures. Therefore the logic of the strategy (or lack thereof) can often be exposed when structured as a narrative.

2.4 *A role for employees.* Leaders may set the direction and destination of the narrative, but it will take the engagement and energy of the employees to get them there. To really engage in the narrative the employees need to see a clear role they can play; a role that they can relate to their everyday working lives. In a good strategic narrative, the employees should be positioned as the heroes of the story.

2.5 *A narrative structure.* A narrative links together different events into a continuous journey. It should have a start, middle and end, and ideally some dramatic tension, or challenge that drives the interest. A strategic narrative should play on these characteristics; for example, using linking words at the start of each section, like 'but', 'so' etc. Include an 'elevator speech' as part of your narrative: four to six headlines that summarize your story.

2.6 *A human and emotional dimension.* Our choices and decisions are primarily driven by our beliefs and feelings. It is therefore important that the strategic narrative engages the hearts as well as the minds of employees. In constructing the narrative try to reflect the emotional journey that the business is on as well as the strategy. Don't be afraid to empathize as well as challenge. Illustrating the core narrative with real-life stories about the way the business affects people's lives, will also give it a powerful emotional pull.

3.0 What is the value of a strategic narrative?

3.1 *To unite people behind a common purpose and direction.* Stories have been used throughout time to unite societies and give them a common purpose and direction. A strategic narrative can do the same for business organizations, leading to greater commitment, discretionary effort, alignment and focus.

3.2 *To create a context for change*: Employees are more likely to engage in change if they believe in why it needs to happen and the benefits it will create. A strategic narrative can set the change within a clear and inspiring journey, helping employees to understand this context and relate it to their own experiences.

3.3 *To link together and make sense of multiple initiatives*: Many organizations have a multiplicity of different corporate messages: purpose, missions, strategic priorities, values, competencies, visions etc, which can be confusing to employees. A strategic narrative can link these together as part of the story of the business journey, improving clarity and understanding.

3.4 *To align leaders so they demonstrate strength and unity*: Employees are far more likely to engage in the business journey, if they have faith in its leaders and believe they are united behind it. A strategic narrative, including the why, what and how of the journey, can be a powerful framework around which to demonstrate this unity.

3.5 *To inspire people, creating pride and camaraderie*: Research in the United States has shown that employees are more likely to be engaged at work if they have pride in the organization they work for and camaraderie with their colleagues. A strategic narrative, and the way it can be brought to life through real-life illustrative stories can stimulate these emotions.

3.6 *To create a personal connection to the strategy*: Again research has shown that employees are more likely to be engaged if they can see a connection between their own work and the business strategy. Every story needs a hero or heroes. The strategic narrative, and the conversation it provokes, can help employees make sense of their roles as the heroes of the business journey.

3.7 *To challenge and change people's beliefs and behaviours*: Human beings make sense of the world using stories and narrative. If organizations want to change their people's beliefs about the business and 'the way they do things around here', then a narrative is a natural starting place.

3.8 *To keep the strategy alive*: A strategy describes a plan of action at a fixed point in time. A strategic narrative describes a journey the business is on. The journey allows for, and actually encourages, learning and adaptation over time, whilst still staying true to the overall direction and desired destination. This in turn makes it more sustainable, especially within a fast changing environment.

Employee voice

Within the first *Engage for Success* report to government, employee voice was outlined in the following way:

> Employees' views are sought out; they are listened to and see that their opinions count and make a difference. They speak out and challenge when appropriate. A strong sense of listening and of responsiveness permeates the organization, enabled by effective communication.

Ensuring your employees have a voice enables them to take part in dialogue across your organization about matters that impact the current and future performance of an organization. If you have a strong employee voice, conversations will take place that are genuinely two-way, and are not about paying lip-service to the concept. Giving employees a voice provides them with the opportunity to positively impact their organization on a variety of levels: the jobs they do, the organizational culture, your products and services, and the way it feels around here.

There are some organizational prerequisites that help to ensure employee voice is authentic and effective, rather than seen as yet another initiative. Like so many aspects of engagement, employee voice at a first glance appears to be a fairly simple and straightforward concept, which should be easy to implement. The reality is quite different. First, there must be good levels of trust within your organization. Employees are not going to express their ideas or contribute to a conversation if trust is low. Employees won't speak up if they feel that their contribution is subject to negative consequences in any way. Employees need to feel safe to speak their minds without fear of any reprisals. You only have to consider the need to reinforce the confidentiality of engagement surveys, or focus groups for example, to see that trust is often difficult to build and all too easy to lose.

Line managers also play a critical role in not only building trust within an organization, but also facilitating employee voice. A report published by IPA and Tomorrows Company (2012), which looks at the role of employee voice to ensure sustained business success, identified some key characteristics of leadership that empower employee voice. They list these as:

- openness;
- good communication;
- approachability.

The report argues that this style of leadership helps to encourage employee voice.

CASE STUDY   Unipart Group

(Originally published as part of the IPA and Tomorrow's Work report on the role of employee voice for sustained business success)

'no problem is a problem'

Unipart is a manufacturing, logistics and consultancy group working in a variety of sectors such as technology, automotive, retail and financial services. Unipart has a particular capability in continuous improvement developed over a period of time. It is a privately owned company and the senior management and executives typically have a long tenure; the chief executive has been in place since the formation of the company.

At Unipart, voice is firmly embedded in the ways of working, and indeed, is viewed as necessary to achieve successful outcomes in many areas. The successful development of the Unipart approach to continuous improvement and change management has led to a widespread conviction and commitment across the organization to employee voice. The 'Unipart Way' provides the principles, tools and techniques to facilitate employee voice, leading to common practices across the Group.

For employees, voice has a clear link to how respected and how valued they feel they are by their managers and the company. Employees believe that consultation and involvement, often by their managers, strengthen their commitment to the site where they work, ensuring its success. The 'no-blame' culture helps to mitigate potentially stressful situations such as performance monitoring or frequent role change, and provides a sense of control through their confidence that they will be involved in any change. This is captured in the concept that 'no problem is a problem'. In Unipart there is an acknowledgement that rather than avoiding problems, they should be actively sought out as opportunities for improvement.

Many of their voice channels are designed to elicit their knowledge to ensure successful innovation and implementation. The idea that employees, and not their managers, are the experts in their area of work supports this form of engagement:

- at an individual level, where people's ownership of their work is expected to generate voice as employees offer feedback and raise problems with line managers;

- at a team level, where teams are expected to take ownership of their work, solve problems and make improvements;

- at a site and divisional level where strong forums are encouraged as a way of management and employees engaging on cross-site issues.

Several factors are significant in enabling employee voice at Unipart. Private ownership has helped the company to take a long-term perspective in developing its approach with its employees, and continues to allow managers relative freedom to act. The decentralized business model devolves much decision-making to the lowest possible level in the organization and makes it feasible for employees to influence that process, thereby making consultation more meaningful and incentivizing involvement.

The leadership and management style works to create an environment in which problems, both personal and performance-related, can be raised and managers act as facilitators to solve problems. Indeed, from team leaders to managing directors, there is an emphasis on knowing employees in a personal capacity – for example, knowing employees' names, personal interests or family context. Both employees and leaders see this as strengthening loyalty and commitment to the leaders and their aims and objectives, and also encouraging employees to discuss problems with production.

In devolving decision-making to the lowest level Unipart demonstrates that several local factors are of key importance; these include authentic leadership, a long-term partnership approach with clients with a commitment from the whole team to meet their needs and the use of a continuous improvement approach to give people the skills and opportunity to enable them to own their own work.

Establishing employee voice: a model for success

In their report, *Releasing Voice for Sustainable Business Success*, IPA and Tomorrow's Company (2012) have developed a model that details all of the critical elements of establishing employee voice within an organization. The model, detailed below, summarizes the factors that influence voice, and is a useful tool when considering employee voice within your own organization. The model highlights:

- the purpose of voice – sustainable business success;
- the outcomes of voice – engagement, commitment and performance;
- the culture and behaviours associated with voice;
- the structures and processes associated with voice.

FIGURE 5.1 Critical elements of establishing employee voice within an organization model

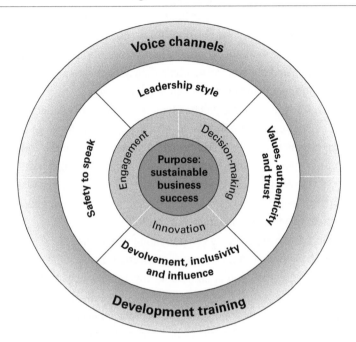

The rise of new technologies are offering more opportunities to ensure employees have a voice within the workplace. In the thought piece below, Michael Silverman talks about the possibilities, and opportunities, presented by the rise of social collective intelligence to unleash the power of employee voice.

Employee voice and collective intelligence

By Michael Silverman, Managing Director, Crowdoscope

Collective intelligence and the rise of social technologies

The internet is giving rise to some remarkable technologies that enable large groups of people to collaborate online. This is having a huge impact in the field of collective intelligence as it provides an opportunity to progress research and practice in this area. There is a need to understand what's important in mass online interactions and discussions because intelligence doesn't just reside within us as individuals – it also emerges from groups of people. Collective intelligence is a broad area and the term is often applied quite liberally to a variety of activities or systems.

In the last 10 years there has been an explosion in both research and interest. The main reason for this burst of enthusiasm is the rapid advance of social and digital technologies in both business and in the public sphere. These changes reflect the rise of a new era for collective intelligence, one that can fully take advantage of both the increasing interconnectivity between people and the increasing computing and storage capabilities of advanced information and communication technologies.

The rise of social technologies has facilitated the rise of collective intelligence because before this it was almost impossible for large and dispersed groups of people to organize themselves and interact. Today, people can participate within technological systems that are increasingly able to orchestrate the collection and analysis of human social activity. This is the frontier of *social collective intelligence:* networks of people and computers acting together in intelligent ways.

Openness and transparency are becoming vital business characteristics within organizations. Elsewhere in society, areas such as digital social innovation and open democracy are growing in prominence. They seek to address how current techno-social trends can be harnessed towards answering some of the most important questions facing modern societies. This desire has resulted in organizations taking a keen interest in social collective intelligence when it comes to employee insights.

There are many areas of work and types of task to which collective intelligence methods can be applied: discussion and commentary, innovation and ideation, competitions and challenges, insight communities, knowledge sharing, workload distribution, collaboration and predicting the future. The open nature of many collective intelligence systems means that these methods are particularly beneficial within organizations in terms of the type of employee voice that is elicited.

Social technologies and the employee voice

Many organizations, in an attempt to be an employer of choice and provide a better experience for their people, are looking to increase employee engagement through employee voice. Vast amounts of literature highlight the relationship between employee voice and organizational benefits. Greater productivity, cohesion and ultimately satisfaction can be seen within a workforce who are offered a voice.

The issue is that many organizations offer little beyond a traditional survey. Broadly speaking, the format of these have changed very little in the last 50 years (except from now being online). This is despite the fact that we have witnessed advancement in social technologies which offer extremely innovative ways to stimulate discussion and elicit voice. Despite good intentions and significant investments, traditional employee surveys often fall short in providing the meaningful insights they set out to.

Our conceptualization of employee voice should evolve in line with these exciting technological and social developments. This includes increased exploratory research into the area of social collective intelligence. Communication, instead of being one-way or two-way, can instead now be multidirectional. Crucially, this means employees can engage in an open forum instead of behind closed doors. This multidirectional approach can be harnessed to encourage collaborative and collective decision-making amongst employees. Communities of employees can work together to provide organizational insights, which offer far more insight than the traditional survey. By having employees interact, to review and respond to how the colleagues feel about certain issues, a company can quickly establish which themes or ideas resonate most with the community. A new form of employee voice emerges which is organized and intelligent.

Instead of being preoccupied with the risks and threats associated with social technologies, organizations should be redesigning their strategies to harness the collective intelligence of their people. Social technologies are here to stay – organizations would be wiser to facilitate the technology in a way that suits their desire to increase employee engagement.

Final thoughts

Collective intelligence is nothing new. Successful organizations have been encouraging collaboration and interaction since the first modern organizations were formalized but few utilize it fully. However, it is *social collective intelligence*, resulting from the rapid development of social and digital technologies, that is both new and exciting in this area. Organizations are only just beginning to appreciate the potential that collective intelligence can offer. There are pockets of good practice appearing as organizations start to implement various collective intelligence activities such as providing employees with a voice. However, these early examples of social collective intelligence are likely to be just the start of the story. Thinking about the future of collective intelligence, developments in human–computer interaction are likely to play a big role enhancing human–human and human–machine interaction. However, for many scientists and entrepreneurs, the ultimate aim is to develop hybrid systems that employ both human intelligence and advanced machine intelligence.

Involvement

Involving employees in your organization is an additional enabler of engagement to the original four published by Engage for Success, which I have included. Whilst some might argue employee involvement falls under the employee voice enabler, it's important to be explicit about the role of employee involvement in engagement, therefore I think it's valid to talk about this separately. If employee voice is all about conversations, dialogue and talking, then employee involvement takes this a step further to facilitate employee action and behaviour. We can give employees a voice via channels such as the staff survey, listening groups, ideas schemes, forums on the company intranet, as well as the way they are managed and led. However, involvement takes this a step further by creating opportunities for employees to actually *do* something different, to contribute, to genuinely get involved in the success of the business. If employees come up with a great idea to improve a product or a service, why not go one step further and give them the chance to actually get involved in the implementation of their idea? Even something as simple as allowing employees to choose the new paint colour or desk style in an office move can contribute towards employees feeling involved in their organization. In a nutshell, involvement ensures employees have the opportunity to engage with the organization.

In my experience however, the practice of involving employees can often be met with barriers. Involving employees can feel counterintuitive to the more command-and-control culture and management styles; however, it is a powerful enabler of engagement. In his book, *The Chief Engagement Officer*, John Smythe (2007) talks about inclusion and co-creation as ways to involve employees. Inclusion involves driving accountability down through an organization, so the 'what' has been decided by the board or the senior team, but employees are involved in the 'how'. This approach allows people with the time and space to figure out what company-wide decisions, changes or ways of working mean for them, their jobs and their development. For example, a company might publicize a new vision, but employees are then given the time and space to consider the ways in which that vision is then operationalized in relation to their day-to-day role. Co-creation on the other hand involves identifying, and then working with those people who can add value if they are included at the outset of a project or a change. For example, if a company is considering changing the way it interacts with customers, it's probably a good idea to involve those employees who deal with customers day to day – often not senior management.

Involving employees doesn't just have to focus on the strategic and operational objectives of the company. There is also a growing body of evidence that makes the link between job design and engagement. For example, Christian *et al* (2011) found certain aspects of a job such as task variety, autonomy, significance and feedback are positively related to engagement in a wide range of research papers. One of the themes that is prevalent in much of the research is autonomy, which was discussed in Chapter 4 as a prerequisite of engagement. In research on call centre employees, Bond (2010) discovered that even a small increase in autonomy resulted in a significant increase in motivation, alongside a decrease in absenteeism and mental distress. In addition, Wrzesniewski and Dutton (2001) in their research looking at hospital cleaning staff, found that those given more autonomy to interact with patients, visitors and others were more satisfied than their counterparts, and felt they were playing a more important role. Autonomy, by definition, provides employees with the freedom to determine their own actions and behaviours and in doing this, employees will experience a high degree of involvement in their day-to-day activities. Equally if we provide employees with the opportunity to get involved with aspects of their job, or projects or the organization, this involvement then facilitates autonomy.

The concept of job-crafting takes this idea a stage further. Job-crafting enables employees themselves to make changes to their own job design. Wrzesniewski and Dutton (2001) define job-crafting as the process of employees redefining and re-imagining their job designs in personally meaningful ways. Wrzesniewski and Dutton argue that experience of meaning at work is malleable; that through job-crafting individuals can:

- change the way they approach the tasks in their work;
- increase or decrease the number and kinds of tasks they do as part of their job;
- change the number of relationships they have with others they encounter at work.

They have a great example of an office cleaner crafting her job by caring for the plants for people who are away or do not have 'green thumbs'. By involving employees in job-crafting their roles, it enables them to take the initiative in small ways: people perform their roles in ways that are meaningful to them, giving them increased sense of purpose and autonomy.

CASE STUDY   Capital One: bringing our vision to life

Capital One is one of the top six credit card issuers in the UK employing around 800 employees out of its Nottingham base. At the start of 2011, Brian Cole, the CEO, launched his long-term vision for the company. The vision is: 'Let's Make Lives Better' and focused on four main goals – including *truly meeting consumer needs* and *having a culture of innovation.*

Launched at the beginning of 2011, early evaluation indicated that whilst the vision was known throughout Capital One, it was very much seen as the CEO's vision by employees. In response to this, we needed to engage employees with the vision, help them understand it and ultimately develop buy-in and commitment. The response to this was to develop an engagement campaign designed to empower employees to own the vision and deliver against it.

The campaign launched with a 'Vision Day' in June 2011, involving all employees. This phase of the campaign deployed a number of tactics including a Vision booklet and stickers asking employees four questions about the vision. Employees were encouraged to answer these and stick them on a Vision wall. Employees also attended an experiential event whereby they were tasked with creating a 30-second viral film to communicate the vision. All of the clips created on the day were posted on the intranet and employees were asked to vote for their favourite.

However, despite great results following this initial phase, Capital One knew it needed to really involve associates to enable them to truly own the vision. What they came up with was the 'Vision Collective'. This involved a group of associates from across the business, who would come together to essentially help other associates to understand and own the vision. The approach was one of viral change: associates were carefully selected to be a part of the Vision Collective. By creating a Vision Collective the aim was to use a viral approach to change, seeking out change agents (or change leaders) to help bring the vision to life. This approach aimed to take the vision from a top-down, programmatic, 'done to' initiative to something owned and driven by associates throughout the business. The creation of the Vision Collective involved recruiting members who have the skills and potential to inspire colleagues to bring the vision to life.

The overall purpose of the Vision Collective was to bring together a group of people from across Capital One to help create the conditions needed for their vision to flourish. This was achieved by:

- recruiting 'change leaders' from across the business;
- establishing the Vision Collective and agreeing roles and terms of reference;
- facilitating a series of workshops/meetings with the group to:
  - agree the purpose and what we wanted to achieve;
  - share a set of strengths-based tools to enable this inquiry with the collective;
  - agree actions;
- putting in place a set of action learning groups to support the group;
- developing a plan which was co-created with the Vision Collective.

This was a very different way of working for many of the Vision Collective and to begin with progress was not as fast as we had intended. However, the group continued to meet and once momentum was gathered there was no stopping them. They have been responsible for a wide range of initiatives, ideas, events and actions within Capital One, all of which have helped to ensure the vision is owned by associates throughout Capital One and is no longer seen at the CEO's vision. The results were amazing: 98 per cent said they understood why the vision was important for Capital One, 97 per cent said this was the right way forward and 89 per cent declared they knew how they could contribute to the vision.

Integrity

Organizational integrity is about ensuring the words of an organization match the behaviours. Whilst this sounds simple enough, many of us have experienced a significant gap between the words and actions of a company. Just consider your company values (if you have them): are they really lived and breathed throughout the organization? What about your company vision: is it really used as a lens for decision-making? Organizational integrity is a critical enabler, not only of engagement, but also trust in the organization and management team. There is no quicker way to erode trust and engagement than to talk about values, and make promises about where the company is heading, that bears little resemblance to employees' everyday working lives.

However, raising any inconsistencies in your company culture and gaps in the words and actions of your leadership team can present a challenge: it's often a difficult message to communicate. One way to overcome this is to conduct employee research to establish if indeed there is a gap. Focus groups are a great way to gather insight from your employees and provide a richness and depth to enable leaders to understand any inconsistencies from the perspective of your employees. Hearing feedback from employees, rather than from the opinion of someone with responsibility for engagement, can make the message more palatable, by presenting an undeniable truth. Once any gap has been established the real work then begins to understand how to close it.

Our engagement pledge template from the Engage for Success team

The Engage for Success team has developed the following engagement pledge template. Getting your leadership team to develop and sign up to such a pledge is a great way to communicate that they are serious about employee engagement. It is a useful tool to then hold leaders and managers accountable, helping to ensure organizational integrity.

Our engagement pledge

<Use this area to input a message from your CEO.>

<CEO name>

<Signed by CEO>

<Photograph of CEO>

The engagement pledge

Why make the engagement pledge?

<Suggested text below>

The Engagement Pledge is a voluntary, company-wide commitment made by leaders and managers in XXXX to effectively engage with their staff. It's a promise that leaders and managers will boost productivity and efficiency by enabling, engaging and releasing the potential of their employees.

We must reinforce our values and goals, focus on performance, and enable our employees to understand how they contribute to our overall success. We are placing even greater focus on engaging all our people, as I know that it is only through our people that we will achieve our vision.

Who makes the engagement pledge?

The engagement pledge is a commitment made by any leader or manager in XXXX.

The benefits of making the engagement pledge

As well as understanding the benefits of an engaged workforce, leaders and managers appreciate that making the engagement pledge will also help unlock the potential of our workforce and lead to a range of business benefits, including:

- being an employer of choice;
- a positive perception by others – clients, employees, community and competitors;
- reduced employee sickness and absenteeism;
- reduction in accidents and wastage;
- improved levels of productivity and efficiency;
- higher levels of customer satisfaction;
- greater sales and profits;
- above average total shareholder return;
- a motivated and engaged workforce.

How do I make the engagement pledge?

That's the easy part! The engagement pledge is for any leader or manager who wants to commit to improving employee engagement with their team, regardless of their starting point on their engagement journey.

There are three easy steps:

1 *Sign the engagement pledge*: The leader/manager expresses an interest in making the engagement pledge commitment. They must submit a copy of their team engagement action plan; once this has been received the engagement pledge certificate will be posted.

2 *Develop an action plan and communicate the commitment*: The certificate should be displayed publicly and all team members should be communicated with about this commitment. Multiple copies can be made and electronic copies can be made available too. The leader/manager must confirm how and when communication was carried out to the team.

3 *Implementation of action plan*: This should be ongoing engagement activity, relevant to your team. The leader/manager will be required to submit quarterly action plan updates for their team. (For support and ideas please see the engagement pledge 'Ideas for action' section of this guidance.)

To discuss in more detail or to make the engagement pledge commitment contact <internal contact who will coordinate this needed>.

How long is the engagement pledge valid for?

The pledge is valid for one year; approximately one month prior to your renewal date you will be contacted to submit evidence of how you have implemented the engagement pledge.

What evidence will I need to submit to renew the engagement pledge?

You will need to send in evidence to show how you have embedded the engagement pledge; this must include your updated engagement action plan along with supporting evidence, such as:

- regular team meetings that include engagement as a topic on the agenda;
- employee focus groups, feedback loops, staff forums, etc;
- training and development for the team;
- talent management;
- contract visits and/or other getting to know the business activity;
- regular one-to-ones;
- performance reviews;
- employee recognition and reward;

- corporate social responsibility (CSR) activity (eg volunteering);

- innovation – activity that generates new ideas and smarter ways of working;

- buddy/coach/mentor activity encouraged – not just top-down, think about peer-to-peer;

- case studies (these could be developed as a result of all the engagement work you are doing);

- award nominations.

<Sample certificate>

Our engagement pledge

Ensuring our people are highly engaged is one of our most important tasks. Our people need to feel their contribution is valued, their views are sought, they feel proud to be part of XXXX and its future and that we live our values every day.

On behalf of [contract name/team name] I [insert name and position] am making a commitment that we shall:

- Listen to our employees' feedback given through the survey and share the results. Act on the feedback. Create an action plan which employees and managers both agree to. Review the progress at least quarterly and inform our employees.

- Personally act as a role model for our values.

- Enable our employees to understand how they contribute to our overall success and to understand XXXX strategic journey.

- Deliver our services efficiently and always aim to give our employees the resources they need to do a good job.

- Actively encourage and support our employes to gain the skills that will meet the needs of our business and will support their future employability.

- Recognize hard work and performance.

- Support the well-being of all our employees.

Signed:

Start date:

Expiry date:

I commend and thank you for the personal leadership you have shown in your commitment to bringing the engagement pledge to life.

Signed by CEO

The engagement pledge: Ideas for action

Here are a few ideas to help you get started with your engagement pledge commitment.

TABLE 5.3   The engagement pledge: ideas for action

Engagement pledge statement	Ideas for action
Listen to employees' feedback given through the survey and share the results. Act on the feedback. Create an action plan which employees and managers both agree to. Review the progress at least quarterly and inform employees	
To personally behave in line with our Governing Principles	
Enable employees to understand how they contribute to our overall success and to understand our strategic journey	
Deliver our services efficiently and give our people the resources they need to do a good job	
Actively encourage and support employees to gain the skills that will meet the needs of our business and will support their future employability	
Recognize hard work and performance	
Support the well-being of all employees	

Getting leaders and managers to sign up an engagement pledge is just the beginning – the real work comes with ensuring words and actions are aligned. However, integrity is not just about aligning behaviours with the company strategy, brand and values. It's also important to evaluate your systems and symbols to ensure they are also aligned, and contributing to, rather than eroding trust and engagement.

Activity

Evaluating system integrity in your organization

This activity enables you to consider the role your organizational symbols and systems are playing in either supporting or sabotaging engagement within your company. Consider the various systems and symbols that operate within your workplace. It might be helpful to consider this in terms of the employee lifecycle, below, but feel free to add in and take away elements as are relevant to your workplace:

FIGURE 5.2   The employee life cycle

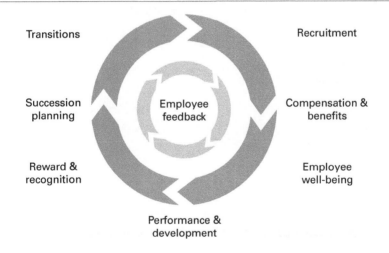

Thinking about your role and your opportunities to impact the engagement of employees within your organization:

- Rate the current employee experience against each stage of the life cycle.
- Does the current situation support or sabotage engagement?
- Is there a gap between words and actions?
- Discuss what the best experience would look like.

- Talk about the role you play and your opportunity to influence at each stage.
- Capture any actions.

TABLE 5.4 Evaluating system integrity

Systems or symbols	Current experience: does it support or sabotage engagement?	Desired future experience	Actions or opportunities?
eg Performance management system			
Office environment			
Employee communication			
On-boarding process			

The vital role of trust in employee engagement
By Hayley McGarvey

Edelman, the global communications firm, provide regular insight on the changing nature of trust, from 33,000+ respondents in 28 countries via their annual Edelman Trust Barometer. The international study looks at who and what people trust, covering a range of themes – including the impact of social media on trust and Donald Trump's governmental changes in the United States, as well as the effects of leadership and management across the globe.

Although the report opens with the assertion that trust has 'stagnated' in 2017 (with little change since 2016), the company's CEO Richard Edelman shares a positive insight in the report's introduction: 'The employer is the safe house in global governance, with 72 per cent of respondents saying that they trust their employer to do what is right'.

While that's great news, Edelman says there are certain expectations of corporate leadership that can't be overlooked if trust is to be improved in organizations everywhere. According to 64 per cent of respondents, building trust should be top of the list for CEOs – ahead of ensuring products and services are high-quality, increasing profits and stock prices, and focusing on whether business decisions are reflective of company values.

The report also found that participants are less inclined to believe information from peers (or 'a person like yourself'), compared to perceived 'experts'. Edelman describes this notable shift as 'a change in the ecosystem of trust, which had become increasingly premised on peer-to-peer discussion'. With a decline in trust in the media, trust in experts to lead the way is increasingly important.

Trust, leadership and employee engagement

In the report, the Edelman team states that 'in order to feel safe delegating important aspects of our lives and well-being to others, we need to trust them to act with integrity and with our best interests in mind'.

We know that trust is a vital element of employee engagement – it forms the basis of the enablers of engagement, and is a two-way street, between employees and their leaders. It might sound cliché, but without it, there's simply no foundation to build upon. As the Edelman report tells us, 'trust . . . is at the heart of an individual's relationship with an institution and, by association, its leadership'.

One of the enablers of employee engagement is integrity; the concept that employees trust that their organization will do as it says, living the values it promotes. People Lab's most recent Spotlight on the Employee Engagement Profession research, found that just 13 per cent of organizations were focusing their efforts in this area. Although participants said they weren't disregarding the enablers (many were focusing on others, such as Strategic Narrative, Employee Voice and Line Managers), integrity fell to the bottom of the list.

Trust is also central to ensuring employees are involved in the organization. Employees must trust their leaders to provide opportunities to involve them – just as leaders need to trust employees to embrace this personal involvement. Without trust, employee engagement can't function, let alone thrive.

SOURCE Adapted from: http://peoplelab.co.uk/the-vital-role-of-trust-in-employee-engagement/

Understanding the science behind the enablers

Employee engagement is viewed by some as a fluffy, intangible pursuit. However, advances in disciplines such as neuroscience have enabled us to back up our activities within employee engagement with science. This knowledge and understanding is crucial in helping to overcome arguments that engagement is a 'nice to have' rather than a prerequisite of commercial success. In my experience, demystifying engagement with the help of psychology and neuroscience gives employee engagement credibility in the eyes of senior stakeholders and others, helping to overcome cynicism.

In the following piece, Hilary Scarlett (2014), of Hilary Scarlett Associates, investigates the neuroscience behind the engagement enablers, and shares some ideas to help improve engagement using this latest thinking to create a brain-friendly workplace.

Thought piece – Neuroscience and the engagement enablers: what helps our brains think and perform at their best?
By Hilary Scarlett

Neuroscience helps us to understand what enables our brains to perform at their best and provides a scientific lens through which to see engagement. It is proving very persuasive with even the most sceptical leaders.

Neuroscience, the study of the nervous system including the brain, is still in its infancy. However, the growth in the number of fMRI scanners over the last two decades is increasing our understanding of the brain. What is particularly interesting for organizational leaders is that we can now apply learning from neuroscience to the workplace. It provides the insights into what helps our brains to focus and think optimally.

This article evaluates the four enablers of employee engagement through the lens of neuroscience, identifying why and how the four enablers help our brains perform at their best. It also demonstrates that improving employee engagement doesn't have to be laborious – often it is many little things that put our brains into a positive state.

Neuroscience

Before exploring each of the enablers, it's useful to set out a few facts about the brain. This will help make sense of some of the points discussed in this article:

- *The fundamental organizing principle of the brain: Avoid threat and find reward.* Although our brains have evolved (especially the prefrontal cortex – the area we use for considered thinking, planning and decision-making), we still fundamentally have the same brain as our prehistoric ancestors. Our ancestors' brains were wired to help them survive: if they had not been structured that way, none of us would be here today. The brain is wired to do two key things: avoid threats (the sabre-tooth tiger) and seek out rewards (shelter, food, warmth). Of these two, from the perspective of survival, it is much more important to avoid threats. Our 21st-century brains continue to be on the lookout for things that might harm us. This is both useful and problematic, as we will explore further on.

- *Our brains like to predict.* Our brains are prediction machines – they want to be able to predict and make sense of what is going on around us. If they can predict, they can keep us safe and conserve energy (the brain uses about 30 per cent of our calorie intake). In addition, because 'thinking' using the prefrontal cortex uses a huge amount of energy and the brain wants to conserve energy, we often rely on past experiences and make assumptions – and these might not always be correct. Change, by its very nature, prevents our brains from predicting and ambiguity is even worse: our brains really don't know what to make of it.

- *Toward and away states in the brain:* Throughout this article, I will be referring to away/threat states and toward/reward states. When we are in a threat state, we can't think or perform well, we're not open to listening or to new ideas and we see the workplace as a more hostile environment than it really is. But take a look at the toward/reward state: to me, this looks like the mindset of an engaged employee: positive, focused and open to change. Neuroscience provides insights into what achieves this mindset and I'll be exploring these in this article.

1 *Leadership/strategic narrative*: The first of the four enablers focuses on leaders and the need for them to create a narrative that provides line of sight between the employee and the organization's goals. Organizations that have a clear story, and that have spent time communicating this narrative have more engaged employees.

This makes sense from a neuroscience perspective. As we know, our brains are prediction machines; although they like a little bit of novelty, they are more comfortable when they have a sense of what to expect. Having a clear story about where the organization is heading enables our brains to predict. Linked to this need to predict, our brains crave certainty. Think about a time when a restructure was announced or your likeable and competent boss announces she is leaving, or you were told that you need to start hot-desking. This sets off our brains – 'What does that restructure mean for me? Will I have a job?' 'Who is going to be my new boss? I really hope X doesn't get the job.' 'Hot-desking? But I like being by the window. Can I still sit with the people I like?' Uncertainty puts our brains into an 'away' state where we become anxious and distracted.

Neuroscience also supports the need for a clear line of sight between us and the purpose of the company. Not only does line of sight give us clarity, it also provides a sense of being valued and of status because our work matters and makes a difference. Feeling valued puts our brains into a positive mindset.

Recent research brings additional insights on what makes a strategic narrative all the more compelling. Adam Grant, Professor at the Wharton School at the University of Pennsylvania, has done some fascinating work in this area. His research has demonstrated that for most people, in most organizations and most lines of work, doing something meaningful means doing something meaningful for others. He describes an experiment amongst fundraisers. He divided the group into two. One group had a short five-minute visit from one of the beneficiaries of the fundraising. The group that had not met the beneficiary continued at the same level of fundraising. However, the group that had met the beneficiary increased their fundraising by 171 per cent and this continued not just in the week following the visit, when you might expect some uplift, but even a month later. So, the strategic narrative is important to employee engagement but one that is about how employees are helping others and is backed up by meeting those beneficiaries, is all the more powerful.

2 *Engaging managers*: Engaged employees have managers who facilitate, empower, recognize and respect them. Neuroscience backs this up and explains why having a manager who respects, stretches and supports you creates a mindset where you can work at your best.

In his book, *Social: Why our brains are wired to connect*, Matthew Lieberman (2013), Director of the Social Cognitive Neuroscience Laboratory at UCLA, sets out the case for why social connections matter so much. Again, it goes back to survival. As mammals we would not survive if we did not have someone to care for us when we are born. So, from our first few moments out of the womb, we are wired to check that there is someone to look out for us.

This need to connect stays with us throughout our lives and this includes in the workplace. Our brains are constantly checking whether we are accepted or rejected, whether we are part of the 'in' group or 'out' group. When we are accepted, our brains are in the 'toward' state and are able to do all the good things that the state enables, but if we feel part of the 'out-group', we are in an 'away' state. Neuroscience has revealed that we process thoughts about people in different parts of our brain, depending on whether we consider them in-group or out-group and not surprisingly, our brains are far less empathetic to those who are in our out-groups. Social rejection has been shown to have a significant impact on our ability to think – managers need to keep this in mind.

It is in the interest of every manager to make sure members of the team feel part of the in-group. I recently worked with leaders in a large UK bank, getting them to think about how they could get their teams to feel part of their in-group. It does not have to be time-consuming and it doesn't have to cost money, but if managers want their team to be able to think and perform at their best, this is essential. Often small actions and gestures can make a real difference – making eye contact, greeting people in the morning, listening to people, focusing on shared goals, buying them a coffee and taking some time to get to know the individual.

As Matthew Lieberman argues in his book, organizations pay far too little attention to the fact that our brains are wired to be social. To perform well at work, these needs must be met. Collaboration, particularly amongst a diverse group of people, has also been shown to be a key ingredient of innovation and the creation of new ideas.

3 *Employee voice*: The third enabler focuses on the employee's ability to speak out and on the organization's being interested in what the employee has to say and responding to those views. Neuroscience provides evidence as to why having a voice matters and again this is rooted in survival. Employee voice is in part about feeling respected and is also about influence. One of our deep needs is to have some control, or at least a perception of control, over our environment. If we have no control, we are helpless and, as in prehistoric times, unlikely to survive. In our 21st-century brains, lack of autonomy leads to higher levels of stress and cortisol. Cortisol is physically damaging and kills brain cells, especially in the hippocampus, which plays an important role in memory. There are many studies that show that we have better health and live longer when we have some influence.

Leaders need to know that when we feel we have no control, we see the same situation as much more stressful. Even a subtle perception of autonomy can make a very significant positive impact on our brain's perception of events: a sense of control is fundamental to how our brain interprets the world. Working with managers in one of the government departments who were closing down offices, we explored where they could give shared decision-making in an environment where most decisions were out of the hands of employees. Managers suggested a range of ideas: asking employees to plan what to keep and what to throw away, allowing them to plan leaving parties, encouraging them to facilitate sessions on what they had learned.

4 *Integrity – espoused and actual values match*: The fourth enabler is all about values and honesty: what an organization says it values must match up with what actually gets recognized and promoted. As mentioned earlier, neuroscience identifies the negative impact of uncertainty on our brain. If we are told one thing, but see actions supporting a contrary value, this creates uncertainty, which leads to a threat state.

This enabler is also about *fairness*, which is an intrinsic motivator. Again this stems back to survival: for our prehistoric ancestors, in order to survive they needed to have their fair share of food, and of warmth from the fire. We see this need today: what child hasn't at some point said, 'But that's not fair!' In the last decade we have seen people prepared to die for fairness: the Arab Spring was an example of people's desire for democracy and the right to be treated fairly and transparently. Neuroscience reveals that fairness is important to all of us and becomes all the more important when we are going through change: if there is transition in the organization then we want to know that we will have our fair chance at keeping our jobs or at influencing some of the outcomes.

Neuroscience underpins the enablers of engagement and helps to explain why they create an engaged mindset. An organization where employees felt unsure of their direction and how their contribution made a difference, where managers were distant, uninterested and disrespectful, and where employees felt they had no influence and could not trust what the organization said it valued, would be an organization where employees would be in a very strong threat state and their brains would be unable to think or perform well.

Neuroscience brings some additional insights to employee engagement: the brain needs to be able to focus to work at its best. This raises lots of questions about the working environment and whether open-plan offices with e-mails constantly popping up, lengthy meetings, and mobile devices always on are actually getting in the way of working at our best. Our drive for efficiency in the workplace has a price and all too often that price is poorer-quality thinking and decision-making as well as negative effects on employee well-being and health.

Neuroscience also provides us with insights into how we think, solve problems and make decisions, and is challenging much of the conventional wisdom in this regard (Lieberman, 2013). Conventional problem-solving approaches have been shown in many cases to reinforce the neural networks in the brain that gave rise to the problem in the first place whereas the adoption of solution-focused, 'learning' mindsets and approaches frequently result in 'breakthrough' thinking.

Neuroscience also recognizes that although certainty, autonomy, connectedness, etc are all important to all of us, we each have different preferences and leaders and managers need to be aware of differing personal intrinsic motivators.

One of the other benefits that neuroscience brings to the movement is the language of science. I have worked with many financial services sector organizations and whereas the language of communication or employee engagement is seen as 'soft', the language of neuroscience is much more appealing. As one leader said, 'I like this. This is science, not the usual "psychofluff" communications and HR people bring.'

Can neuroscience teach us about how to spread the work on employee engagement? I believe it can. We are receptive to new ideas when we are in a toward/reward state so we need to make sure that the people we are speaking to do not feel criticized, threatened or wrong.

Key to all this is that people have to reach their own insight: insight in itself is rewarding, more memorable and lasts longer. We need to help leaders reach their own insights about employee engagement, by giving them some space to think about moments when they have felt really excited by work or times when they have seen their teams fired up. Neuroscience also shows us that small actions, conscious or subconscious, can make a big impact on our sense of engagement. Creating a more engaging workplace does not have to be difficult but it does need awareness of what helps the brain and what hinders. Neuroscience provides the evidence to support the instinctive beliefs of good leaders and managers.

Sometimes leaders and managers just need more encouragement in their good practices, for example, that taking time to talk to a team member is not just a 'nice' thing to do, it is actually helping to get the brain into a positive state where it can think, innovate and work better.

TABLE 5.5 Creating a brain-friendly workplace: questions to ask yourself and leaders

We know that:	So:
The brain craves certainty	What more can you tell people?
	Do you have regular communication times and processes in place to help the brain predict?
	Do you explain the rationale behind important decisions that affect people, wherever possible?
	Most performance management, reward and talent management processes create unwanted and unintended states of uncertainty. How can we change them to create a 'toward' state?
A sense of some control has a major impact on reducing stress	What are you already doing to involve people? Can you do more?
	Where else can you pass down responsibility?
	What happens when you are under pressure – is there a tendency to micro-manage? How can you better manage your emotions and continue to delegate?

(continued)

TABLE 5.5   (*Continued*)

We know that:	So:
Our brains are wired to be social and social rejection has an impact on our IQ	Would all your team members say they feel part of your 'in-group'? When did you last speak to each team member? What can you do to remove any barriers to people feeling part of your in-group? What steps can you take to connect with each one? Are you trusted and do team members trust each other? Do you know what matters to each member of your team, what motivates (and what frustrates) them?
Having a sense of purpose and doing good for others is hugely motivating to our brains	When did you last communicate the direction and purpose of the organization? Have you connected employees to the beneficiaries of their work in the last few months? Does everyone recognize the value of the contribution they make and feel appreciated? Do you reward the activities and behaviours that really matter?
Fairness is fundamentally important	Would people say that they are fairly treated in comparison with others? Fairness is not about treating everyone the same way – do people understand and accept the rationale for why some groups might be treated differently from others (eg home working, flexitime etc)? Are people held accountable for their actions and behaviours, irrespective of position in the organization? What assumptions do you make about others? How justified are they and how might things differ if you adopted a different frame of reference?

(*continued*)

TABLE 5.5 *(Continued)*

We know that:	So:
Status matters – we all compare ourselves with others whether we recognize it or not	Do people feel listened to and are their views and opinions genuinely valued? Do individuals receive full credit for their ideas and contributions, irrespective of who they are? Could you do anything more to reduce status barriers in your organization?
Competitive advantage often depends on speed of action and quality of thought	Are decisions delegated to the lowest appropriate level and are employees trusted to use their judgement? Do your organizational practices (multi-tasking, back-to-back meetings, infrequent breaks, mobile expected to be always on, etc) prevent good quality thinking and decision-making? Is your default position about solving problems as opposed to finding solutions?

Conclusion

The paradox of employee engagement is that while it appears to be a straightforward concept, actually making any significant progress to improve engagement continues to elude many organizations. In my experience companies often struggle to know where to begin and the challenge can seem overwhelming. In this chapter we have broken engagement down into a number of enablers to help provide a framework to improve engagement. The enablers offer a practical way to break down the challenge to engage your workforce into more manageable chunks. Evaluating your current activity against the backdrop of the enablers also provides focus for your engagement activity and helps to prioritize your strategy and plan.

Employee engagement tools and techniques

06

Introduction

One of the most common questions I encounter when working with companies to engage their people is: 'What can we do practically to improve engagement?' This chapter will provide some answers to this question. Here I'll share various tools and techniques I have used over many years of working within this field. What they have in common is that they are all tried and tested: I know that they work! You'll be able to see how and where they fit into the enablers' framework discussed in the previous chapter, and also how they take the psychology of engagement into practical application.

Taking a strengths-based approach to employee engagement

One of the themes that runs throughout the tools and techniques discussed here will be that of a 'strengths-based' approach. In Chapter 4 we talked about the positive psychology of engagement, understanding why it is that engaged people outperform others. As a reminder, engagement is a lead indicator of business success rather than a lag indicator: engagement comes first. Drawing on the science of happiness we talked about the need to create opportunities for positive emotion and experiences, and that when we experience these states we release higher levels of dopamine, which in turn switch on learning centres helping us to work harder, better and smarter.

So why is it then that conversations on engagement often begin with analysis of all that is wrong with our workplaces? Strategies designed to engage employees more often than not begin by evaluating problems, looking at what erodes engagement, and then asking how we can fix these problem areas. This approach is referred to as a *deficit approach* to employee engagement, and is compounded by over-reliance on the results from the annual staff survey as the starting point for action. This approach tends to take the bottom five or so areas from the survey and task managers and teams to work on these areas to improve engagement. It's very rare that companies look at the positive findings from the survey and ask how they can learn from this insight. This is the approach I used in my early days of working within the field of employee engagement: going around the survey cycle and focusing on trying to fix all those areas that scored poorly. However, after a few years of trying to fix the broken areas, I found that this approach wasn't really working. Sure there would be some improvements in certain areas, but overall, whilst a huge amount of effort and resources were going into tackling the problems, the solutions just weren't sustainable. By chance I read an article about a technique called *appreciative inquiry* (Berrisford, 2005), which changed the way I approached employee engagement and has informed my work ever since.

What is appreciative inquiry (AI)?

Don't let the name put you off! The concept of AI was originally developed by Cooperrider *et al* (1995) at Case Western Reserve University. Essentially AI is a simple, strengths-based philosophy and approach, which argues that there is just as much to be learned by understanding what works, and what could work, in various situations, instead of always focusing on all that is wrong and how issues and problems can be fixed. When I first came across AI, I recognized immediately the potential of this tool for developing engagement. I recalled various meetings and workshops on engagement I had attended over the years, where the conversation had started by looking at everything that was wrong and how we could fix it: this approach felt counter-intuitive to developing engagement. The approach itself was not in any way engaging and was often quite depressing! People left these sessions feeling fairly helpless about their current situation, overwhelmed by how much was wrong and needed fixing in order to improve and develop engagement amongst their teams and the organization in general. It only takes a few cycles of this approach for the organization to develop learned helplessness when it comes to engagement. If you begin to hear phrases like 'nothing will ever change', and 'here we go again', coupled with a drop year on year in survey response rates, you know you're in this place within your own organization. On discovering AI, I wondered what might happen if we started a conversation by understanding what actually works, and what engagement looks and feels like for our people.

How does AI work?

AI provides a simple framework to follow to enable groups, teams and the organization to have different conversations about engagement. The methodology is based around what is known as the *5-D cycle*.

FIGURE 6.1   Appreciative inquiry (AI) '5-D' cycle

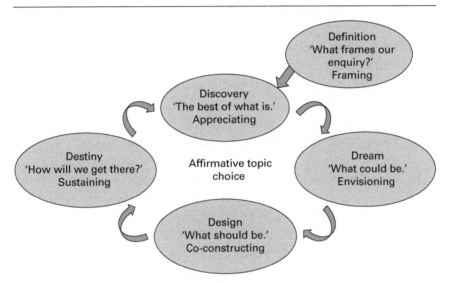

The 5-D cycle offers a simple process to follow when planning any AI intervention. The inquiry takes place by following the cycle through its entirety in the following way:

1 *Definition*: This stage sets up the topic for the AI intervention, essentially framing the inquiry. There are a number of ways in which this can be done. First, if there is a problem or issue that the company wishes to tackle with respect to engagement, this would then be reframed. So for example, if you have an issue with stress or absence you'd like to delve deeper into using AI, you might choose to define your topic as 'promoting well-being' or 'creating a great place to work'. In addition AI can be used equally well when there isn't a problem as such, but simply an area you want to explore further, such as developing an engaged workforce.

Once the topic for AI is defined we then move onto the process itself. Essentially, participants are taken around the cycle, and given the opportunity to talk in depth about each stage. Questions are often drafted before the session to prompt stories and discussion at each stage, but flexibility is helpful. What is great about this process is that it can be run in small groups, with teams, or in large-scale summits with hundreds or even thousands of employees.

2 *Discovery*: Once the topic for the inquiry has been established the process begins with the discovery phase. This part of the process is all about reflecting on 'best of' or positive experiences, by collecting stories from participants. So for example, within the context of engagement, participants might be asked to share stories about times within their work life when they were really engaged, in order to understand what was happening and what the conditions that made this experience possible were.

Questions are prepared in advance to elicit these stories, anecdotes and experiences: at the heart of this process is *storytelling*. Insight is uncovered about the topic but in a positive and appreciative way. In essence, rather than focusing on what isn't working, this phase asks what has worked previously and what we can learn from this.

In my experience this is an incredibly simple but powerful way to get an organization thinking about engagement. By asking people to share stories about times when they loved their jobs the whole focus and feel of the discussion is positive and optimistic. I often use these types of questions to introduce the topic of engagement to people. Very quickly people realize there are common themes throughout the stories they are hearing, which reflect earlier points I made around the need for autonomy, mastery and purpose as prerequisites for engagement. In over 10 years of hearing stories from people about times when they were highly engaged, with hundreds of people, I have never once heard anyone say they loved their job or felt engaged because they were paid a lot, or because the coffee was great, or they had a lovely office, or a big bonus. People tend to talk about being valued and appreciated, having autonomy, a great boss and team, for example. In addition, the experience people have from talking about times when they loved their jobs is engaging in itself. People recall positive memories and experience the emotions they felt at the time: they remember what it felt like to be engaged and are therefore often more motivated to help create a workplace where they can once again have similar experiences. This is a far more productive way to begin a conversation on engagement than focusing on what isn't working and what the company or team scored badly on in the recent employee engagement survey.

3 *Dream*: Once participants have spent time thinking about current or previous experiences within the theme of the AI intervention, they then move onto the dream phase. This section focuses on what *could* be, and asks that participants envision a future that is different from today. This phase is all about the art of possibility, really encouraging participants to focus on what *could* be, challenging them to stretch their thinking and allowing themselves to get excited about a different future. Questions or activities are designed to inspire participants to create a clear and tangible view of where they want to be, and to enable them to describe this future in detail.

The dream phase builds on the learning and discussion from the discovery phase, encouraging participants to create something new. So for example, if the theme for the AI intervention is to create a great place to work, the dream phase would encourage participants to imagine that anything is possible and create a future great place to work for their organization. Questions would be asked, such as: 'What will it look like? What will it feel like? How will it be?'

Using creativity and expressive forms in the dream phase works really well and takes people out of their usual patterns of thinking. For example, in the past I have asked groups to create a mood board or visual for a future great place to work. I have provided art materials to enable groups to do this. Inevitably, there are those groups who get stuck into the activity, who have fun with it and create some really inspiring pictures of the future. However, sometimes groups can feel more uncomfortable with the exercise, so play it safe by writing a bulleted list on a flip chart or similar. There is a stark difference between the two approaches, which the groups notice immediately. Those who have embraced the task generate some great thinking and ideas and perhaps most importantly, energy and motivation to change things. Conversely, those groups who stick to the tried-and-tested bulleted list produce the same answers they have always come up with. Interestingly, I never need to point this difference out to the groups I work with – it's clear for them to see. They reflect on the differences and make the point themselves.

4 *Design*: Next comes the design phase which moves thinking on from what *could* be, to what *should* be. This stage of the process enables the participants to build on their learning and conversations from the previous stages to begin planning and prioritizing what would work well. Questions are asked around what needs to change in order to bring to life their thoughts, ideas and visions from the previous stages. Changes are identified and the seeds of plans and projects are put into place.

In my experience, by following the cycle of AI, by the time you reach this stage participants are far more open about what is possible, and what is within their own ability to change than they might be if the more usual deficit approach is followed. On reaching this stage, it's rare to hear: 'It'll never work' or: 'What's the point? Nothing will ever change.'

5 *Destiny*: The final stage of the AI cycle is destiny. This stage really focuses on what needs to happen in order to deliver or act upon the design discussed in the previous stage. This stage looks at how participants can be accountable for activities and plans they are going to personally take forward, be responsible for or even experiment with. This stage really emphasizes the potential and value of small changes participants can make today in order to move the organization closer to where they want to be.

AI as a tool for engagement

AI is a powerful tool to use within engagement: whether using it as a framework for engagement *per se*, or using it to look at aspects of engagement such as promoting well-being at work, or authentically recognizing employees. Its power lies in the fact that it encourages participants to talk about, and share, real-life experiences and stories, looking at what has already worked in the past or is working today. These real-life stories and experiences are a great foundation for imagining future possibilities, which then don't seem so far-fetched or overwhelming.

From a psychological perspective, given that AI is strengths-based, the process itself generates positive emotions and experiences; it is an engaging process in itself. The process also sets out a clear purpose at the outset and facilitates autonomy amongst participants; they contribute their own stories and ideas and develop their own solutions.

Finally, having a group work together to imagine future possibilities is an excellent way of both involving employees, and giving them a voice: both enablers of engagement. It also makes sense, checking that people are on the same page and there is motivation to move in the same direction.

The 'Make the Difference' toolkit: using AI to develop engagement

Whilst I'm an advocate of using AI to develop and improve engagement, the terminology involved with this approach does not always hit the mark with stakeholders, managers and employees. For some organizations talking about 'dream' or 'discovery' leaves them cold and switches them off from the approach before you have even begun. On realizing the potential of AI to develop engagement, I wanted to find a way to use the fundamental principles, but within an approach that was more palatable to the organizations I was working with. So I developed the 'Make the Difference' toolkit, which takes the best of AI and delivers a straightforward, flexible tool to develop engagement.

The 'Make the Difference' toolkit is a simple and easy-to-use set of activities that outlines a particular way of asking questions and envisioning the future. This approach acknowledges the contribution of individuals, by asking about their own personal engagement, rather than assuming we know what is best for them. This approach creates meaning by drawing on individuals' and team stories of success. As you'll see from the diagram below the stages are taken from the AI 5-D cycle.

The essence of this toolkit is set out in the following pages and is an abridged version of the full intervention. Within each step are various tools and materials to allow you to run sessions for that particular stage of the process.

The five toolkit steps

The five toolkit steps are as follows:

1 *Introduction and employee survey review*: The purpose of this stage is to set the scene for your focus on employee engagement, explaining what it is, and why it matters for your organization. You can integrate the toolkit into your employee survey process or simply use it as a stand-alone activity.

2 *See the difference*: This stage encourages reflection on what has worked for employees in the past and how you can learn from these experiences.

3 *Imagine the difference*: This stage enables employees and managers to create a shared view of what the future could be like.

4 *Shape the difference*: The purpose of this stage is to facilitate agreement on what the employee engagement plan for the team or group should look like.

FIGURE 6.2   Appreciative inquiry: the 5-D cycle

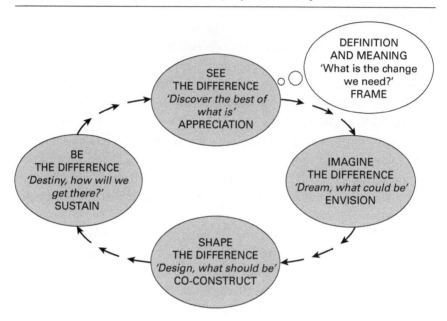

5 *Be the difference*: Finally, this stage is designed to ensure everyone in the team or group takes accountability for the changes agreed, encouraging regular review and monitoring of the team engagement plans.

The toolkit user map below (Figure 6.3) summarizes the toolkit stages.

The toolkit is designed to help you make the transition to transformational engagement within your company by embedding engagement into your organization as an ongoing activity or focus rather than a once-a-year survey. Typically, I recommend that managers use the tools contained here to facilitate conversations about engagement with their teams. However, the tools also work well with those teams who have responsibility for engagement. The 'Make the Difference' approach is different to the usual deficit approach to employee engagement in a number of ways:

- Given that the toolkit is based on AI, it is strengths-based, so rather than asking what is broken, the tools included here will facilitate dialogue on positive experiences, when people have been highly engaged. This enables employees and managers to focus on what works for them rather than on what does not work.

- The toolkit provides a clearly defined, step-by-step process for people managers and others to follow with their teams. For each step, the toolkit explains what people managers need to do and provides them

FIGURE 6.3 Toolkit user map

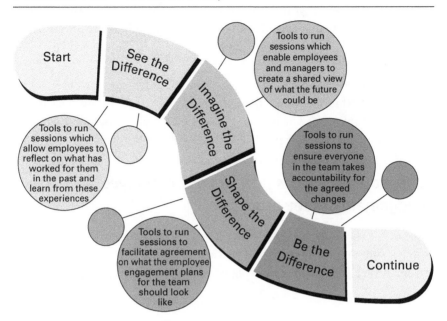

with the tools and guidance they need. This then enables ongoing dialogue between managers and their teams on engagement, rather than a once-a-year discussion in response to the teams' survey results.

- The toolkit can be used in a modular way. Lack of time to focus on engagement is often cited as a barrier and it can be difficult to take people away from their day jobs, so the tools can be used in any way that suits the manager. That might be in half-day workshops or in 20-minute huddles.

- By using the toolkit, managers will develop their skills and knowledge of employee engagement. The toolkit will enable managers to really understand what drives engagement within their own team and therefore take action to improve it.

Using the toolkit: introducing the tools

The tools contained within the following pages give you a flavour of how the toolkit can work. You can develop further activities that are relevant to your own organization. The tools can be used flexibly – you can use them in a bite-size approach if it's difficult to get people together for large chunks of time, or you can add a few of the tools and activities together to create a workshop lasting from a few hours to a couple of days. I'd recommend using a session plan to help you schedule your overall approach and sessions you are planning to use. Take a look at the example (Table 6.1) to give you some ideas. The timings given here are for guidance only; you can choose to extend the time or reduce the time to suit your own circumstances.

Over the following pages you'll see 'how-to' guides for various sessions you can use within the 'Make the Difference' approach. Please refer to the mini-guide (Table 6.2), which gives an overview of which tools and activities to use within each stage of the 'Make the Difference' framework.

Using your toolkit as part of your employee engagement survey process

You can use the tools as part of your employee engagement survey process, or as a stand-alone intervention. If you are intending to use the tools as part of your survey process the following information will be of help.

TABLE 6.1   Sample 'Make the Difference' session planner

Item	Timing	Materials needed	Facilitator
MAKE THE DIFFERENCE INTRODUCTION SESSION (approx running time 60 mins)			
Intro to engagement presentation	30 mins	Slides	
A great place to work?	30 mins	Paper and pens	
SEE THE DIFFERENCE SESSION (approx running time 90 mins)			
Our team results	30 mins	Slides from your report	
Peak experience	30 mins	Paper and pens	
What matters to me	30 mins	Cards or flip chart	
IMAGINE THE DIFFERENCE SESSION (approx running time 30 mins)			
Imagine the future – mood-board exercise	30 mins	Paper and pens	

(continued)

TABLE 6.1   (*Continued*)

Item	Timing	Materials needed	Facilitator
SHAPE THE DIFFERENCE SESSION (approx running time 30 mins)			
Mind the gap	30 mins	Paper and pens	
BE THE DIFFERENCE SESSION (approx running time 30 mins)			
Team reflection	30 mins	Paper and pens	

TABLE 6.2   A quick guide to the tools

Make the Difference stage	Tools you can use
1.0 Introduction	Tool 1 – Introduction to engagement – part 1 Tool 2 – Introduction to engagement – part 2 Tool 3 – Great place to work
2.0 See the difference	Tool 4 – Assessment of engagement from personal stories (peak experience tool) Tool 5 – Understanding of personal engagement of team members ('what's important to me' card-sort exercise)
3.0 Imagine the difference	Tool 6 – Mood board tool Tool 7 – Transform my workplace tool
4.0 Shape the difference	Tool 8 – Mind the gap tool Tool 9 – Clues, hunches and themes tool
5.0 Be the difference	Tool 10 – Team reflection Tool 11 – Action planner

What you need to do

The guidance here is intended for managers who are running sessions with their teams on their employee survey results. The guidance provides a brief overview of the steps managers need to take to get the most out of the survey process and use it as a springboard to build engagement within their team. It is recommended for use when managers have received their team survey results.

Interpret your employee engagement survey report: how-to guide for managers

You can provide the following guidance for managers:

You will need to make sure you prepare fully for your feedback session with your team. There is some guidance below on how to read your report, but most importantly you will need to ensure you make the time to talk through the results with your team, and involve them in action planning. You are not required to come up with actions and solutions yourself – this is something you need to do in partnership with your team.

Reading your report

- *Get the big picture*: Examine your results, comparing them to your business area, the company and the benchmark to understand your results in context. Focus on the results for those questions that relate to the engagement of your team.

- *Highlighting your areas of strength and your areas for development*: Understand those areas in which your team is performing well and those areas in which they are not.

Strengths and development areas: Good questions to ask:

- Where are your strengths?
- What are your high scores?
- Where have you improved most?
- Where are your opportunities for improvement?
- Where have you seen decreases compared to last year's results?
- What surprises you about these results?
- Develop a story: Examine your report to get a sense of your strengths and opportunities. It can be useful to develop a brief summary or story of your report, one you can share with your team. A verbal description of where you are can be much more enlightening than a list of numbers.
- Get into the details: Every survey is different but it can be useful to examine comparisons and benchmarks if you have this data.

- Consider the context: What has happened within your business last year – and what will happen in the near future? Does anything in the outside world have any impact on the results?

Preparation tips

Having taken the time to respond to the survey, employees will be interested to hear about the results and, more importantly, to discuss and agree what actions are going to be taken as a result of their feedback:

- Give your team access to the reports before you meet to help them prepare and formulate their questions and ideas properly.

- Consider what expectations your team will have for the meeting and the issues that are likely to be raised.

- Consider whether you will need the support or assistance of your HR department for in-depth knowledge on the employee engagement survey, its tools, process, and follow-up process.

'Make the Difference' toolkit: individual tools

In the following pages, I have provided actual tools and activities that can be used as part of the 'Make the Difference' approach. They are intended to be used by managers with their teams, but can also be simply adapted to be used with other groups.

Introduction tools

The following set of tools is aimed at managers having initial, scene-setting conversations with their teams about engagement within your organization. They are intended to provide a warm-up to the topic of engagement and are part of the definition and meaning stage of the 'Make the Difference' approach.

TOOL 1: introduction to engagement (Time: 20–30 minutes)

Use the first five minutes to set the scene. Explain what will happen in the session, then use the following warm-up exercise (see also Chapter 1):

- Ask everyone to spend one minute individually writing down all of the words that come into their mind when you say 'engagement'.

- Then after the minute, ask everyone to select the one word that really resonates with them.
- Then ask everyone to read out their one word.

Outputs

This exercise will demonstrate the personal nature of engagement. It means different things to different people – what makes me love my job is probably different to others in the room. It's also a good way of getting people to begin thinking about what the term means.
   Explain:

1   *If you are using the 'Make the Difference' toolkit as part of your survey process:* We are taking a different approach to action planning this year; that's why we're using this toolkit. We recognize the survey is a useful starting point for a conversation about engagement but it is only part of the story. We'd firstly like to thank everyone for taking the time to complete the survey; your input is really valuable to better understand engagement. But what we'd like to do is spend some time better understanding engagement. These sessions are all about finding out what is important to us as a team, and to you as an individual, and what we can do to improve our working lives – so let's begin.

2   *If you are not using the 'Make the Difference' toolkit as part of your survey process:* We recognize the vital role that an engaged workforce has on the performance of our business. We are therefore going to be spending some time talking about engagement within our team – what it means to us and most importantly how to improve it. These sessions are all about finding out what is important to us as a team, and to you as an individual, and what we can do to improve our working lives – so let's begin.

TOOL 2: introduction to engagement presentation (Time: 15–20 minutes)

It's important to explain to employees what engagement means to your organization and why you are focusing on it. I recommend drafting a few slides on this topic, which can be used by everyone within your organization. You could use a cascade process to communicate this information to help ensure consistency of messages.

Objectives:

- to communicate the background to engagement within your organization and the purpose of these sessions;
- to introduce engagement, what it is, why it matters and how to achieve it.

TOOL 3: a great place to work (Time: 30 minutes)

Engagement can be a difficult term to understand – what we actually mean when we talk about engagement is really about making this a great place to work. So we're going to spend some time talking about what this means to us.

This session will provide insight on what engages individuals and teams in a way that is more open than the survey, rather than making assumptions about what engages people.

Teamwork

Ask your team to get into pairs and discuss:

- what a great place to work should feel like;
- what a great place to work should look like;
- what makes a great place to work;
- what it is and what it isn't.

After 10 minutes in pairs, ask each pair to share the outputs from their discussion, then have a wider group discussion.

Time to talk

Instigate a group discussion. Talk about the outputs from each pair:

- What are the similarities?
- What are the differences?

- Are there any surprises?
- What are their general observations about the responses?
- Is there anything as a team we can action now?

Action

Use the stop, start, continue model to begin to capture actions as you go through your 'Make the Difference' sessions.

TABLE 6.3   Sample 'stop, start, continue' model

	STOP	START	CONTINUE
ME			
TEAM			
BUSINESS			

See the difference activities

The next set of tools are intended for use within the 'see the difference' stage of the 'Make the Difference' approach. Again the guidance below is written with managers in mind. In these activities managers will be using a variety of exercises to enable their team to assess the current situation in regard to engagement:

- *Tool 4*: Assessment of engagement from personal stories (peak experience tool);
- *Tool 5*: Understanding of personal engagement of team members (what's important to me card-sort exercise).

TOOL 4: peak experience exercise (Time: 20–30 minutes)

By recounting personal stories of engagement your team will be able to reconnect with what really engages them at work. This will help your team get to the heart of what really engages them and also discover that often this is within their power to influence.

This session will help you understand what engages and motivates your team.

Activity

Ask your team to think about a time when they were really engaged at work – why they loved what they were doing. In pairs, spend 10 minutes interviewing each other (5 minutes each).

Use the following questions:

- Can you tell me about the most valued or engaging experience you have had in your work-life? A time when you really loved your job?
- What were the conditions that made it possible?
- How did these experiences make you feel?

Ask team members to capture an overview of the story, what made it possible, and how it felt, and to also capture any key themes they observe emerging. They will then feed back each other's story to the whole group. When they do this you will capture the key themes on a flip chart.

TABLE 6.4   Peak-experience capture template

	THE STORY	WHAT MADE IT POSSIBLE	HOW IT FELT
ME			
MY PARTNER			

Outputs

As team members are recounting their stories, capture the key words that they feed back. Typically this will include themes such as:

- valued;
- pride;
- confidence;
- autonomy;
- trusted;

- teamworking;

- great manager;

- challenging work;

- success.

This exercise allows people to reconnect with the emotional side of engagement; by telling their stories, team members remember what it feels like to be engaged in their work. Much of the feedback we have an opportunity to influence ourselves, both individually and as a team. This is also a great exercise to get your team in a positive state of mind to talk about engagement.

Discuss and explain

When everyone has fed back their stories take a look at the words you have captured:

- What are the group's observations of the words you have captured?

- What can you do to influence this as a team and create an environment where some of this comes to life?

- So what are your actions? (Please capture any actions in the stop, start continue template as per the previous exercises.)

TOOL 5: what matters to me – the card sort (Time: 20–30 minutes)

Our team survey results are only part of the story in understanding what engages us as individuals and as a team. First, they were taken at a particular moment in time; things might have changed since then. Second, the questions are pre-determined. The survey makes some assumptions about what engages us. However, we want to keep this discussion more open to better understand how we can improve engagement within our team.

This session will facilitate conversations about what engages individuals and ensure action plans are focused on the right actions to improve engagement.

What you'll need

You'll need to make up some cards: 10 cards for each team member. Cards should contain the following information:

TABLE 6.5   Card-sort template

[Insert your Company Logo] What is important to me at work? .... Rank this from 1 – 10 (1 is the most important) Rank:.. How well does this organization perform against this? Really well　　　Not at all 1　　2　　3　　4　　5

Activity

Ask each person to think about what is really important to him or her in order to be engaged at work. If they get stuck ask them: 'What makes you want to jump out of bed in the morning and actually look forward to coming to work?' If required you can include specific attributes from the survey, eg 'communication', 'my team', 'pride', etc as prompts.

Ask them to write down their top 10 list and capture this on their cards, one item per card, and then rank:

- their 'top 10' in order of importance (1 being most important – 10 being least important);
- how the company performs against this (1 being performs really well against this, and 5 being performs really badly against this).

Talk about it

Ask the group to feed back what they have captured, then discuss what is important:

- Look at the similarities and the differences.
- Identify the areas for action.
- Is this very different to what the survey told us, or quite similar?

Write it down

Capture any actions in the stop, start, continue template as per the previous exercises.

Imagine the difference tools

The following set of tools is intended for use within the 'imagine the difference' stage of the 'Make the Difference' approach. Again, the guidance below is written for managers to use with their teams, but can be easily adapted for other scenarios. In these activities managers will be using the tools to enable their team to envision the future:

- *Tool 6*: Mood board tool;
- *Tool 7*: Transform my workplace tool.

TOOL 6: mood board (Time: 30 minutes)

Evidence shows that when we are clear about what we want to achieve we are much more likely to achieve it. Please use the exercise below to get your team to create a vision for the future – what it will feel like to work here if we make the improvements to our engagement we've been talking about so far.

This session will help you and your team create a collective vision of the future.

What you'll need

To run this exercise you'll need:

- A3 card, one per group for their mood board;
- old magazines;
- glue;
- art materials (optional);
- pens.

The mood board

In this exercise, ask team members to get into groups of four and to pick a date in the future. Ask them to imagine that you've made all the improvements you have been talking about – that this is a great place to work.

To help them do this you can use the following questions:

- What is a typical day like?
- What is good about working here now?
- What has changed?

Time to talk

Then ask the groups to create a mood board using the materials provided to communicate their vision of the future. Ask them just to use images if possible. Also stress that anything is possible; they need to imagine there are no constraints and anything can happen! Allow 15 minutes to complete this task. Groups will then be asked to feed back their mood boards to the wider team.

Discuss

In the discussion, ask:

- What are the common themes?
- How does the future vision make you feel?
- What can we begin to action now to try to get us moving towards this?

Write it down

Please capture any actions in the stop, start, continue template as per the previous exercises.

TOOL 7: transform my workplace (Time: 60–90 minutes)

This session will help you and your team create a collective vision of the future.

The challenge

Make a short film: *Transform my workplace.*

The brief

Transport yourself into the future, to a place where this is the best place in the world to work. What will be happening? What will it look and feel like here? We want you to 'transform your workplace' and make a short film to communicate your ideas.

In groups you'll be given a flip cam and a blank storyboard to help you design your film. You'll have just 40 minutes to make your film, and then you'll be asked to play your film back to the rest of the group.

What you'll need

To run this exercise you'll need:

- *Packer video cameras*: Alternatively people can use their smart phones to make short films.
- Card and pens: To map out your storyboard.
- *Write-up tips*: To create a great film (on reverse).

Talk about it

Some questions to ask the group:

- What are the common themes?
- How does the future vision make you feel?
- What can we begin to action now to try to get us moving towards this?

Write it down

Please capture any actions in the stop, start, continue template as per the previous exercises.

Tips for creating a great film
Producer

The producer's role, like any good project manager, is to get your team working together and develop your concept.

Director

The director is responsible for directing the filming once the concept has been agreed, script written and storyboard produced.

Scriptwriters

Responsible for taking the concept and bringing it to life, writing step-by-step instructions for all involved in your shoot, along with any words, lyrics or actions to be delivered by your cast.

Storyboard artist

Working with the scriptwriters you create a visual reference guide for the film to help brief your director and cast.

Location managers

Responsible for finding the right location/locations to shoot your film clip.

Stage manager

The stage manager works with the director to help get the cast into position.

Camera operator

The camera operator films all the action.

Although you will have individual responsibilities, the closer you work together, the better the final result. When the films are complete, spend time viewing each other's films.

Shape the difference tools

The following set of tools is intended for use within the 'shape the difference' stage of the 'Make the Difference' approach. This time, the tools are designed for managers to guide their teams towards creating a plan of action to improve engagement, building on their learning and reflection from the previous stages. However, it should be pointed out that action is encouraged in earlier stages via the use of the 'stop, start, continue' approach: teams shouldn't wait until this stage to make any changes or implement any action, this should be happening already. Moreover this stage helps to really focus teams on what else needs to happen to move them forward and improve their engagement:

- *Tool 8*: Mind the gap tool;
- *Tool 9*: Clues, hunches and themes tool.

TOOL 8: mind the gap (Time: 30 minutes)

Once the current situation and the desired future are identified, a gap analysis can be done to determine what action is needed. This session takes you through your current state and desired future and helps you identify the gaps that need to be filled.

This session will help you conduct a gap analysis for engagement.

Filling the gap

Remind your team about themes emerging from the previous sessions:

- Where we are today (from 'see the difference').

- Where we want to be (from 'imagine the difference').

Divide your team into two groups and ask them to discuss and document:

- how near we are to where we would like to be:
  - when this is a great place to work; and
  - listing all the areas we are performing well in;
- how far away we are from where we would like to be:
  - listing all of those areas we need to develop in.

Then look at what the 'gap' is. Talk about what the gap tells us and therefore what our thoughts are on areas for action as a team.

Time to talk

Undertaking a gap analysis is a great exercise to fully analyse and understand what we do, how we do it and what we can do to make things better. Discuss and identify the gaps as a team.

What to do

Please capture any actions in the stop, start, continue template as per the previous exercises – by now you should be developing a comprehensive action plan for your team.

TOOL 9: clues, hunches and themes
(Time: 45 minutes)

This session will use the evidence and insights you have gathered so far to help you to build your action plan. To run this session you will need: sticky notes (Post-it® notes), a flip chart pad and pens.

Capture the clues

First, ask your team to capture the 'engagement clues' they have gathered so far on the Post-it® notes provided – one clue per sticky note. The clues must be based on fact and not opinion, so for example:

- *I have seen... people smiling a lot more recently.*

- *I have heard... that Joe is leaving because he can't work flexibly here.*

- *I read... a recent report that showed our employee turnover is up.*

- *I know... that I intend to be here in a year's time because I love my job!*

Once you have gathered all of the clues, stick them up onto a wall and ask your team to read through.

What are the hunches?

Now ask them to interpret what these clues mean: What are their hunches about? What do they see on the wall? This is where their opinions and interpretations are sought, for example:

- *I believe we're seeing more people smiling around here because we have a great new boss who really values what we do.*

- *I think that our employee turnover is up because morale has taken a dive following all the recent changes we have gone through.*

Capture all of the hunches onto a flip chart and review and discuss them as a team:

- Who agrees/disagrees?
- Why is this happening?
- What is within our sphere of control?

Theme findings

As you are discussing the hunches you need to capture the themes emerging. For example, many of your hunches might lead to a theme that is: 'We need to get better at managing the people-side of change.'

When capturing the themes, try to focus them into areas for opportunity, so rather than say: 'We're really poor at managing the people-side of change', flip this to: 'We will focus on getting much better at managing the people-side of change, and what we need to do is…'.

In response to your themes, capture any arising actions. Throughout this exercise ask: 'What can you do about the situation?' and: 'How can we influence it?'

Write it down

Please capture any actions in the stop, start, continue template as per the previous exercises to build up your team action plan.

Be the difference tools

The following set of tools is intended for use within the 'be the difference' stage of the 'Make the Difference' approach. The final stage of the 'Make the Difference' approach is about empowering employees to take action and accountability for at least some of the changes they have identified throughout the process:

- *Tool 10*: Team reflection;
- *Tool 11*: Action planner.

TOOL 10: team reflection (Time: 30 minutes)

It's good to make time to think about actions and behaviours that can positively impact upon engagement, in particular what individuals and teams can do differently to improve their engagement.

This session will give your team the space to reflect on previous discussions and consider how they can impact engagement.

Activity

Split the team into threes and ask them to consider the outputs and actions from all of the previous sessions you have run. Ask them to discuss and consider the following:

- How does our future vision make you feel?
- Identify the three commitments you can make to achieve the changes you want to bring about.
- List the top three things that need to change, and ideas for how you would change them.
- List any actions you need to take.

Talk about it

Ask the group to feed back and capture the outputs in a central place. Ask for feedback and discussion from the rest of the team as each group feeds back.

Write it down

Please capture any actions in the stop, start, continue template as per the previous exercises.

TOOL 11: action planner

This session will set measurable action plans for your team to improve employee engagement.

Activity

Ask your team to look back through the stop, start, continue templates you have filled in together through your 'Make the Difference' journey and agree your engagement action plan. Some things to think about:

- What do you want engagement to deliver for you and why are you focusing on engagement?
- Use your action points from previous exercises.

TABLE 6.6   Action planning template

Action	Owner	Timescale

- Pick no more than five action points.
- Please avoid arbitrary target setting, such as: 'Improve dimension x by y per cent.' Link actions and improvements you are looking for to business goals.
- Empower your team to own their actions; not all actions need to be owned by the line manager.

Outputs

You should by now have a full and complete action plan, which has been developed by your team.

And finally: keeping the process alive

Moving from transactional engagement to transformational engagement requires ongoing dialogue on engagement, a culture where engagement is in the DNA of the company, rather than seen as an annual stand-alone activity. The 'Make the Difference' toolkit provides a great set of tools to enable these conversations to happen, but the real power of the toolkit is in keeping these conversations and actions alive. To help achieve this we recommend managers nominate an 'engagement champion' from their team.

Their role would include:

- documenting the actions from your workshop;
- reporting progress;
- keeping engagement on the agenda;
- working with HR to ensure any major issues are fed back up the line.

There are many reasons for an organization to survey its employees, and here are some of the main benefits:

- Surveys can help confirm what we already know.
- Surveys can identify what we didn't know.
- Surveys can dispel organizational myths.
- Surveys provide employees with a confidential feedback process.
- Surveys can help target improvement activities.
- Surveys allow organizations to track improvements in results over time.

However, you do not have to rely on surveys to tell you how your people are feeling within your organization. The best way to keep your finger on the pulse is to empower and encourage managers to speak to their teams on a regular basis. Engagement updates can be built into weekly/monthly/ quarterly meetings. This will remind employees that it is still on the list of priorities.

It's important also to close the feedback loop, linking actions taken back to engagement activities and discussions. When changes are made and success is achieved, make sure to explicitly link what has been done to the feedback received: you can never overstate this.

Top tips for managers running 'Make the Difference' sessions

Very often, managers believe they need to have all the answers – that's why they *are* a manager isn't it? It can feel quite different for managers to involve their teams in developing ideas and plans to improve and develop engagement. Below are a few tips and guidelines you may wish to share with managers or others who will be facilitating 'Make the Difference' sessions:

- This is an opportunity to find out what your team thinks. You can start the conversation, but you should allow them to do most of the talking.

- Don't arrive at your session with a prepared action plan. The whole point of this part of the process is to get your team's feedback and collectively decide on actions. It is best to avoid pre-empting their responses.

- Involve *all* of your team in the conversation; try to avoid letting one or two people dominate. Do not let a minority of your team members decide the direction of the session. Once people have had their say, invite others to participate. Reiterate that the session is to allow *all* team members to contribute. This can result in a richer and more innovative action plan.

- If you're looking at your survey results with your team, try to avoid getting caught up in a discussion about maths. There may be disagreements about the exact meaning of some numbers in the report. You can then move this conversation towards interpretation to construct a story and a thematic summary.

- Emphasize the positives as well as the negatives. Very unhappy teams may require a few minutes at the beginning of the session to get certain feedback 'off their chest'. It may be beneficial to allow some time for this at the beginning of the meeting, but ensure that you return to the task at hand. When a team member offers a complaint, you can counter this by inviting the person to make a suggestion for improvement. Ask your team to reframe negative statements into something they want to move towards instead.

- Keep it simple by focusing on two or three items for action to begin with, and discourage your team from attempting to solve everything at once. It may be advisable to restrict actions to this number of items, but then allow for additional initiatives further down the line once actions are completed.

The World Café approach

The World Café (2008) is a further example of a strengths-based approach that works well to develop engagement. It is a powerful social tool for engaging people in conversations that matter and is a great way to engage employees. It's based on the understanding that conversation is the core process that drives personal, business and organizational life and is more than a method, a process or a technique – it's a way of thinking and being together sourced in a philosophy of *conversational leadership*. Drawing on seven integrated *design principles*, the World Café is a simple, effective and flexible format for hosting large group dialogue. Whilst the approach doesn't specifically use AI, there are obvious similarities and I have often used AI and the 5-D design principles to design Cafés I have run with organizations.

World Cafés tend to be run with large groups of people, and take the form of a summit run over a single day or a couple of days. They make a great alternative to the usual employee conference by involving participants in the conversation, rather than talking at them for hours. The World Café can be modified to meet a wide variety of needs. Specifics of context, numbers, purpose, location, and other circumstances are factored into each event's unique invitation, design and question choice, but the following design principles comprise the basic model.

How to run a World Café: guidelines for success

Conducting an exciting Café conversation is not hard – it's limited only by your imagination! The Café format is flexible and adapts to many different circumstances. When these guidelines are used *in combination,* they foster collaborative dialogue, active engagement and constructive possibilities for action:

1 *Set the context and clarify your purpose*: Pay attention to the reason you are bringing people together, and what you want to achieve. Knowing the purpose and parameters of your meeting enables you to consider and choose the most important elements to realize your goals, eg who should be part of the conversation, what themes or questions will be most pertinent, what sorts of harvest will be more useful, etc.

2 *Create hospitable space*: Café hosts around the world emphasize the power and importance of creating a hospitable space – one that feels safe and inviting. When people feel comfortable to be themselves, they do their most creative thinking, speaking and listening. In particular, consider how your invitation and your physical set-up will contribute to creating a welcoming atmosphere. Create a 'special' environment, most often modelled after a café, ie small round tables covered with a checkered tablecloth, butcher-block paper, coloured pens, a vase of flowers, and optional 'talking stick' item.

3 *Welcome and introduction*: The host begins with a warm welcome and an introduction to the World Café process, setting the context, sharing the Café etiquette, and putting participants at ease.

4 *Small group rounds*: The process begins with the first of three or more 20-minute rounds of conversation for the small group seated around a table. At the end of the 20 minutes, each member of the group moves to a different table. They may or may not choose to leave one person as the 'table host' for the next round, who welcomes the next group and briefly fills them in on what happened in the previous round.

5 *Explore questions that matter*: Knowledge emerges in response to compelling questions. Find questions that are relevant to the real-life concerns of the group. Powerful questions that 'travel well' help attract collective energy, insight and action as they move throughout a system. Depending on the time frame available and your objectives, your Café may explore a single question or use a progressively deeper line of enquiry through several conversational rounds. Each round is prefaced with a question designed for the specific context and desired purpose of the session. The same questions can be used for more than one round, or they can be built upon each other to focus the conversation or guide its direction.

6 *Encourage everyone's contribution*: As leaders we are increasingly aware of the importance of participation, but most people don't only want to participate, they want to actively contribute to making a difference. It is important to encourage everyone in your meeting to contribute their ideas and perspectives, while also allowing anyone who wants to participate by simply listening to do so.

7 *Connect diverse perspectives*: The opportunity to move between tables, meet new people, actively contribute your thinking, and link the essence of your discoveries to ever-widening circles of thought is one of the distinguishing characteristics of the Café. As participants carry key ideas or themes to new tables, they exchange perspectives, greatly enriching the possibility for surprising new insights. After the small groups (and/or in between rounds, as desired) individuals are invited to share insights or other results from their conversations with the rest of the large group. These results are reflected visually in a variety of ways, most often using graphic recorders in the front of the room. Through practising shared listening and paying attention to themes, patterns and insights, we begin to sense a connection to the larger whole. After several rounds of conversation, it is helpful to engage in a *whole group conversation*. This offers the entire group an opportunity to connect the overall themes or questions that are now present.

8 *Listen together for patterns and insights*: Listening is a gift we give to one another. The quality of our listening is perhaps the most important factor determining the success of a Café. Through practising shared listening and paying attention to themes, patterns and insights, we begin to sense a connection to the larger whole. Encourage people to listen for what is not being spoken along with what is being shared.

9 *Share collective discoveries*: Conversations held at one table reflect a pattern of wholeness that connects with the conversations at the other tables. The last phase of the Café, often called the 'harvest', involves making this pattern of wholeness visible to everyone in a large group conversation. Invite a few minutes of silent reflection on the patterns, themes and deeper questions experienced in the small group conversations and call them out to share with the larger group. Make sure you have a way to capture the harvest – working with a *graphic recorder* is recommended.

If you're interested in running a World Café I would highly recommend taking a look at their website: **www.theworldcafe.com**. On the site you'll find a host of useful resources, a World Café community you can join, videos, case studies: everything you'll need to run your own Café.

Involving employees: using an employee-led approach to engagement

For engagement to be sustainable, it needs to be led and owned by employees from within the business rather than HR, or internal communications or even your head of engagement. So far we've talked in depth about the critical role leaders and managers play in developing engagement. However, employees who are further down the hierarchy also have a critical role to play. The concept of employee networks, or champions, or change agents has been around for some time and used to great effect in many organizations. Essentially this tactic gives responsibility for engagement, not just to leaders and managers, but to those employees in the organization who may not officially have 'manager' within their job title.

This approach works well for a number of reasons. First, research shows that people are more likely to trust 'a person like me' or 'a regular employee' than the CEO or board of directors. Edelman (2017) publish their *Trust Barometer* report annually, which details a range of insight on trust and is a useful resource to understand the shifting sands of who we do and don't trust. So taking an employee-led approach to engagement capitalizes on this insight, that employees are more likely to trust others like them or regular employees than directors. Second, using an employee-led approach can also help to facilitate autonomy. By giving a group of champions autonomy to develop and lead on your engagement agenda this not only contributes to increasing their own engagement, but also sends out a message to others within your company that autonomy is encouraged and supported. Using an employee-led approach also facilitates purpose and mastery, the other two dimensions of self-determination theory, discussed in previous chapters. Setting up a community such as this involves working with them to establish their purpose, and more often than not developing their engagement skills to ensure they are equipped to fulfil the role that has been jointly identified. Finally, I have found that this approach to engagement is more sustainable and helps to embed engagement into the culture of the organization. Engagement is owned by employees, and whilst membership of the group may change, the group itself continues, often for many years, helping to ensure engagement is a constant area of focus.

Undertaking an employee-led approach to engagement: creating a community of engagement leaders

The following guide provides you with some top tips:

1 *Defining the role and responsibilities of the group*: The roles and responsibilities of an employee-led group will very much depend on the context of what you are trying to achieve within your own organization. However, to help you think about the types of skills and capabilities that make a good engagement representative take a look at the role profile below, which we have developed to help companies recruit the right people. This role profile has been designed to outline the role of engagement champions. This role profile focuses on creating a great place to work (GPTW). The work of an engagement champion within this context will be integral to ensuring this happens – they will be passionate about employee engagement, and the role engagement plays in the creation of a GPTW.

2 *Recruiting members*: Once you have defined the roles and responsibilities of the group, it's important to get the right people involved from the outset. There are a number of ways you can recruit members:

- Advertise the group and the role itself and recruit members as you would for any role within your organization.

- Have an election-based approach, where potential candidates campaign to be elected onto the group.

- Ask for volunteers to sign up to be a part of the group via a company-wide communications campaign.

TABLE 6.7 'A great place to work': role profile for engagement champions

Role purpose: what is the purpose of the role?	Accountabilities: what are the deliverables?	What is needed?
To work alongside steering group in identifying ways in which we can make the organization a better place to work by sharing ideas, planning activities, implementing and evaluating actions to improve the way we work on both a local and virtual level. This role will contribute towards the wider objective of helping the organization to attract and retain the best quality staff The role involves regular communication with frontline employees to understand what they value most in their jobs, to identify where the organization may be falling short and to jointly come up with innovative solutions as to how we might address any issues Although you will work as part of a virtual team, much of your time will be spent focusing on the continuous improvement of your own site You will be enthusiastic and energetic and will enjoy motivating others. You will be an ambassador for 'a great place to work' and will play an important part in keeping the vision alive	To play a lead role in developing engagement through: • attending regular meetings to review progress against plan and to prioritize next steps • leading engagement sessions for local employees and reporting back on progress and achievements to date • facilitating group discussions, remaining positive when dealing with difficult people or situations by building rapport and displaying confidence when influencing others • generating and collating creative ideas as to how we can make this a better place to work, to feed back into the wider team • making recommendations on areas for improvement and possible solutions • driving forward local activities and being involved in these as appropriate • building trust and developing good working relationships with other engagement champions • demonstrating a desire for success and actively seeking opportunities where they will be able to add value	Key know-how: • To have a good understanding of the overall objectives of engagement within our organization • To have an appreciation of the role of frontline employees in understanding the issues faced • To be able to critically evaluate the effectiveness of local/group initiatives introduced as a result of 'a great place to work' • To effectively manage stakeholder relationships along with the ability to build rapport and develop good working relationships with others Personal skills: • To take the initiative and demonstrate commitment to the overall vision • To actively contribute towards creating a great place to work • To be confident when delivering sessions to small groups • To have good communication and facilitation skills • To remain calm when dealing with conflict/difference of opinion • To be passionate about what we can deliver and be able to engage others in the vision by talking positively about the benefits to both employees and the business • To display energy and enthusiasm for engagement

- Ask teams or business units to put forward their own representative.

- Or you can pick people yourself if you think this would give you the best result.

3 *Establishing a purpose*: Whilst roles and responsibilities may have been set prior to the formation of the group, involving the group in defining their purpose once formed is ideal. This can be done within the first meet-up of the group and helps to give the group direction for their activities. It can be as simple as a one-line statement or a more in-depth terms of reference – whatever works for you.

4 *Developing the team*: It's important to ensure that engagement champions (or whichever term you use to define members of the group) have the right skills to fulfil their roles. At the most basic level I would recommend running an on-boarding session that provides some of the basics of engagement: what it is, why it matters and how you do it. It's important that this group feels like engagement experts and has the knowledge required to overcome criticism.

5 *Defining success criteria*: Success criteria should be demarcated with the team to define from the outset. Not only will this enable you to track and monitor progress but also to help the team to view the difference they are making to the organization. It also enables reporting back up the line to demonstrate the value-add of this approach to senior management.

6 *Rewarding and recognizing team members:* Employees undertaking this additional role need to be valued and recognized for the additional contribution they are making. Some organizations choose to do this formally, actually assigning part of an employee's freedom to work (FTW) to their champions role, building in objectives to their appraisal process and linking bonus to performance. For other organizations employees undertake this role above and beyond their day job, and it's important that in such cases employees are valued and recognized. This can be via formal channels such as the company awards scheme or more informally, for example via a thank-you letter from directors with a gift.

A network of engagement champions can make a significant and sustainable difference to engagement within an organization. The network itself also helps to facilitate autonomy, mastery and purpose with those involved, developing their own engagement. This approach helps to empower a small but influential group of employees to own, develop and deliver your engagement strategy at a local level, making small but significant changes.

CASE STUDY AXA PPP Healthcare

With corporate bees, Zumba® classes, electric vans, French lessons and a whole range of flexible working patterns in use, AXA PPP Healthcare takes employee engagement very seriously. AXA PPP Healthcare is part of the AXA Group, a worldwide leader in financial services. With 2,300 employees, this part of the business specializes in healthcare, providing affordable plans that offer peace of mind for customers and their families. They have been recognized as one of the 'Top 25 Best Big Companies to Work For' – for the third year in a row now – and have been awarded the 'Positive about Disabled People' symbol from the Department of Employment.

AXA PPP Healthcare has embraced employee engagement for many years, recognizing it as a critical driver of business success. Back in 2000, AXA ran its first global employee opinion survey. In AXA PPP Healthcare, the data revealed a keen interest in corporate social responsibility issues among employees, specifically within the local community. A committee of volunteers was set up to build relationships with local community organizations and charities, to organize fundraising efforts and encourage employee volunteering. It proved such a success that shortly afterwards a full-time role was created to manage the activities, working alongside the 'Hearts in Action' committee. In 2014 over half the employees took part in at least one day's volunteering and over £170,000 was raised for various charities by employees.

Employees have also driven behavioural change in the area of environmental responsibility. 'Greenwatch' volunteers persuaded employees and management to make dramatic changes to support the environment, ranging from encouraging recycling by setting up recycling stations (everything from paper cups to bras!), dramatically reducing paper consumption and introducing electric vans, photovoltaic units on every building, light sensors, and a lift-sharing scheme. The team has even set up four beehives on the roofs of the AXA offices within Tunbridge Wells, looked after by employees who have been specially trained. The honey produced is sold to employees for charity.

As a healthcare company, AXA PPP Healthcare practises what it preaches, and in addition to employee assistance programmes, occupational health and mental resilience training, employees are encouraged to get fit with Zumba® and Bokwa® classes, relax with meditation and yoga classes, give blood, have free mole scans and flu jabs, learn sign language and have life-coaching, among other benefits. Employees also get involved in any campaigns being run for corporate clients, such as sun awareness, bowel cancer awareness and mental health initiatives, and enjoy a health and well-being room where they can de-stress and relax.

What is really interesting about the AXA PPP Healthcare story is that their engagement activity is predominantly driven and led by their employees. The beehives came about after an employee put the idea to management and was given the green light to go ahead. Autonomy features heavily in the company: if employees have good ideas to improve not just their workplace, but products and services as well, they are actively encouraged to pursue this and make it happen. For example, the Ageing Well and Dental hubs on the corporate website were developed by the employees who came up with the original idea. This approach supports integrity within the business; employees are encouraged to come forward with ideas, but unlike many organizations, they then see these ideas come to life.

Although there is an engagement strategy, the company strongly believes that it is the proactive involvement of its people that drives the best ideas. The various sports and social clubs are testament to this – most companies would not dream up a knitting club (which crochets poppies for Armistice Day). It is not just down to employees, though: many of the directors happily get involved, offering their services as dinner-party chefs, coffee waiters or babysitters to the highest bidders in the annual charity auction. It is this culture of involvement that makes AXA PPP Healthcare a great place to work.

Using a viral change approach to engage employees

I am a huge fan of the work of Leandro Herrero (2008) and his work on using a viral change approach to develop engagement within organizations. This approach builds on the employee-led change approach discussed previously to bring about change, in this case, a more engaged workforce.

Within his book, *Viral Change*, Herrero makes a compelling case for an alternative approach to the traditional large-scale change methodologies we are all familiar with. In essence, he argues that change happens when people start to do things differently, to behave differently, and that these behaviours spread in a way that is more akin to a virus than to a formal cascade down the company hierarchy. But what is really interesting about this approach is that it calls for the identification of small, tangible, concrete, non-negotiable behaviours to bring about the desired change within an organization. These behaviours are then role-modelled and spread by small groups of highly connected, highly influential people within an organization. Leandro argues that approaching change in this way is much more effective than the usual top-down, campaign, or programme approach.

There are a number of reasons using a viral change approach can work well for engagement. First, this approach relies on defining the small behaviour changes you need to realize your goal. In our case we are looking at how to improve or develop engagement within the workplace. It is helpful to consider small behaviour changes when looking at engagement: the term 'engagement' can feel unwieldy, abstract, and often poorly defined within organizations. Taking the time to figure out what behaviours will change for employees to be engaged is a very worthwhile pursuit. For example, I worked with a client who had a very disengaged workforce: only 25 per cent of employees reported that they were engaged at work as measured by their annual employee survey. When looking at how to go about improving engagement, the team involved felt overwhelmed by the enormity of this task and where to start. We used a viral change approach with this client, starting the process by recruiting and developing a group of engagement champions. Working with this group we spent a significant amount of time understanding what would be different if the workforce was highly engaged, specifically, how would people behave? One of the themes that came out was that people weren't very friendly, no one said hello in the morning when they came into work, and people just didn't talk to each other. The champions agreed the company needed to talk more. Breaking down the task of improving engagement into small, well-defined behaviours gave the champions confidence and belief that they could begin to change their workplace and make improvements.

Which brings me on to the second reason a viral change approach works well for engagement: it promotes autonomy, mastery and purpose, which underpin engagement. Working with the champions, we enabled them to figure out the purpose of engagement by defining the behaviour changes required. In addition they were tasked to solve the problem – what behaviours needed to change – which in turn contributed to their autonomy. And finally they were tasked with doing something about this, with role-modelling the behaviour changes they had defined, which in turn gave the champions mastery experiences.

The champions agreed that they could get the company talking more by committing to the following behaviours:

- On arriving at work each day they would say 'good morning' and speak to at least three people as they walked to their desk.
- At least three times a week they would take lunch in the cafeteria and speak to colleagues.
- Once a day they would get up and go to speak to a colleague rather than e-mail them.
- At least once a week they would start a conversation at the 'whiteboard' area in the break-out space about the topic of the week with other

colleagues (the whiteboard area was a large white board where each week a question was posed and employees were encouraged to write up responses or other questions).

There was some scepticism from certain members of the group that these actions would make any difference. However, what happened was that very quickly reports began to filter back that things were feeling different, people were talking more, and the office felt friendlier. The champions were pleasantly surprised at just how effective this approach was to changing the culture of the organization very quickly. Of course this is just one example to bring to life how viral change can work as a technique to improve and develop engagement. In this example the champions group worked on developing engagement for over a year and there were many other examples of behaviours they defined and role-modelled, helping to spread them across the organization. With this particular client, their engagement index score moved from 25 per cent to 89 per cent in just 12 months, providing us with a very compelling case for using viral change.

Developing employee voice

There are a number of tried-and-tested tools and approaches that can be used to ensure your employees have a voice. In summary there are three main approaches:

1 *The representative structure approach*: This refers to approaches whereby employee representatives meet managers on a regular basis, either via scheduled committees, or through more ad hoc arrangements. The essential characteristic of this approach is that participation is not direct between employees and their managers but is mediated through representatives. This includes structures such as trade unions, staff council or employee works councils.

2 *Specific communication channels, which are designed to give employees a voice*: These can include channels such as ideas schemes, forums on your company intranet, listening groups and many more.

3 *A more informal approach, which is part of your company culture and your DNA*: For example managers naturally ask for their team's opinions, a coaching culture could be in place, employees are consulted on change and decisions which impact them and many more.

What all of the approaches have in common is that they capture views, thoughts, ideas and opinions of employees. This might be on an individual level or views can be aggregated to provide the collective voice of the employee. Over recent years we have witnessed more emphasis on individual voice and a relative decline in collective voice. For example, there has been a steady decline in union membership in more recent years, although they are still an important channel for employee voice in certain sectors such as public services.

Representative structure approaches

Approaches include:

- *Partnership schemes*: Such as European Works Councils. This approach focuses on common ground and mutual gains, seeking to approach issues in a spirit of cooperation rather than through traditional adversarial relationships.
- *Joint consultation*: This approach focuses on issues where there is common interest to all parties involved. This can include non-union as well as unionized workplaces.
- *Collective representation*: This approach involves negotiations, which lead to joint regulation of pay and other conditions of employment between employer and employee representatives.
- *Employee forums*: This approach involves groups of non-union or mixed groups of union/non-union employees meeting with management for consultation and information sharing.

Communication channels designed to give employees a voice

Approaches include:

- *Two-way communications*: This includes any communication channel that allows employees to respond and feed back. This could involve face-to-face briefings, for example, leaders' Q&A, or online discussion forums.
- *Suggestion or ideas schemes*: This approach can include the formal company suggestion scheme, or a more ad hoc approach to gathering employee ideas about a specific issue or topic.
- *Attitude surveys*: Questionnaire surveys (electronically or paper-based), designed to discover staff's opinions and attitudes with particular aspects of work.
- *Project teams*: Groups of individual employees brought together on a regular or ad hoc basis to discuss issues or specific aspects of work.

It's worth mentioning here that the rise in social media channels has led to another significant shift and *the emergence of 'social voice'*. This change has been driven both by the development of technology and by changes in wider society, which has become more individualistic and more networked. Social media has enabled individual employees and groups of employees to express their views upwards to management, across to other colleagues and outwards to customers and the general population in a less structured and hierarchical manner. This can be done either via the companies' formal social channels or informally via websites such as Glassdoor, which enable employees to anonymously rate their workplace and CEO. Whilst social media is a new and unfamiliar tool for many employers, there is no doubt that we will see a rise in the use of this channel of communication in the future. This is a topic we will revisit in Chapter 9 given the potential significance for the future of employee engagement.

It's important to provide a variety of ways for your employees to make their voices heard. Running an annual employee opinion survey is not enough: imagine what would happen to a company that only sought the opinions of their customers once a year. In order to move to transformational engagement companies need to continually listen to employees, harness their feedback and insight and act on it. This should be ongoing and embedded into the organizational culture, not something that is done annually. Providing a good channel mix to enable employees to make their voices heard helps to achieve this. The Involvement and Participation Association (IPA) provide the following guidelines:

- Employees need to be able to express their views both individually and collectively, therefore voice channels need to strike a balance between the two.

- Using a variety of tools ensures that the organization gets a broad perspective that is representative of their staff as a whole.

- Channels have to be fit for purpose. For example, direct and instantaneous voice channels are more effective for the sharing of ideas to promote innovation, while more structured and formal channels, such as trade unions or staff forums, are better suited to consultations on redundancy, reorganization or restructuring.

- Employees tend to have preferences about which channels they wish to use. Some may be happy to speak up at team or union meetings, others might not feel comfortable.

- Using approaches to voice that do take into account the growing use of social media, or those that prevent effective bottom-up communication between employees and managers/senior leadership or between employees within an organization represent missed opportunities. Companies need to make conscious choices around how they provoke and stimulate employee voice. Using a variety of appropriate channels, analysing what is being said and identifying specific suggestions for action to follow through and feeding back demonstrates the organization's commitment to voice and therefore encourages employees to participate more fully. Understanding and embedding this cycle creates a self-reinforcing or virtuous circle to achieve effective voice.

Taking a big-picture approach to your strategic narrative

Whilst it may be somewhat of a cliché, a picture really does paint a thousand words. Engaging employees in your strategic narrative is rarely a straightforward exercise. Working with senior leaders to understand the company's strategic narrative can involve complicated numbers, financial ratios, market and industry knowledge and a whole lot more. Translating this complex information into something employees can engage with is a challenge. Over the years I have often used a 'big picture' approach to overcoming this challenge. This approach involves translating the company strategy into a visual or series of images to enable employees to understand where the company is heading and why.

Below is a case study from Big Picture Learning and EDF Energy to illustrate this approach and how it works.

CASE STUDY   Leading the energy change

EDF Energy is one of the UK's largest energy companies and the largest producer of low-carbon electricity, producing around one-fifth of the nation's electricity from its nuclear power stations, wind farms and coal and gas power stations. The company supplies gas and electricity to around 6 million business and residential customer accounts and is the biggest supplier of electricity by volume in Great Britain.

The need

In January 2009, British Energy was acquired by EDF Group and work began on bringing together EDF Energy and British Energy – and refreshing the vision, mission, ambitions and values of the new company. Results from the November 2009 employee engagement survey showed employees were keen to learn more about the company's direction and new business activities – and how they could play their part in 'Leading the energy change'.

The solution

The first EDF Energy 'Our Compelling Story' learning map was developed with the company's 70-strong Senior Leadership Team and was used as the basis for manager-led workshops across the company from March 2010. The large, visually rich picture contained information about EDF Energy – celebrating the past, conveying the present and painting a picture of a new and inspiring future. It gave teams of 8–10 people the opportunity to explore content in a challenging and enjoyable way, using interactive learning materials such as discussion prompts, card matching exercises, a jigsaw puzzle and quizzes. Using this approach helped to encourage discussion and understanding of key learning points, tapping into the knowledge and opinions of everyone involved. The 'solutions focus' of supporting materials ('What's working already?' 'How can we make things even better?') facilitated positive and constructive debate.

Four sections covered the core content:

- **What we're all here for:** Our vision and mission; industry context and challenges.

- **What we need to stay focused on:** Our ambitions, milestones, metrics.

- **How we need to work together:** Bringing our values to life for each team.

- **What we need to do:** Our biggest hopes; actions needed to move us forward.

More than 14,788 employees (some 96 per cent) took part in the original series of workshops and content was also used as part of induction for new employees.

Key outcomes

Post-session reactions from participants were hugely positive:

- I enjoyed my 'Our Compelling Story' session (93 per cent).

- Participating in the session was a good use of my time (87 per cent).

- Our session leader encouraged everyone to get involved (98 per cent).

- Our session leader was well-prepared for running the session (98 per cent).

- I'm looking forward to playing my part in 'Leading the energy change' (91 per cent).

FIGURE 6.4 EDF Energy big picture

Furthermore, survey results in November 2010 showed a solid improvement in positive responses for engagement drivers (eg leadership, change management, communications):

- I believe strongly in EDF Energy's ambitions (+9 per cent).
- I believe EDF Energy's Executive Team has a clear vision for the future (+8 per cent).
- What kind of job is EDF Energy's Executive Team doing in providing leadership? (+9 per cent).

There was also a statistically significant difference between the responses of people who had attended a workshop versus those who hadn't. These results, coupled with local success stories, assured EDF Energy's Executive Team of the return on their investment and a second chapter of 'Our Compelling Story' – a continuation of the original picture – was launched in September 2013. This programme is achieving similarly positive results; people who have attended sessions report higher levels of engagement and feel much more 'connected' to EDF Energy. Those who have attended both workshop sessions and can see how they are contributing to the journey report the highest levels of engagement.

Part of 'the way we do things around here'

Having 'Our Compelling Story' on office walls makes it easy to explain what EDF Energy is all about, how business areas fit together and how individuals can contribute to the company's success. It is used in conversations between employees, partnering companies and visitors alike. The second 'big picture' now provides the backdrop to a digital site with over 30 interactive hotspots to support the sessions, providing an accessible online resource which continues to bring EDF Energy's journey to life.

Conclusion

Within this chapter I have outlined a range of practical tools and techniques that can be used to improve and develop employee engagement. I have deliberately selected those approaches that I have first-hand experience of using successfully. Using a strengths-based approach to improving and developing engagement is one of the most effective ways to ensure engagement objectives and improvements are sustainable.

Planning and action

07

Introduction

It may sound obvious, but research shows that those businesses that are happy with their engagement efforts have a robust strategy and plan in place. A recent report, *The State of Employee Engagement*, published by Smith and Henderson and HR Zone, in association with Saba (2014), found that fewer than one in five companies have a defined business case that describes the benefits of improving employee engagement for their organization and only one-third of businesses have a strategy or plan for improving engagement. However, those businesses that do report higher levels of buy-in from senior leaders and managers. They are also more satisfied with the results of their engagement programmes. Ensuring that you formally record and communicate your engagement strategy and plan is therefore critical to ensuring your success.

In this chapter we'll take a look at what a good engagement plan looks like and the steps involved in creating your plan. We'll also look at how you then communicate your plan to achieve stakeholder buy-in, as well as discussing the common pitfalls and barriers to implementing your engagement plan.

In Chapter 3 we introduced the strategy roadmap as a useful tool to summarize your employee engagement strategy. By following this template you should now have an overall vision, purpose and direction for your engagement plan. In addition you should also have considered the business case for engagement within your own organization, considering how your engagement goals and outcomes are aligned with your organizational strategy. Getting to this point provides a robust foundation on which to build your engagement plan – what you are going to do to achieve your goals and outcomes. In Chapters 5 and 6 we talked about how you actually go about improving engagement, and shared various tools and techniques. At this point you should be considering what is going to be included in your plan to achieve your engagement goals and outcomes. In the following pages we'll share with you some thoughts and ideas on how to document all of these strands into a coherent plan and get people to support it.

Developing your plan: a step-by-step guide

There is no right or wrong way to document your engagement strategy and plan – there are, however, some critical elements that should be included. Below is a simple diagram which outlines the key steps to pen your plan. Over the following pages we'll walk through each of the key steps of a good engagement plan; however, please bear in mind that your strategy and plan should align with your organizational goals so will ultimately be unique to your company.

FIGURE 7.1   The employee engagement planning cycle

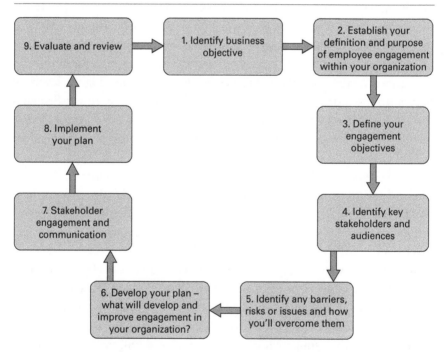

Identify your business objectives: answering the 'why' question

Your employee engagement strategy and subsequent plan should always begin by understanding the business context and strategy, seeking to understand how an engaged workforce will help you achieve you business goals. Some useful questions to ask at this stage are:

- How will focusing on employee engagement help you achieve your organizational strategy and goals?
- Why is it important that you focus on employee engagement?
- What will happen if you don't?
- Is there a clear business case for focusing on employee engagement?
- What are the business outcomes or benefits of focusing on engagement?
- Do you have an obvious engagement problem?
- Is there a 'burning platform'?
- What are your competitors doing in this space?

In Chapter 2, we talked about the business case for employee engagement, the compelling body of evidence that links engaged employees to a range of desirable business outcomes. The alignment of engagement to business outcomes tends to focus on the following areas:

- reducing employee attrition;
- reducing employee absenteeism;
- improving productivity;
- improving customer experience;
- building a culture of innovation;
- increasing sales performance;
- successful change programmes.

The first step of any engagement strategy or plan involves figuring out why you want to develop an engaged workforce.

Example

The following example is taken from an actual engagement strategy and plan. The company in question was specifically having problems with employee turnover and absence. The plan was to focus on improving engagement across the company to address these business outcomes.

Overall aim – to create a great place to work.

The primary objectives of the engagement strategy plan are to:

- reduce employee attrition by 8 per cent in 12 months;
- reduce employee absence by 4 per cent in 12 months;

- establish this company as an employer of choice, which will be measured via recruitment metrics;

- maximize the performance of our employees through improved productivity, which will be measured by operational metrics.

In achieving these objectives, the following benefits will also be realized:

- make it easier to recruit the best people and retain, motivate and develop our people;

- build on profitability by increasing staff productivity;

- produce high-quality products and services;

- less resistance to change as trust is built up both ways so employees are more attuned to, and more likely to accept, continuous improvement;

- generate excitement and enthusiasm amongst employees by creating a vision of the future that they want to aspire to.

Establish your definition of purpose of engagement within your organization

In earlier chapters we discussed the need to define what you mean by employee engagement within your organizational context. Within this section of your plan you need to outline what you mean by employee engagement and how you will talk about engagement within your organization. In Chapter 1, we provided a number of different definitions of engagement and a case study to illustrate how Bard developed their own definition of engagement. To help you do this, you might want to consider the following questions:

- What do we understand by the term 'engagement'?

- What would a highly engaged workforce look like and how will it be different from today?

- What experiences do we have of being highly engaged: what are the common themes and the conditions that made this experience possible?

The first two stages of the appreciative inquiry approach, discussed in Chapter 6, provide a useful framework to help you figure out what you mean by engagement within your own organization:

- Step 1: the best of what is:
  - Discuss your experience of being highly engaged, and capture the learning from this.
- Step 2: imagine the future:
  - Think about what sort of organization you want to be, what the future will look and feel like when you have a highly engaged workforce.

If you choose to use terms such as 'employer of choice' or 'great place to work', use this stage in your planning process to define what this means to your organization. Terms such as these can be helpful to talk about engagement more widely in the organization, and are often preferred to using the term 'employee engagement'. However, they can also be wholly intangible, therefore it's important to be crystal clear about what 'a great place to work' means within your organizational context. By doing this you avoid raising unrealistic expectations: some employees may interpret a great place to work to mean that your company will introduce a Googleplex-style workplace complete with slides, funky break-out areas and free food! It's important to establish your definition at the beginning of the process.

Define your engagement objectives

By now you have established why you are focusing on engagement, the business outcomes you are looking to impact and what you mean by employee engagement. The next step of the planning process is to set your engagement objectives. Some useful questions to ask yourself here include:

- How can engagement contribute to the business outcomes we have identified? For example, how might a highly engaged workforce result in lower employee attrition or absence? Or how can improved engagement create a culture of innovation or improved customer experience?
- What is it we need employees to think, feel, believe or do to develop and improve engagement? For example, if we wish to reduce employee attrition we need employees to believe this is a great place to work, somewhere they want to stay.
- What level of engagement are we aiming for?

Example engagement objectives The following are examples of engagement objectives taken from real engagement strategies and plans:

- to improve engagement, as measured by the annual survey engagement index, by 15 per cent within 12 months;

- to make the *Sunday Times* 'Best 100 Companies to Work for' list;
- to attain Investors In People Gold standard;
- to engage employees in the vision and strategy of the business;
- to involve employees in creating a great place to work.

Identify key stakeholders and audiences

Employee engagement doesn't fit neatly into one area of the organization. Even if your organization has a position that includes employee engagement in the job title, engagement is never the sole responsibility of an individual or even a team. Therefore a critical stage of the planning process is to identify your key stakeholders and audiences, conducting an in-depth stakeholder analysis and engagement plan.

The diagram below details the evolution of employee engagement within organizations:

1 Initially employee engagement is an area of focus for the company, most often in response to the annual engagement survey. At this stage it is reactive and involves working on issues raised within the survey. Typically an individual or team will be given responsibility for looking after the survey process and capturing actions arising, often as an add-on to their day job.

2 After a time the organization begins to recognize the need to align engagement with the overall business strategy. At this point HR and the executive team will be more involved in the engagement agenda; however, it is still predominantly reactive and still responsive to outputs from the survey. Within this stage, engagement begins to feature as part of the organization's business strategy and is beginning to be recognized as an enabler for business success and a differentiation from competitors.

3 At this point the organization is beginning to recognize that engagement is not the sole responsibility of a single team or function. There is a realization that engagement has the potential to support and contribute to the business strategy. Other teams and departments are brought in to work on the engagement agenda – for example facilities management to help ensure the work environment supports engagement, or internal communication to help ensure employees understand and buy in to the organization's vision and strategy. Engagement activity is no longer something that happens in response to the annual survey, but is a continued area of focus for many different parts of the business.

4 Finally we see the organization move into what we call the *consortium approach*. It is at this stage that organizations are operating in the realm

FIGURE 7.2 The evolution of employee engagement

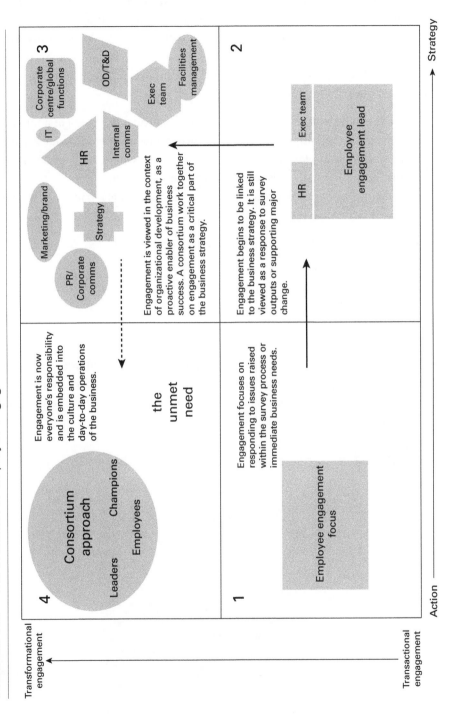

of transformational engagement. Here, engagement is the responsibility of everyone within the organization; it is proactive and embedded into the culture of the company. It may be that there is no longer a need for the annual survey, given that employee feedback is sought and harnessed in an ongoing way. It is a given that employee engagement is a vital component of the business strategy.

Therefore in order to move towards transformational engagement a number of different stakeholders and audiences need to be involved in your engagement strategy and plan. It's important to consider where your organization is currently, and who needs to be involved in your plan.

Some useful questions you might want to ask to help you identify who you need to involve are:

- Who do we need to make it happen?
- Who do we need to support us?
- Who needs to be informed?
- Who do we need to reach?
- Who does this affect?

There are a number of excellent stakeholder-mapping techniques that can help you with your stakeholder engagement plan. One of the most used and helpful techniques is to map stakeholders on a power/interest grid, detailed below:

FIGURE 7.3   Understanding your audiences: the persona approach

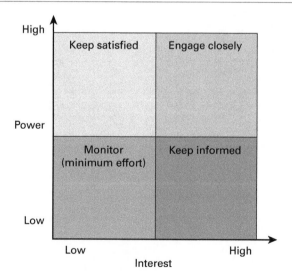

Stakeholder analysis can sometimes result in a very complex stakeholder map and engagement plan. The *persona approach* offers a more pragmatic way to understand and segment your key stakeholder groups. The approach has been popularized in recent years within the field of developing user-centred software, design and websites.

Personas are essentially fictional characters that are created to represent a specific stakeholder or audience group. The personas are developed to represent the goals, behaviours, attitudes and needs of a stakeholder group. Details of each persona are usually captured in a one- to two-page description, which brings the persona to life and makes them as realistic as possible.

There are a variety of ways in which personas can be developed. At one end of the spectrum, you can undertake a full-scale research process to understand audience segments. However, the approach I recommend is to create a 'lightweight' persona. This approach involves running a workshop to brainstorm and agree your key audience segments. For example, below are segments I developed with a client when considering their employee engagement strategy and plans:

- senior management;
- line managers;
- online employees;
- field-based employees;
- sales teams.

Once the key segments are agreed, you then need to bring each segment to life with a persona. This process involves creating a fictional character, or persona, to represent each segment. Each persona is then brought to life by considering questions such as:

- Who are they: age, gender, life outside of work, interests, focus etc?
- Where do they work?
- How long have they been with the company?
- How do they feel about working here?
- Where do they want to go with their career?

These questions help to get to know each persona. See the example below for an extract from a persona. The purpose of building personas is to enable you to target communication effectively to each of the segments you have identified. Building your personas also helps you to get closer to your audience and stakeholder segments, considering how they feel and their employee experience – all of which is useful insight to inform your overall engagement strategy and plan.

Persona – Line Manager
Name – Carly
Age – 30

About – Carly is a new line manager; she has been in the job for six months, after being promoted. She has been with the company for three years and this is the second company she has worked for since graduating with a degree in business administration.

Carly is an enthusiastic and keen manager. She really wants to do the best by her team but she has not received any training or development to help her, so she is feeling a little unsure of her capabilities. She is very social, is friends with her team and regularly socializes with people from work. She is engaged with the company, committed to the vision and purpose and wants to make a difference. However, sometimes she is unsure about how to communicate the information and messages she receives. She has great potential to be an advocate for the employee engagement strategy and plan but currently has no knowledge of the plan or the contribution she could make.

Identify barriers, risks and issues

Any good planning process involves evaluation of the factors that might get in the way of implementation. Given the well-documented problems companies have in realizing improvements in employee engagement this is especially relevant. Of course whilst we have included this as a discrete step in the planning process, in reality assessment of barriers and risks should happen throughout the entire process. There are a number of questions which can help to begin to identify potential barriers, risks and issues:

- What will stop us achieving our engagement objectives?
- What might get in the way?
- Who might get in the way?
- What are the risks involved, and what could be done to mitigate them?
- What will happen if we do nothing?

There are therefore some common barriers to creating an engaged workforce that you may encounter, and therefore worth exploring a little further here.

Current economic climate Set against a backdrop of austerity, defined by redundancies, pay freezes, lack of bonus or rewards, and dwindling pension funds, it can be difficult to understand how companies begin to improve engagement. It's difficult to feel highly engaged if you are surrounded by such doom and gloom, and this context can also be used as an excuse to put engagement on the back burner until things improve. However, it's precisely when times are tough that companies really need engagement. The case study below illustrates this.

CASE STUDY

In 2009, when the recession was really beginning to bite in the UK, I worked with a client operating in the home improvement space. We initially began working together to focus on creating a great place to work in order to improve engagement within the company and positively impact employee attrition and absenteeism. The approach we took was the strengths-based approach detailed in Chapter 6, using a network of champions to spread viral change throughout the company. We began to have success using this approach, but as the recession took hold the goalposts changed. Now the business was looking at making compulsory redundancies in light of a less than favourable sales forecast for 2009. However, given the success of the engagement activity and a forward-thinking HR director, the company decided to share the issues facing the organization with the group of champions. The executive team met with the champions and the situation was discussed at length. Essentially there were three possible solutions on the table: make redundancies, cut the working week or reduce pay. The champions made a compelling case to opt for the pay cut option, and the pay cut they were considering was not insignificant: it was 10 per cent for each and every employee. The executive team were somewhat sceptical that employees would go for this but supported the champions' request to travel across the company communicating the discussions that were had, the decision to cut pay and the rationale behind this. The company then voted on whether or not they would take a voluntary pay cut of 10 per cent. An astounding 87 per cent of employees voted yes: they would take the pay cut if required. What was more remarkable though was that as the year progressed the gloomy sales forecast did not come to light. Whilst their industry market was down around 25 per cent for that year, they actually exceeded their targets by 12 per cent, and it was never necessary to implement the pay cut. Engagement scores on the annual survey also improved significantly from less than 50 per cent to 94 per cent.

Lack of a definition and purpose If you are following the advice in this book this won't be an issue for you. However, there are companies who have a vague notion they want to improve engagement but they don't know why and they don't really know what they mean by engagement. It's impossible to make any real change or improvements if you have not clarified what you're working on and why.

Managerial resistance When talking to managers about the role they play in engaging their teams, one of the most common lines I hear is: 'I just don't have time for this.' Managers play a critical role in engagement so getting them on board is crucial. However, when managers are being asked to do more with less, it is an understandable reaction to yet another task on the never-ending to-do list, and one that can feel overwhelming for many managers. My approach when working with organizations is to focus specifically on managers' own engagement. If we expect managers to play a lead role in engaging their teams, they first need to be engaged themselves. Again, taking the strengths-based approach outlined in Chapter 6, I often work with managers to focus them on their own engagement, encouraging them to think and talk about times when they were highly engaged. What often happens is that managers say they have lost touch with what it feels like to be engaged and that revisiting these experiences reinforces how crucial this is to their overall well-being and happiness at work. By taking managers through the 'Make the Difference' framework detailed in Chapter 6, it enables them to understand what needs to change within their working lives in order to engage again. All too often, managers are tasked with improving engagement with little or no thought to their own engagement, so treating managers as a special, discrete group of stakeholders is important.

Paying lip-service to engagement Integrity, or matching the 'say' with the 'do', is cited as one of the key enablers of employee engagement. Employees see straight through grand gestures made to create great places to work, or become an employer of choice, that are not quickly backed up with action. This is a common barrier to engagement, whereby the top team know they should be focusing on improving engagement, but are just not committed to putting in the resources required. For example, I have lost count of the number of times I see organizations that have a healthy budget for the engagement survey but no budget for what happens after the results are in. Or companies who are reluctant to free up resources to focus on engagement, expecting employees to take actions above and beyond their day jobs. Some companies are happy to use the champions approach but are then reluctant to give champions the necessary time to fulfil their roles successfully. This is a challenging barrier to overcome. It requires tenacity and resilience on behalf of those people who are focusing on engagement to stick with it. Demonstrating the value being added and the difference they are making is key, ensuring senior leaders hear about progress and wins. Documenting engagement objectives that align with your organizational strategy is key – measuring progress and reporting on this is a good way to get people to sit up and take notice. Bringing in external speakers from other organizations can help: hearing their stories can inspire confidence that focusing on engagement will improve performance. Organizing 'seeing is believing' tours to companies you know your senior team admires can also be a useful technique to inspire and facilitate action.

Over-reliance on the survey Putting too much emphasis on the survey process is another familiar barrier to employee engagement. Some companies see the survey as a panacea for improving and developing engagement but the survey is a means to an end, not the end itself. There are a number of problems associated with over-reliance on the survey. First, if employees see little changing as a result of the survey process they quickly lose faith and confidence in this approach. Year on year response rates dwindle and employees become cynical that the survey delivers any real change. Second, managers and leaders can become too focused on the data itself, analysing differences between teams, even becoming competitive about their results compared to other team results. The data can be a distraction from the overall purpose of the survey: to understand current engagement and put in place actions to improve it. Third, employees can suffer from 'survey fatigue', whereby employees run out of steam when talking about engagement and filling in yet another survey. Finally, if your survey results are good or great, the survey can result in complacency when it comes to engagement with a lack of motivation to keep focusing on the topic, given everything is okay.

In my experience the way to overcome over-reliance on the survey is to ensure it is seen as just one element of the overall engagement strategy, rather than the engagement strategy itself. The survey needs to be positioned as part of the 'evaluate-and-review' step within the planning cycle. By doing this, the survey process is integrated into the overall engagement strategy and plan.

Leadership capability The Engage for Success movement and Ashridge Business School have recently been investigating the barriers to engagement amongst business leaders. They published a research paper in 2013, which can be found on the Engage for Success website that details their findings (Armstrong and Ashridge Business School, 2013). The research looked specifically at employee engagement through the eyes of a CEO, and they highlight leadership capability as one of the major barriers to employee engagement. The following summary is an extract from the research report and is produced with kind permission from Engage for Success. The summary found the following aspects of leadership behaviours to cause problems for employee engagement:

- *Fear of feedback*: The CEOs interviewed talked specifically about the relationship between engagement and feedback, and their anxieties about giving and receiving negative feedback. Some CEOs, particularly those from large corporates, surfaced a fear that by exercising engaging styles of leadership within their area of the business, this would be viewed as 'weak' or 'holiday-camp' leadership within other parts of the organization. This suggests that in some organizations engaging leadership is yet to be fully appreciated, and those who lead engagement in this way may be perceived to be mavericks as opposed to mainstream leaders. Other CEOs surfaced a perception that by engaging with people it creates more problems than it solves, by raising expectations that cannot be met, particularly in the current economic climate.

- *Double-edged nature of leadership*: This theme emerged as a result of CEOs talking about the challenges of leading engagement. Many felt engagement was one of the most difficult parts of the leadership task and that engaging leadership requires them to walk a fine line. Some surfaced internal conflicts, such as feeling engagement draws them close to people, but despite this closeness, they must still be able to take tough decisions when necessary.

Conversations about the duality of engaging leadership also included some CEOs talking about the pressure to project confidence to the rest of the organization, whilst at the same time being able to admit they do not have all the answers. Others talked about having to be resilient yet emotionally attuned; decisive yet giving 'voice' and having to project certainty despite an uncertain climate. These tensions make engaging leadership a difficult task.

- *Finding new ways of leading*: Some CEOs talked about there being no 'one way' to lead engagement. Instead, they argued, engagement is about leaders discovering their own unique leadership style that is congruent with their own purpose and values, and works within their own organizational contexts. For one CEO, engagement was about leading with truth and honesty. For another, it was about fostering deep relationships at work.

  Some of the CEOs interviewed described current leadership models, which value attributes such as control and toughness, as deficient. Instead, some called for different ways of leading, where people, not financial results, become the heart of organizational performance.

- *Challenges of self-awareness and self-enquiry*: To lead with passion and purpose, CEOs acknowledged that this requires deep levels of self-awareness and ongoing processes of self-enquiry. Despite the need for self-awareness, some CEOs admitted that it was difficult for them to reach 'true' self-insight when conversations and feedback in their organizations do not stem from a place of honesty and deep mutual trust.

  Feedback is pivotal in unlocking leader self-awareness, but some talked about how it made CEOs feel 'deeply uncomfortable' to ask for feedback in this way. Others believed that even if they asked for feedback about themselves, they would not be told the truth because hierarchy would prevent it. Many CEOs saw corporate conversations as hierarchically driven.

  Some CEOs described engagement emerging from 'deep trusting relationships'; however, to forge these kinds of relationships, it takes a certain kind of leader.

Leadership capability can be a barrier to successful employee engagement for all of the reasons above, but in addition it's often because organizations simply expect managers and leaders to somehow know *how* to engage employees. There is very little development focused specifically on equipping managers to engage their teams. Dedicated leadership development, which looks at how managers and leaders can engage their teams, is required to overcome this barrier. I have worked with many organizations over the years doing just this: helping to demystify engagement for leaders and providing them with a simple toolkit to help them develop engagement with their teams.

Culture and systems It's often the case that the culture and systems of an organization are not set up to support employee engagement and get in the way of engagement activity. The Engage for Success and Ashridge Business School research (Armstrong and Ashridge Business School, 2013) on barriers to engagement highlighted many such barriers. Often organizations promote outdated leadership models, which reward and promote those with skills such as order, control and toughness. Leadership skills that support employee engagement such as emotional intelligence, coaching skills and storytelling are often not recognized or rewarded. Leaders are often taught that they need to have the answers, be in charge and control a team, which is not congruent with critical aspects of engagement such as building autonomy and mastery.

Within my work I deliver a lot of coaching training and development for managers and leaders. Without exception managers I work with always struggle with enabling others to come up with answers to their problems. Their entrenched leadership model is that they as a manager of a team need to solve everything and have all of the answers. There is a change going on, with more and more leaders recognizing the need to engage teams and use coaching as well as directive management styles; however, the dominant leadership style in many organizations remains a barrier to employee engagement.

Organizations are all too often focused on the short term, with immediate results driving the business. This focus on immediate results can drive behaviours that sabotage employee engagement. Investors are interested in the financial results of a company, not how engaged their employees are, so it is little wonder that the CEO and their team focus on the financials rather than how people feel about working there. This is, again, a difficult barrier to overcome. However, once again by aligning engagement objectives to organizational outcomes and strategy you can begin to make the business case for focusing on engagement and deliver some impressive return on investment. With one of my clients, we were able to link engagement activity to significantly reduced employee turnover and absenteeism, which enabled a compelling return on investment (ROI) story to be shared across the business.

Develop your plan: what are you going to do to achieve your engagement objectives?

Clearly your plan depends completely upon your engagement objectives. In previous chapters, we have discussed the enablers of engagement as well as sharing a range of tools and techniques that are of help when considering the action you need to take. Some points which will help when planning your activities are:

- When considering our engagement objectives what do we need people to think, feel, believe and do? Then use these responses to identify action that needs to be taken.

- Prioritization: Sometimes there is so much that needs to be done it can feel overwhelming. Using a tool to prioritize your actions can help, for example you might want to use a speed of implementation/cost matrix detailed below.

FIGURE 7.4   Implementation/cost matrix

When considering your plan you will need to ask yourself: 'How much will this cost?' It is useful to use a cost-benefit analysis to do this, which will help you to convince budget-holders of the benefits to engagement activity rather than simply focusing on the costs. The costs and benefits associated with improving employee engagement will depend on what you want to achieve and your engagement objectives. If you can, work out both what your proposal programme of action will cost but also the potential payback in financial terms. There are, of course, some engagement strategies, such as talking to and listening to staff, that do not need to cost anything significant. A full-scale leadership development programme will certainly have a greater cost involved, but if poor leadership is the problem, then the longer-term benefits could far outweigh the costs.

Stakeholder and audience engagement and communication

Having identified your key stakeholders and audiences already you now need to focus on selling your strategy and plan to them. To be successful, your employee engagement strategy and plan needs buy-in and commitment from the most senior people in your organization, through to managers and key influencers. It is helpful if senior leaders publicly demonstrate their commitment to employee engagement, by both role-modelling and 'walking the talk'.

Some points which are helpful to consider:

- Is there a collective understanding of what engagement means to your organization and why you are focusing on it? If not, what communication needs to happen to achieve this?

- Based on your stakeholder analysis, work out different messages for different audiences and stakeholder groups.

- What do you need each stakeholder group to do to help achieve the engagement objectives and therefore what communication will they need to receive?

- Using the engagement curve below, figure out where stakeholder groups are on the curve and adapt your communication and messages accordingly.

When planning your communication to stakeholders and audience groups a simple communication-planning template as detailed below can be helpful to guide you through the process.

Implement your plan

After all the careful consideration and planning which has accompanied the development of your engagement strategy and plan, the time has now come to put it into action. In an ideal world this process is straightforward, but often real life gets in the way. When implementing your plan there are some pointers which can help you ensure you stay on track:

FIGURE 7.5   The engagement curve

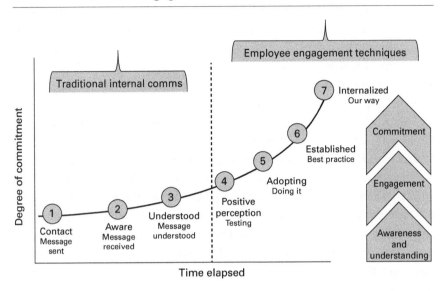

TABLE 7.1   Communication-planning template

Who? Audience	Why? Objectives	What? Messages & content	How? Channels	When? Timing	How did it go? Evaluation

- Consider how you know the plan and actions are heading in the right way.
- Is your plan achieving your objectives?
- Does the plan need any amending in any way?
- Are you getting in any feedback from employees regarding your activity?
- Are there any other competing priorities that are getting in the way?
- Is there anything else happening in the organization which you need to be aware of?

What will help you implement your plan is the ability to remain flexible: to change direction or activity if required rather than doggedly sticking to your original plan. For example, I was working with a client many years ago on their engagement strategy and plan. We were working on improving employee engagement with the aim of improving overall customer experience, ultimately to stem the customer losses the company was experiencing at the time. There was a range of activity happening, involving development and communication of the company's strategic narrative, leadership development, and a renewed focus on living the company values. However, as roll-out of the plan began we started to pick up feedback from employees. We heard themes such as: 'here we go again' and: 'guess what they want us to do now'. Rather than ignore these rumblings we decided to open up the conversation with employees. We set up a series of *listening groups*, each with a different theme, which was based on the feedback we were getting: for example we named one 'Here we go again'. We invited employees to come along to these groups to talk about their concerns, but more importantly we asked them to be a part of the solution. We brought in senior management to facilitate the groups, rather than relying on HR or internal communications, which helped to give the activity credibility: we were taking this feedback seriously. The sessions were set up so that participants could get everything off their chest at the beginning of the session, but the second half of the session was based around an appreciative inquiry process. The listening groups were well attended, and demonstrated that the company was listening to employees. They enabled constructive conversations to happen and helped to ensure the plan of activity remained on track. If we had stuck to the original plan this activity would not have happened, but by remaining flexible and responding to employee feedback quickly we averted some serious derailing.

Evaluate and review

The final phase of the planning cycle is the *evaluate-and-review* phase. However, there is a question as to whether this should be the final step of the planning cycle or the first step. In my opinion, it is valid to both kick off the planning cycle with evaluate and review and also end the cycle here as well. The employee engagement survey is the most well-known and used way of evaluating engagement, and if you have access to employee engagement scores at the beginning of the planning process it provides a useful benchmark for subsequent activity. The next chapter is dedicated to measuring engagement. In it, we will go into detail regarding approaches to measuring engagement, but also ways in which you can demonstrate your impact and evaluate your activity against objectives.

Conclusion

The planning cycle provides a useful framework to help you develop your employee engagement strategy and plan. Taking a formal approach to developing this is critical to overcome criticisms of engagement being 'fluffy' or intangible. Following each of the steps enables you to link engagement activity to business goals and outcomes, helping to demonstrate the value an engaged workforce can bring to an organization.

08 **Measuring engagement**

Introduction

There is now an entire industry based around the need to measure employee engagement. Within this chapter we will look at the various types of employee engagement measurement available and understand how to select a method of measurement that is right for your organization. We will also look at some of the exciting developments happening at a macro-level and how policy makers are becoming increasingly interested in how we can measure and track engagement or well-being/happiness. Finally, we will outline how you can show the impact of employee engagement and demonstrate the value you add, by evidencing return on investment.

The employee engagement survey

The employee engagement survey is now a familiar tool in most organizations, with the CIPD reporting that around 80 per cent of large organizations measure engagement. Data from your employee engagement survey is useful to understand where your people are, how engaged they are and what is and isn't working in order to improve engagement. In the previous chapter we discussed how the review/evaluate stage is a crucial element of the overall employee engagement planning cycle. However, before you can measure engagement, you have to understand what it means for your organization: we can't measure what we have not clearly defined. As discussed in Chapter 1, there are at least 50-plus definitions of employee engagement, and often an engaged workforce is something that you feel as soon as you walk into the organization.

However, in order to measure employee engagement, you need to define exactly what it means. This is why your engagement definition is so important. As you will see from the wide variety of employee engagement survey approaches that exist, different survey providers are often measuring slightly different things. It's therefore critical to ensure you know what you are trying to measure before embarking on any survey.

The employee engagement survey is useful as a foundation for insights for action; however, it is only a small part of the overall engagement jigsaw: it is a means to an end not the end itself. As employee engagement has developed over the years, the engagement survey has become increasingly used to understand exactly how employees are feeling, and the extent to which they are engaged or disengaged. Employee engagement action plans are very often in response to survey findings aimed at developing engagement within organizations.

There are a whole range of different survey tools out there, and exactly which aspect of engagement these tools measure will vary. For example, some measure the level of engagement as a scale or percentage, often in the form of an 'engagement index'. This approach can be helpful in that it enables benchmarking to take place. Other tools identify the key drivers of engagement via regression analysis. Some look at the preconditions of engagement and others measure the outcomes of engagement. Whilst there are overlaps in the various survey tools available, most of them do differ slightly. Time and effort must be taken to understand what it is you wish to measure and why.

Employee engagement survey providers

There are a wide variety of employee engagement survey providers. The list below is by no means exhaustive but it does provide an overview of some of the different definitions or models of engagement and underpinning survey solutions provided by the different survey vendors. Survey providers have, over the last few years, been developing technology to provide solutions which offer continuous listening rather than an annual survey approach. Understandably, given the sizable value of the engagement survey market, suppliers are keen to protect their intellectual property with respect to their questionnaire design and actual items (questions) used. Therefore it has not been possible to publish the question sets used by different providers here, but you can use the information below to give you some idea of the approaches taken by some of the survey providers out there, using this as a basis for further exploration into solutions available.

1 *IBM Kenexa*: IBM Kenexa view employee engagement as a desired state (Macey and Schneider, 2008), and measure it via an equally weighted combination of four individual elements: pride, satisfaction, advocacy

and retention. They argue that an engaged workforce is one where employees have pride in the company, and are satisfied with their organization as a place to work, and also, who advocate for and intend to remain with their organization. Employee engagement is viewed as a result of organizational policies and practices and leadership and managerial behaviours that precede the state of employee engagement. They argue employee engagement itself precedes the display of discretionary effort that promotes heightened individual, team and organizational performance. They have a set of four specific questions that measure engagement within their survey solution, looking at pride, satisfaction with the organization, employee advocacy and intention to stay with an organization.

2 *Aon*: Aon's model of engagement is the 'say, stay, strive' model, which argues that employees are considered to be engaged when they display the following three engagement behaviours:

- **Say:** speak positively about the organization to others inside and out.
- **Stay:** display an intense desire to be a member of the organization.
- **Strive:** exert extra effort and engage in behaviours that contribute to business success.

Their survey design is based upon this model, seeking to identify key drivers of these behaviours and therefore where to direct resources to develop engagement.

3 *Gallup*: Gallup developed its Q12® engagement survey in response to studying data for thousands of organizations to understand correlates of worker productivity and performance. Gallup consultants analysed hundreds of questions in hundreds of surveys before developing the 12 questions with the highest correlations to external measures.

Topics covered include workplace expectations, supervisory relations and even working with a best friend. Each of the 12 questions is rated on a five-point scale and fits into one of the following four categories:

- basic needs;
- management support;
- teamwork;
- growth.

An engagement index is then generated which is based on the combined ratings from the ratings across all 12 questions. Employees are then segmented into one of the following three categories:

- **Engaged** employees work with passion, have a strong connection to the organization, they work hard to innovate and improve.

- **Not-engaged** employees do the work expected of them, but do not put in extra effort.

- **Actively disengaged** employees aren't just unhappy, but are spreading their unhappiness to other staff.

The Q12® database, with 5.4 million responses, is one of the largest employee benchmarks available.

4 *ORC International*: ORC International also use the 'say, stay, strive' model of engagement, evaluating aspects of the employee experience which drive these three factors. Within their model 'say' refers to employee advocacy, 'stay' refers to employee commitment and 'strive' refers to discretionary effort.

The academic viewpoint

Whilst the engagement survey industry has been growing in recent years, so too has academic literature aimed at defining what engagement is and how to measure it. There are now a variety of measures of employee engagement, which have been developed and rigorously tested within the world of academia. However, they are much less commonly used within an organizational context than the consulting firm's measurement tools.

In Chapter 1, when discussing the different definitions of engagement, we made reference to the term being used in the following ways:

- to refer to a psychological state (eg involvement, commitment, attachment, mood);

- to refer to a performance construct (eg either effort or observable behaviour, including pro-social and organizational citizenship behaviour);

- to refer to a disposition (eg positive affect);

- or a combination of the above.

The definition or perspective you choose to adopt will inform the measurement tool you then use. There are three predominant scales for measuring engagement that have come out of the academic world:

1 the Maslach Burnout Inventory – General Survey (MBI-GS);

2 the Utrecht Work Engagement Scale (UWES);

3 the Job Demand – Resources (JD-R) model.

The Maslach Burnout Inventory – General Survey (MBI-GS) was developed following the Maslach Burnout Inventory (MBI). The MBI model was initially developed to measure burnout of individuals who work with other people (Schaufeli and Bakker, 2004). The model included three dimensions:

- exhaustion, which measures fatigue without referring to other people as the source of one's tiredness;
- cynicism, which measures indifference or a negative attitude towards work in general, but not necessarily other colleagues;
- [lack of] professional efficacy, which refers to both social and non-social aspects of occupational accomplishments.

This approach to defining and measuring engagement argues that burnout and engagement are at opposite poles of a continuum that is entirely covered by the MBI. Therefore energy, involvement and efficacy are argued to be the direct opposites of the three dimensions of burnout detailed above. The measure therefore assesses engagement via the opposite pattern of scores on the three MBI dimensions. Low scores on exhaustion and cynicism, and high scores on efficacy will indicate engagement.

The second measure of engagement as a psychological construct is the 17-item Utrecht Work Engagement Scale (UWES), which was later shortened to nine items (Schaufeli *et al*, 2006). This approach to measuring engagement argues that engagement is a more persistent state, which is not focused on a particular object, event, individual or behaviour. This approach views burnout and engagement as opposite concepts but argues that they should be measured independently with different instruments. This approach views engagement as a positive, fulfilling, work-related state of mind that is characterized by vigour, dedication and absorption.

Vigour is characterized by high levels of energy and mental resilience, the willingness to invest effort in one's work, and persistence even in the face of difficulties. *Dedication* refers to being strongly involved in one's work and experiencing a sense of significance, enthusiasm, inspiration, pride and challenge. Finally, *absorption* is characterized by being fully concentrated and happily engrossed in one's work, whereby time passes quickly and one has difficulties with detaching oneself from work.

A third measurement scale to come out of academic literature is the Job Demand – Resources (JD-R) model (Demerouti *et al*, 2001, and Bakker and Demerouti, 2007). The model argues that job demands (eg physical demands, time pressure, shift work) are associated with exhaustion whereas lacking job resources (eg performance feedback, job control, participation in decision-making, and social support) are associated with disengagement.

It is interesting that these instruments to measure engagement are not much used within organizations and yet they are based on sound academic theory and have been rigorously tested. If you are considering how you want to measure engagement within your organization, these instruments are well worth a look and are easily accessible.

Running your employee engagement survey – things to consider

If you are thinking about running an employee engagement survey, use the points below to help you get the most out of a survey initiative. They are equally useful if you already run a survey, but want to ensure you are getting the most from it.

1 *For what purpose?* Make sure you are clear about why you are running a survey and how this insight can be used to inform your overall engagement strategy and plan. What will you do with the results and how can you ensure the survey report won't just gather dust on a shelf somewhere? There are many approaches to running a survey; the all-employee annual survey is not the only way. For example, some companies survey a sample of employees at more regular intervals across the year to run shorter 'temperature' checks. Other organizations don't actually do a survey at all, choosing to go down a qualitative route instead and run regular focus groups to understand how their people are feeling and how engaged they are. For some companies it's all about the external benchmark, or getting on a 'best of' list. There is no single correct way to gather insight about engagement; just be sure that you explore all of the options.

2 *Begin with the end in mind* (in the words of Stephen Covey, 1989): Be clear about what a successful employee engagement survey project looks like and what insights will be useful. For example, some companies want to understand the drivers of engagement from their survey process, while others simply want to view aggregated data from each question. Think about how you want to splice and dice the data; the design of your research needs to be built in up front to enable different segments of data to be viewed. If you are choosing to work with an external survey provider work out what success looks like and be really clear about what is important to ensure the smooth running of any employee engagement survey project.

3 *What are your priorities?* Considering your priorities for the survey process is useful to help you decide whether or not you wish to use an

external supplier or run the survey yourself. Using an external supplier has many benefits, for example use of the latest technology, ease of reporting, confidentiality of responses, ability to benchmark and access to the latest best practice research and approaches. However, it's useful to revisit your objectives for running the survey to understand how important these aspects are to you. If you simply wish to get an understanding of how employees are feeling at a particular moment in time you might wish to use a tool such as Survey Monkey or Question Pro to run the survey yourself. However, be mindful that there is considerable technical skill involved in writing good questions and designing research, so ensure that a qualified member of your HR team, or other, is involved with this process.

4 *Consider the ideal employee experience*: When conducting a survey you are asking employees to take the time to complete the survey, so it's a good idea to think about how you can make this a positive experience for them. To avoid 'survey fatigue', the survey experience for employees needs to be positive. From the way the survey is positioned, to how participation is encouraged, through to the way in which results are communicated back to employees and the role they will have in action planning: these elements should all be considered to help make the survey experience a good one for your people.

5 *What role do you want your managers to play in the survey process?* Getting the support of your managers is an important aspect of the overall survey process, therefore you need to consider how you involve them in the process. You need your managers on board with the engagement survey, to champion it and encourage their teams to participate. Therefore communication with managers throughout the survey process is important. Consider what support you require from your managers and what they will need from you in order to fulfil their role effectively. How will you support managers in making sense of their results and discussing them with their teams? The 'Make the Difference' toolkit discussed in Chapter 6 is one way you can provide a toolkit to help managers use the survey results in a positive way with their teams.

6 *Useful questions to consider if selecting an external employee engagement survey provider*:

- Does their definition and model of employee engagement work with your definition and model?

- Do their key driver questions align with your company strategy and focus?

- Is there an opportunity for their survey design to be tailored to fit your organization or is it an off-the-shelf solution?
- Will their survey design include open response questions to collect employee comments?
- How has their tool been validated and tested?
- Does their tool allow for any external benchmarking?
- Are they able to offer translation services if required?
- Can they offer multi-format surveys if required, eg online and paper?
- Can they provide different cuts of the data as required, eg by department, team, manager etc?
- What reporting tools do they offer and how easy are they to use?
- What type of statistical analysis do they offer?
- Have they got any recommendations from other clients?
- What action planning support do they offer?
- What is the cost? Be sure to enquire about any extras such as requesting further data cuts, or special reports.

Common survey themes

Despite the wide variety of different definitions of employee engagement, different models used and survey solutions on offer, there are some key themes that the majority of surveys will include. The Society for Human Resource Management (SHRM) Foundation in the United States identified a number of common themes, which are used to measure employee engagement by survey providers. They include:

- pride in employer;
- satisfaction with employer;
- job satisfaction;
- opportunity to perform well at challenging work;
- recognition and positive feedback;
- personal support from line manager;
- effort above and beyond the minimum;
- understanding the link between one's job and the organization's mission;
- prospects for future growth with one's employer;
- intention to stay with one's employer.

Different survey providers will also include different items (questions) to analyse the key drivers of engagement: that is, what elements of an employee's work experience can be linked to those questions used to measure actual engagement. Typically these types of questions include areas such as:

- work-life balance;
- diversity;
- pay and conditions;
- communications;
- leadership;
- managers;
- environment;
- training and development;
- reward;
- recognition;
- colleagues;
- career opportunities;
- job;
- brand;
- company reputation;
- customers;
- performance management;
- policies and procedures;
- goals and objectives;
- operating efficiency;
- health and safety;
- quality;
- and more...

Typically it is when considering the potential drivers of engagement that the survey grows into a beast! There are usually only a small number of questions used to actually measure engagement of employees, depending on which model or provider you use. However, often when discussing which parts of the employee experience you want to measure to understand drivers of engagement, the numbers of questions asked becomes unwieldy.

There is an opportunity here to go back to the purpose of the survey: what is it you're trying to measure and why? Do you simply want to understand how engaged your people are, or is it important to look at what is driving engagement as well? When looking at which questions to include to understand drivers of engagement it is useful to consider the engagement survey within the context of the wider business strategy. For example, for a retail company with brand and customers at the heart of its strategy, questions relating to these areas are important to include; for a manufacturing company questions around quality and governance might be important.

Talking point: a critique of the employee engagement survey approach

There is no doubt that data and insight regarding employee engagement within your organization is a critical part of the engagement strategic planning process. It's vital to understand how your employees are feeling, how engaged (or disengaged) they are, and what action needs to be taken to improve engagement. You also need to be able to track and monitor action taken to understand what works and inform your plan. However, over the years the employee engagement survey has taken centre stage for many organizations looking to improve engagement. As stated previously, the employee engagement survey is a means to an end not the end itself. If used wisely the survey process and the insight provided can be invaluable, but often over-reliance on the survey process results in a transactional approach to employee engagement. This approach involves putting the survey process at the heart of engagement activity, it is a reactive way of approaching engagement and can feel like a tick-box exercise: once the action planning has finished the company forgets about engagement until it's time for the next survey.

I believe that companies have become over-reliant on the survey because it provides a false sense of security, giving the illusion that something is being done about engagement. Improving engagement can feel like an overwhelming task, but undertaking a survey gives confidence that something is happening to tackle engagement. Survey feedback always involves providing the results in the format of charts, data and engagement indexes. This can feel like a comfortable and familiar place for many senior leaders who operate in a world of management reports and numbers. The survey takes something which is predominantly about feelings, emotions and behaviours and then uses the language of data and numbers to communicate findings. This is, I believe, part of the reason why companies have become over-reliant on the survey and why we still see transactional engagement as the predominant approach in organizations today.

So whilst data and insight are important to improve engagement, there are a number of problems that you need to be mindful of when using an employee engagement survey:

1 *Definition problems*: We have already talked at length regarding the challenge of defining employee engagement before you can measure. However, I would go one step further. In my experience engagement is very personal, and whilst there are common themes in the different definitions, in reality what defines engagement, and what drives engagement can differ from company to company. Each engagement survey provider will explain why their model is the right model and back this up. But in my experience there is no substitute for undertaking qualitative research to understand:

   • how your organization wishes to define engagement;

   • what drives engagement for your employees.

   Undertaking qualitative research to answer these questions will then allow you to build a bespoke measurement tool, which will be valid for your organization, ie it will measure what it is supposed to measure.

2 *Obsession with response rates*: Many companies still seem to be obsessed with improving their response rates to the annual survey, to such an extent that this can often be seen as a key component of their engagement strategy: to improve survey response rates by X per cent. I'm unsure where this preoccupation with response rates began, but again I believe this could be because it offers a useful diversion from the real challenge of actually improving engagement. That is, if we focus on improving response rates, and we have success in this area then it feels like we're making progress, right? Wrong. Common sense would say that higher response rates are better, the more people filling out the survey the more engaged they must be. But this, of course, is not true. I have seen many engagement surveys over the years with 80 per cent-plus response rates but low engagement scores. When you look at

best-practice social science research, what we actually need is a representative sample of employees to ensure that the findings we observe can be generalized to the wider population. Therefore as long as we sample in the correct way, and the sample is large enough, this is enough to give us what we need. The question of sample size has long been debated within social science, but there are some helpful sample size calculators which you can find on the internet which take account of:

- your total population size, ie number of employees;
- the margin of error you're willing to tolerate, usually between 3 per cent and 6 per cent.

They then provide a calculation for how many responses you need to have; either 90 per cent, 95 per cent or 99 per cent confidence level.
To illustrate:

- population size: 10,000 employees;
- margin of error: 3 per cent;
- sample size:
  - 90 per cent confidence = 703 responses;
  - 95 per cent confidence = 965 responses;
  - 99 per cent confidence = 1556 responses.

You'll see for this example that you're looking at a 10–15 per cent sample size for the results to have a low margin of error and high confidence level – this is nowhere near the 80 per cent-plus response rates companies go after.

The same tools also provide a calculator to work out how many surveys you'll need to send out to generate the required response rate.
To illustrate:

- If we are going for 95 per cent confidence, we need 965 responses back.
- Our predicted response rate is 35 per cent.
- Therefore we will need to send out 2754 surveys to ensure we reach the necessary response rate.

Finally the tool then calculates the accuracy of your response rates.
To illustrate:

- Population size is 10,000.
- We actually had back 2460 completed responses from the 2754 surveys we sent out.

- That gives us:
  - an error level of 1.4 per cent at 90 per cent confidence;
  - an error level of 1.7 per cent at 95 per cent confidence;
  - an error level of 2.3 per cent at 99 per cent confidence.

You can see from the example above that with a population of 10,000 employees, an approximate response rate of 25 per cent comes with a very low error rate and a high confidence level. And yet I'm sure many CEOs would be disappointed with a 25 per cent response rate. Again this comes back to establishing the purpose of the survey and understanding what a higher response rate will actually give us.

Finally before we move on, a quick word on sampling. In order to be able to generalize any findings to the wider population we need to ensure we take what is known as a probability sample. A probability sample means that everyone within the population, ie employee base has an equal chance of being included in the sample. The easiest way to achieve this is to send the survey to everyone. Or you can select a sample of employees to send the survey to, as detailed by the worked example above; you just need to ensure you use probability sampling methodologies so that you can generalize the results once they are in.

3 *Mind your language*: One of the challenges of using a survey is that of the semantics and language involved. For example, often surveys will ask questions about senior leadership: depending on where employees sit in the hierarchy this will mean different things to different people. Establishing questions with as little ambiguity as possible is a real challenge. Often this ambiguity and differences in interpretation become clear in the survey follow-up process. For example, when running focus groups to delve deeper into issues raised within the survey it becomes clear that employees have interpreted certain questions in very different ways.

4 *Obsession with benchmarking*: In addition to obsessing about response rates, in my experience, senior leaders are also obsessed with external benchmarking. Making the *Sunday Times* 'Best 100 Companies to work for' list, or the top companies in the Great Place To Work list, are often set as employee engagement objectives. Whilst this motivation does provide a burning platform to enable a focus of resources on engagement, very often making the list eclipses the purpose of engagement itself, to improve the business and create a competitive advantage. The objectives and plan are at risk of being

short term when the focus is to benchmark. I would prefer to view making a list as a benefit of having a focused engagement strategy and plan, rather than the plan itself.

5   *Deficit approach*: Finally, one of the major problems with placing the survey process at the heart of your engagement strategy and plan is that it encourages a deficit approach to engagement. Action planning often focuses on fixing those areas in which the business performed poorly, rather than learning from the insight about the organization's areas of strength. When focus groups are run after the survey process there are rarely questions asked about what we are doing well in and how we get more of this. Very often the post-survey discussion and action planning – looking at the bottom scores and coming up with ways to improve them – are quite depressing processes. This in turn results in an engagement survey process that is actually quite disengaging. Even when companies are performing really well, when it comes to engagement, the action planning process will often still focus on those areas that could be better.

You've done the survey – what next?

One of the major crimes committed when it comes to the survey process is not really knowing what to do with the results. The IPA reported in 2007 that less than half of organizations within the UK knew what to do to encourage engagement. A poorly executed survey follow-up plan is one of the quickest ways to erode engagement, and trust, in the survey process. This is why we sometimes see response rates dwindling year on year, and hear employees say that nothing happens as a result of the survey.

Once the results are in, and the analysis has been completed, it's important to communicate the findings to employees as quickly as possible. The survey process can often be quite lengthy; sometimes months can pass by between filling out a survey and hearing about the results. Please see Chapter 6 for some tools and techniques designed to help managers feed back the results to their teams.

After the survey findings are in, it is helpful to run some qualitative research to delve deeper into areas of interest arising from the process. Often the survey process raises more questions than it answers, and senior leaders seek to answer the 'why' for some of the findings. For example, why is it that managers have a higher engagement index than non-managers, or why is it that employees are proud to work here but we have a high percentage of people indicating they aren't intending to be working here in 12 months' time?

There are a range of qualitative methodologies which can be used to further explore the data from the survey process:

- focus groups;
- follow-up interviews;
- World Café event;
- online discussion forums;
- lunch session with senior leaders;
- facilitated team discussions.

Depending on the topic for the qualitative research it is sometimes preferable to use an external facilitator to ensure objectivity and confidentiality. For example, if bullying within the workplace has been flagged as an area of concern, it's preferable that a third party runs a session to explore this further.

Once the results have been communicated, the process typically moves into the action-planning phase. Action planning tends to happen at different levels within the organization:

1 Key organizational themes are identified and then actions to address them planned at the senior team level.

2 Department themes are identified for various business units and departments. Sometimes project teams are put in place to work on these actions.

3 Teams can identify matters affecting them from the survey that they are able to action themselves and formulate a team action plan to address these issues and themes.

Actions are often recorded in a single place and someone, typically HR, has responsibility for tracking and monitoring actions and reporting progress.

Top tips for successful action planning

Once the results are in and have been shared across the organization, action planning takes place. This is where the real work begins, to actually do something with the findings from the survey:

1 *Identify the issues or themes you want to address*: More is less in this context: try to pick a few areas to focus on, and avoid trying to fix everything at once. You might want to focus on:

- Areas highlighted as key drivers of engagement: this could be drivers that you have scored poorly on and therefore need to action, or drivers that you have scored strongly on and therefore wish to maximize on.

- Areas that are either above or below benchmarks: either internal or external.

- Ask your team what is most important to them and which areas they would like to take action on.

2 *Understand the issues*: Before you plan any action you need to fully understand the issues or themes you have chosen to work on. Work with your team to delve deeper into those areas you are going to focus on. If it's an area of strength, why is this, what works well, and what can you do more of? If it's an area for development, why is this, what isn't working and what needs to change?

3 *Developing your action plan*: This is where you can really involve employees in coming up with an action plan. Appreciative inquiry is a useful framework for developing an action plan, helping to understand what needs to change to address the issue raised. Actions should be simple, tangible and concrete, for example capturing an action such as 'improve trust within our team' is too abstract and difficult to action. When capturing actions consider how you will *know* when they have been implemented, and capture any measures if required. This will help you to ensure actions are tangible.

4 *Check the action plan feels right*: Once the action plan has been agreed, reflect on what is in it. Does it feel right? Will the actions improve the employee's experience of working within your organization? Are the actions concrete and tangible enough? Will you be able to measure and track progress? Is there anything missing?

5 *Embed the action plan into 'business as usual'*: Try to encompass your action plan into your objectives or work list. The aim is to try to integrate improving engagement into the culture and daily operations of the

business. It should not be the case that the action plan is reviewed monthly by a team or a project group, but it should be something that is discussed and worked on continually.

6 *Track and measure your progress*: To avoid employees feeling like nothing happens as a result of the survey process it's important to track and measure your action plans. Are people doing what they said they would do? Is progress being made?

7 *Communicate progress*: Ensure stakeholders are kept up to date with the progress of actions undertaken. Try to incorporate actions into the management reporting process, or scorecards, to make this business as usual.

8 *Celebrate success*: Finally, make sure that any successes or wins are celebrated and communicated widely. Progress, no matter how small, gives employees confidence that they can trust the survey process and that it is possible to make positive changes.

Survey 2.0: the rise of technology to measure engagement

The employee engagement survey will certainly be around for a few years yet, but the way the survey is used to measure and track employee engagement is changing. We are beginning to see companies moving away from an annual survey. In their 2017 'Spotlight on Engagement Report', People Lab found that the number of companies running an annual engagement survey dropped from 80 per cent in 2016 to 55 per cent in 2017. What they found was that companies are looking to measure engagement on a more regular basis, seeing an increase in the use of pulse checks. Advances in technology mean that we can now measure engagement more regularly, or in real time far more easily, rather than waiting for the results of an annual survey. The types of tools and applications that measure customer experience in real time are increasingly being used within the workplace. Research indicates that around 9 per cent of companies are already using an employee app to measure engagement, and 18 per cent are planning to implement one in the near future. This is a much-needed and welcome development for employee engagement. Transformational engagement is characterized by employee opinions being sought, harnessed and acted upon continually, rather than annually; therefore these technological advances will help organizations move towards this.

Companies such as Culture Amp, Hive, TINYPulse, Peakon, Thymometrics and others are changing the way the survey works. Solutions typically enable employees to complete surveys in a few minutes from a range of devices: desktop, tablet or smart phone. Some of these new technologies also offer solutions for capturing employee conversations and other qualitative data, going beyond the traditional survey approach. The results then appear immediately on a dashboard or scorecard for review, enabling real-time tracking of employee feeling and engagement. In essence these new tools are enabling companies to collect data iteratively, rather than once a year. These new solutions are making it easier for companies to ensure employee feedback is continuously sought, harnessed and acted upon. What is less straightforward is knowing where to begin when selecting a solution provider; the number of companies offering real-time employee feedback is growing almost weekly! The guidance outlined earlier on what to consider when running an employee survey still applies, whether you're running an annual survey or want some way of collecting feedback regularly.

An alternative approach to the employee engagement survey

Ideally your employee engagement survey should be based upon the specific requirements and context of your organization. An alternative approach to the survey process is to begin with a qualitative research phase to explore and discover:

- what engagement means to your organization;
- what the drivers of engagement are for your organization.

One of the ways in which you can do this is to begin with a series of 'peak experience' workshops. This approach is detailed in full within Chapter 6 but in essence employees are asked to recount stories about times when they were highly engaged. Capturing the themes that emerge from these workshops should then inform the basis of your quantitative survey design. By switching the process around you can ensure that your survey is asking the right questions of your employees. For example, it might be that for one organization the opportunity to innovate, be creative and have autonomy is important for engagement, whereas for another organization a focus on governance, clear objectives and quality might be more important.

Beginning the process with workshops of this nature also provides a positive experience for employees when discussing and thinking about engagement. Rather than focusing on what is not working, employees reflect on what it felt like when they were highly engaged and therefore more motivated to improve engagement within their company.

With one client I worked with we started their engagement insight process in this way, using a facilitated card-sorting exercise to enable employees to consider what being engaged at work meant to them and what really mattered to them at work. A group of 'champions' were initially trained to facilitate this process. Champions then worked alongside line managers to run similar sessions with their teams. Almost immediately changes started to happen. The process itself opens up lines of communication between managers and their teams. Employees often report that it is a positive experience to engage in a conversation about what is important to them at work, rather than someone in an ivory tower assuming they know what is going to engage them. Straight away they feel that they are being listened to. One particular example I recall was that of a call centre employee talking to his team about how frustrating it was that on working shifts at the weekends the vending machines were often empty and there was nowhere nearby to buy food. He said it would be really helpful to have a microwave in the kitchen area. The manager replied that that was easy to fix and came in the next day with a £25 microwave. The manager asked why the team member had never brought up this issue before to which the team member replied, 'You have never asked me before what matters to me at work.' While this may seem like a small gesture, it was a big deal to that employee, not just having the microwave itself but the gesture of really being listened to, and trusting that something might happen as a result of his feedback.

On completing workshops, employees gathered their cards from the workshop and on returning to their desk they received an e-mail with a link to a survey, which asked them to input the results of their card-sorting exercise. This was the *quantitative* phase of the process. Employees reported that the exercise felt far more meaningful and relevant given they had already spent time talking about what engaged them with their teams.

Managers were provided with a toolkit, similar to the 'Make the Difference' toolkit detailed within Chapter 6. This enabled managers to have ongoing conversations with their teams about engagement, starting with the initial card-sorting exercise. When the results came through from the quantitative phase of the process, this was simply another piece of the engagement plan they were working on and in many ways the data served to simply reinforce the conversations and actions that had been happening since the process began.

The findings from the initial card-sorting exercise also enabled a subset of questions to be developed which were then used in regular, monthly 'pulse check' surveys to track and monitor the climate and culture within the organization.

Simply by turning the process around, and beginning with the qualitative phase, we found that we were able to achieve much better results from the survey process, which then linked to desired business outcomes. In addition this approach fast-tracked the move towards transformational engagement.

CASE STUDY An alternative approach to the employee engagement survey: Charles Stanley

In 2015, investment management firm, Charles Stanley, one of the longest established firms in the City of London, recognized the need to modernize, and began a transition from a traditional investment management business mode, to a more holistic offering of wealth management. To ensure success, a great deal of change would be required across all aspects of the organization, including restructuring the company, amending ways of working and influencing a cultural shift.

The new CEO, Paul Abberley, identified three key areas of improvement to support the organization's strategic objectives:

- customer satisfaction;
- shareholder satisfaction;
- employee engagement.

Focusing on employee engagement was a new direction for the firm, as previously the company operated a more traditional 'top-down' management approach.

The 'Great Place to Work' project was launched with five main objectives:

1 To understand the current level of engagement within Charles Stanley.

2 To identify areas for improvement now, during change and in the future.

3 To track progress against employee engagement during the business transformation.

4 To set future benchmarks, so employee engagement could become an ongoing measure as one of the organization's KPIs.

5 To introduce a sustainable model for employee engagement for Charles Stanley going forward.

From the outset Charles Stanley were keen to ensure they did not make assumptions about what engaged their people. They wanted to ensure that they asked the right questions, which would enable them to work on the right areas in response to feedback from the survey. Therefore, the project began with workshops involving both employees and stakeholders, to understand what engagement meant to them, and critically the conditions that made engagement possible. The workshops involved over 200 employees, who shared their thoughts and views using activities based on the 'Make the Difference' approach detailed earlier within Chapter 6.

The insight gathered from these workshops then enabled a bespoke survey to be developed, ensuring that the right questions were asked. The survey was used as not only a mechanism to measure current levels of engagement but also as a benchmarking tool enabling progress to be monitored. It was the company's first ever survey and provided a good understanding of what areas needed focus in order to improve the working lives of employees and staff, and highlighted what needed to be done to move the company towards being a great place to work.

Analysis of the findings included the following actions:

- The launch of focus groups, to gain a deeper understanding of the trends found in the survey feedback. These groups were also an opportunity for employees to make their voices heard within the company.

- Management development training to ensure managers had the skills, capabilities and tools to develop and improve engagement with their teams.

- The launch of a manager's toolkit, providing managers with a simple set of tools to ensure employee engagement became integral to the organization and not just focused on the survey.

- The creation of eight specific work streams, facilitated by the project team, but led by employees. These were aimed to explore and improve specific areas identified in the survey. These work streams included areas such as reward and recognition and client experience.

Each work stream came up with a plan and a number of actions, both quick-wins and longer-term solutions. What was crucial though was that these work streams were led by employees, rather than taking a top-down approach.

This whole project instigated one of the most in-depth reviews of the organization to date. As a result, Charles Stanley was able to put a number of 'fixes' in place, as well as make some fundamental changes to how they do things.

The survey has continued to run since and year-on-year, over a three-year period, the results have improved. Some of the key successes include:

- A 17 percentage point increase on the Employee Engagement Index compared to the first year's survey; from 56 per cent in 2015, to 67 per cent in 2016 and 73 per cent in 2017.

- A 40 percentage point increase in the responses to 'My work gives me a feeling of personal accomplishment'.

- Improvements in 95 per cent of the items included in the survey, with a number of questions showing 30 percentage point gains.

The company has also seen a positive correlation between the areas which have shown significant improvements and the project work streams that were set up after the first year's survey. For example, there were improvements against all questions relating to Client Experience and Reward & Recognition.

As well as fantastic employee feedback, the business in itself has been turned around and returned to profit. And in 2016, Charles Stanley was awarded three Investors Chronicle FT awards and six Defaqto 5 Star Ratings across the following services: Bespoke Discretionary Management, Collective Portfolio Services (direct custody), DFM Model Portfolio Service, Collectives Portfolio Service (on platform), PanDynamic Model Portfolios and PanAsset Model Portfolios.

In 2017, Charles Stanley was awarded the 3D ARC award, won business culture leader at the Business Culture awards, won the 'Brilliance in Employee Engagement' award at the HR Brilliance awards and in February 2018, won the HRD 'Distinction in Employee Engagement and Experience' award.

Client satisfaction has also been measured and Charles Stanley is pleased to report that at the time of going to print, it has a Net Promoter Score of 54.6 per cent (the industry average is 36.5 per cent). Even the manner in which the digital offering has been designed has specifically been to ensure optimum client outcomes and a delightful service. In February 2018 Charles Stanley Direct won the Best Direct Platform for Customer Service at the Platforum Awards in February 2018. This whole case study helps to demonstrate that if you get it right with your people, everything else follows!

The macro-view: a look at how the policy makers are getting involved with employee engagement

The Engage for Success movement (2009) was originally tasked by the Labour government in 2009 to answer the following questions about employee engagement:

- What is it?
- Does it matter?
- What are the characteristics of engaged organizations?
- What are the barriers?
- What could government and its delivery partners do to help?

Specifically the group was tasked to look at how employee engagement could help the UK out of recession. The movement describes itself in the following way:

> Engage for Success is a movement committed to the idea that there is a better way to work, a better way to enable personal growth, organizational growth and ultimately growth for Britain by releasing more of the capability and potential of people at work.
>
> We want to grow awareness about the power and potential of employee engagement. We want to provoke people to think and to learn more about it. And above all we want individuals and organizations to take action, secure in the proof that it works and passionate about its importance.
>
> We provide evidence, case studies and points of view about how employee engagement drives performance and productivity to achieve growth, to make the case for action. We support people in the workplace with practical tools and ideas they need to take action, and we hope to inspire people to get involved in our movement by facilitating access to like-minded communities, experts and leaders.
>
> The movement is widely supported across the UK, involving the public, private and third sectors in the belief they can learn a lot from each other. Organizations supporting the movement account for more than 2,000,000 people.

There can be little doubt that this movement has influenced some of the developments happening at a macro level within employee engagement. For example, the Office for National Statistics now conducts a well-being survey, asking the following questions:

- Overall how satisfied are you with your life nowadays?
- Overall to what extent do you feel the things you do in your life are worthwhile?
- Overall how happy did you feel yesterday?
- Overall how anxious did you feel yesterday?

The Measuring National Well-being programme began in November 2010 with the aim to 'develop and publish an accepted and trusted set of National

Statistics that help people understand and monitor well-being' (see Office for National Statistics, 2018 for latest study). The programme has developed a set of 41 headline measures, organized by 10 'domains' including topics such as 'health', 'what we do' and 'where we live'. The measures include both objective data (for example, number of crimes against the person per 1,000 adults) and subjective data (for example, percentage who felt safe walking alone after dark). Measures are updated with latest data in March and September each year. Whilst 'well-being measurement' is not the same as 'employee engagement measurement', I think it is interesting to observe that how people feel about living within our society is now viewed as an issue of importance for the government.

When considering the well-being of our society it is worth noting that since 1970, the UK's GDP has doubled, but people's satisfaction with life has hardly changed. It is reported that 81 per cent of Britons believe that the government should prioritize creating the greatest happiness, not the greatest wealth (New Economics Foundation, 2009).

> Gross National Product measures everything, except that which makes life worthwhile. *Robert F Kennedy*

Rises in GDP over the last 35 years have not resulted in increased human well-being. In response to this issue the New Economics Foundation developed their National Accounts of Well-being measure. This measure is a new way of assessing societal progress, providing a cross-cutting and more informative approach to policy-making. The measure contains both personal and social dimensions and looks at feelings, functioning and psychological resources. More information can be found at **www.nationalaccountsofwellbeing.org**.

The synergies between measuring well-being at a national level and engagement at a work level should not be ignored. The developments at policy level in measuring well-being are of relevance to developing employee engagement at work. For example, both well-being research and engagement research report that money is not a key driver of either. The focus on well-being at a policy level also indicates that governments are taking the well-being and engagement agenda seriously.

Measuring your impact

As well as measuring engagement itself it's also important to measure the impact of your strategy and plan. Improvements in engagement could be a part of that measurement, but you might wish to consider other ways in which you will demonstrate the value added of your engagement strategy and plan.

The engagement objectives you have set should define how you will measure the work you are doing and demonstrate the value you are adding. Typically evaluation falls into the following categories:

- *Process evaluation*: This is an assessment via audience perceptions. Examples of process questions include:

  - The engagement workshop was a good use of my time.

  - My facilitator did a good job of answering any questions arising.

- *Impact evaluation*: This measures the immediate effects of any engagement activity. Impact evaluation tends to look at areas such as employee understanding, buy-in and commitment to activities or plans. Examples of impact questions include:

  - I understand why we are focusing on engagement.

  - I believe that this direction is right for our company.

- *Outcome evaluation*: This measures the longer-term impact of engagement activities on desired organizational outcomes. Outcome evaluation tends to look at behavioural outcomes, or business outcomes you are aiming for with your engagement strategy and plan. Examples of outcome measures include:

  - reduction in employee attrition;

  - increase in productivity;

  - increases in employee referrals.

When considering your measurement plan, you will also need to think about the approach and methodology you will use. It is not always necessary to run a full-scale quantitative evaluation programme: sometimes qualitative methods are the right answer. The table below summarizes the different approaches.

Finally, the Holy Grail of demonstrating the impact you have via your engagement strategy and plan is whether you can evidence any return on investment (ROI). Essentially this involves undertaking a cost-benefit analysis of the activity. It can be a challenge to claim that specific business outcomes are directly as a result of engagement activity but I believe this should not stop you trying. With one particular client, we worked on a 'great place to work' programme, using the alternative survey approach detailed in Chapter 8. At the end of the 12-month programme we had significantly

TABLE 8.1   Quantitative and qualitative research summary

	Quantitative	**Qualitative**
Objective	To quantify data and generalize results from a sample to the population of interest To measure the incidence of various views and opinions in a chosen sample Sometimes followed by qualitative research, which is used to explore some findings further	To gain an understanding of underlying reasons and motivations To provide insights into the setting of a problem, generating ideas and/or hypotheses for later quantitative research To uncover prevalent trends in thought and opinion
Sample	Usually a large number of cases representing the population of interest. Randomly selected respondents	Usually a small number of non-representative cases. Respondents selected to fulfil a given quota
Data collection	Questionnaires, online, telephone, face to face, experiments, secondary data	Interviews, focus groups, content analysis, conversation, observations

decreased employee turnover, which we were able to put a financial gain against. At the same time the company had also observed a significant increase in sales. They had a team of analysts look into this, fearing that mistakes had been made with forecasting. However, the answer that came back was that this increase in sales performance was down to the 'great place to work' programme. Again we were able to put a ROI figure against this. I believe it is easier to claim any benefits from your engagement activity if you have a clearly stated strategy, plan and objectives from the get-go. If you are emphatic that you are aiming to reduce employee turnover, and then your measurement demonstrates that this has happened, it is easier to claim that this must be at least in part down to your engagement strategy and plan. The more we can evidence the financial benefits of engagement activity, the easier it will be for engagement to be taken seriously, and invested in, within our organizations.

Conclusion

Measuring engagement is not without its challenges given the lack of a single, universally agreed definition. By working out what engagement means to your organization though, you can then figure out how you will measure it. The time has now come for companies to shift their focus from the employee engagement survey to what happens after the survey. If you're unsure where the focus is within your organization, take a look at any budget you have to run a survey versus any budget you have to *action* the results of the survey – the answer is often quite telling.

Technological advances are enabling companies to understand how their people are feeling in real time which is a welcome advancement and I believe these new technologies will really take hold within the next few years. However, whilst it is important to measure engagement and understand what drives it, the real work begins once we have this insight, in taking action to improve and develop it.

The future of employee engagement

Introduction

Employee engagement has been on the HR and management agenda for about 15 years now. When I first started talking to senior leaders and other stakeholders about engagement, my focus was on establishing the business case – convincing people it was a worthwhile area to direct resources to. Fast forward 15 years and it's very rare that I have to do this – the majority of people I work with are on board with the need to focus on engagement. Interestingly though, the conversations I have with people about what engagement is are still strikingly similar to those I was having 15 years ago. In some ways we have come so far and yet in others it can feel like Groundhog Day.

So what about the next 10 years? What does the future of employee engagement hold? Where will employee engagement go next and will we ever land on a universally agreed definition? In this chapter I'll share with you some thoughts of my own about where employee engagement might be heading and you'll also hear from a couple of thought leaders within the industry about where they believe we're headed.

Predictions for the future of employee engagement

The Engage for Success movement, in association with the CIPD and the Institute of Employment Studies, published a thought leadership series on the future of engagement, which is still well worth a read (MacLeod and Clarke, 2009). The collection covers a wide range of perspectives from academics through to practitioners and consultants, covering themes from employee voice to how engagement is changing. Here are some thoughts of my own, on where engagement should go next.

Employee engagement practice – implications for future practice

When thinking about the future of employee engagement, I started with my observations of current practice and what needs to change to move the discipline on. These observations are based upon research I have formally conducted with a range of companies to understand how they approach engagement and what they do, as well as my general observations of the industry.

What needs to change

1 *Defining employee engagement and what drives it: The 'ivory tower' approach versus involvement*: Most companies don't consider consulting their employees to find out what engagement means to them. They define engagement and its drivers in an 'ivory tower' and measure it predominantly via an impersonal survey. If engagement is reliant upon alignment of individuals' values with organizational values, and is a process by which individuals become involved in the success of the organization, then the ivory tower approach is fundamentally flawed. My observations are that this approach feels very much like a parent/child relationship. I liken this approach to somebody telling me what happiness means, regardless of my own definition, and then telling me they know what can be done to make me happier. When I spent some 10 years in the corporate world as an employee myself, I actually found this approach, and the assumptions being made, at best annoying and at worst quite insulting, that somebody believed they knew what engagement meant to me and how my own engagement could be improved. I wanted to be involved in this discussion, give my thoughts and opinions and be involved in improving my own engagement. Very few organizations consider the personal nature of engagement, often taking a 'one-size-fits-all' approach. I think the time has come to challenge this approach.

2 *The need for a collegial approach*: Many companies experience problems with the implementation of their employee engagement strategy, arising from the many different stakeholders playing in the engagement space, coupled with a lack of real ownership. Even where some collaboration exists this relates primarily to relationships between functions such as HR, internal communications, organizational development (OD), learning and development and to a lesser extent, marketing. There is a need for a more collegial approach to take engagement strategy to

implementation. A truly collegial approach is characterized by collective, shared responsibility by each of a group of colleagues with minimal supervision from above. The absence of such an approach is one factor that prevents many companies from turning employee engagement strategy into action.

3 *Turn up the listening*: Listening to employees is different from demonstrating two-way communication. To move on from 'two-way' communication (a term only ever heard in the corporate world), to authentic listening, organizations need to do more than simply run an annual survey or an ideas scheme for example. Organizations, and the people that work within them, need to get much better at listening for engagement to improve.

4 *The say-do conflict*: Many companies talk about their leaders' commitment and enthusiasm for engagement. However, the paradox is that when probed many companies report that although leaders are committed they simply do not have the time to engage employees. Is this a convenient excuse or the truth? What leaders are saying and what they are actually doing are in conflict. For engagement to improve in companies we have to work on matching our words and our actions.

5 *Involving employees*: There is still a belief that change starts from the top and cascades down the organization. This idea is being challenged via the work of people like Leandro Herrero; however, many companies still put a lot of faith in the top-down cascade. Companies are still wary of *truly* involving employees, other than in a superficial way, eg 'name the new intranet'. Some organizations are trying out employee-led change via the use of 'change champions', but we need this to become the preferred approach to see real improvements in employee engagement.

6 *Happiness is still a dirty word in organizations*: Despite a growing body of evidence that happiness at work can lead to positive business outcomes, it is still a dirty word in many organizations. Zappos famously grew from a shoestring start-up to a US $2 billion company by creating a business model fuelled by happiness. In Chapter 4 we outlined the case in detail for focusing on happiness at work: happier people are more productive, healthier people, more likely to stay, and the list goes on (*Harvard Business Review*, 2011).

Shawn Achor, author of *The Happiness Advantage* (2011), makes a compelling case that the greatest competitive advantage in today's economy is a happy and engaged workforce. Some of the business outcomes he cites are increasing sales by 37 per cent, productivity by 31 per cent, and accuracy on tasks by 19 per cent. As discussed in Chapter 4, happiness is a prerequisite of success, not simply a result. And yet few companies focus on creating a happy workforce. In the future I think we need to reclaim the word 'happiness' and view a happy workforce as a desirable business outcome.

7 *The deficit approach is still dominant*: Analysing problems and poor performance is still the dominant approach when it comes to employee engagement. It is interesting that engagement is considered to be a positive psychological construct, like happiness, well-being and flow, and yet the research and practice then takes a deficit, problem-solving approach. There seem to be very few companies who are asking what works well, what 'good' looks like and how we can use a strengths-based approach to improve and develop engagement.

8 *The survey still rules*: The employee engagement survey is still the preferred method of measuring and analysing engagement within organizations, but surely if we are serious about improving engagement we need to move with the times and find better ways to do this. Sites such as Glassdoor have ensured companies are now much more transparent than they used to be; how it feels to work in an organization is no longer a well-kept secret.

In addition the way companies collect survey data is still predominantly annually, or maybe monthly, via an online tool, or a hard-copy questionnaire. However, with the rise of smart phones and tablets, even wearable devices, surely this is set to change?

Big data is also a term we are familiar with, meaning the ability to pull in data collected from a variety of sources to reveal deep insights. However, once again employee engagement is behind the curve in utilizing these developments. There are many advances in technology and the way data is used that could really help us improve engagement.

9 *The rise of social media*: Social media has become an increasingly important feature within our lives. However, research into the ways in which social media impacts our psychological well-being is still scarce. This is particularly true of research that looks at the impacts of social media used within the confines of an organization, referred to as Enterprise Social Networks (ESN). Use of ESN is on the rise within organizations, with many commentators arguing that ESN will become an essential communication tool of the future (Gose, 2013). However, to date there is little published research that specifically investigates if, and how, ESN impacts employee engagement. Intuitively it seems that social media could present a huge opportunity for employee engagement, enabling more collaboration, feelings of connection, conversation and more.

So what? My recommendations for future practice

1 *Get personal*: It is important to have a shared definition and meaning of what employee engagement is and what it is there to deliver inside your organization. Don't assume that even if you are using the same words, you mean the same thing. Take time to have conversations across your organization to understand what engagement means to people and what can improve and develop their engagement at work. This doesn't haven't to be an onerous process, for example simply tasking managers to run 'peak experience' sessions with their teams can be a great way to start having these conversations and involve employees in improving engagement. We cannot assume that a select group can understand and know what motivates individuals within an organization. Your insight might be that people want to be recognized more; you might then ask a select group to design and implement a glittering awards scheme and event, when actually all people wanted was a 'thank you' for a job well done.

2 *The collegial approach: Time for new management thinking*: With no clear ownership of employee engagement, a collegial approach will enable movement from strategy to action. Companies must get comfortable with the idea of colleagues collaborating, with shared and collective responsibility with minimal supervision from above to make engagement happen. Take action by setting up your employee engagement coalition, involving people from across the business.

3 *Stop talking, start listening*: The time has come to banish the term 'two-way communication' – what does it mean anyway and would people use it outside of the corporate world? Get back to basics and understand that people want to be treated as human beings, and be listened to. Creating opportunities for people to have their say and feedback are valid but on their own can actually erode engagement if employees do not feel they are being listened to. We all understand what it means to be listened to, for someone to really hear and understand what we're saying; applying this in the working world should not present the challenge it seems to. There are many ways in which this can be achieved, but one of the most successful I have used is to introduce a coaching culture. Training managers to use coaching to have conversations with their teams is an incredibly effective way to turn up the listening within organizations.

4 *Unblocking the leadership barrier*: If your leaders are talking about being committed to engagement but then saying they simply don't have time don't ignore it. Leaders, both those named on the org chart and those who have informal but nonetheless significant leadership roles, impact engagement significantly. Engagement presents a new management philosophy and requires new and different skills from leaders. Leaders saying they don't have time to engage are actually saying they don't have time to lead and addressing this issue will have powerful implications not only upon successful engagement but on the performance of the company as a whole. Take action by building engagement training into leadership development programmes, or run stand-alone engagement development sessions for your leaders.

5 *Involving is at the heart of engagement*: Involving employees is often a challenging concept for senior leaders – they fear at best unrealistic expectations and at worst anarchy. Involving employees is shifting management thinking and for those organizations brave enough to try, it has profound and far-reaching impacts on the business. Turning the triangle on its head by using a process of employee-led change presents a huge opportunity for engaging employees and for organizations who are serious about engagement. Future practice should seek opportunities to involve employees wherever possible.

6 *Reclaiming happiness*: The research shows clearly that happy employees are good for business. I believe the time has come to stop shying away from talking about happiness at work. If we can back up the need to focus on creating a happy workforce with the compelling evidence that exists we can begin to change the way happiness at work is viewed.

7 *Taking a strengths-based approach*: There are a range of tools and ideas contained within this book to help you take a strengths-based approach to improving employee engagement. Start by looking at what you are currently good at: ask why this is the case and how you can use these strengths to improve engagement within your organization. Next time you run action planning in response to your survey findings just try using appreciative inquiry as a framework and see the difference this makes.

8 *New technologies will impact the way companies listen – is the end finally in sight for the annual engagement survey?* We have seen a significant increase in engagement apps and platforms, designed to capture and manage employee feedback. We have also seen an increase in the use of wearable devices. These technologies and solutions are making it easier to capture data and insight in real time. Because of this, we're already seeing an increase in companies moving away from an annual employee survey and moving towards ongoing listening strategies to not only capture more meaningful data but improve their employee voice. These advances mean that companies are finally able to move from a transactional approach to engagement to a more transformational approach.

9 *Embrace enterprise social media (ESN):* Social media is here to stay and, I believe, offers a great opportunity for engaging employees. Keep up to date with the latest developments, find out what other companies are doing and ask your employees how they feel about using social media at work.

10 *The revolution is coming – automation will change the way we work – everywhere!* The continued automation of work is beginning to cause a real stir. According to a recent study by Oxford University, all the developed nations on earth will see job loss rates of up to 47 per cent within the next 25 years. Although modernization cannot be held responsible for the full hit, it certainly will play a very large part. We've seen an increase in productivity apps, innovations in machine learning and now we're seeing how automated vehicles will revolutionize the way we move goods and people. Glassdoor have also predicted automation, in all forms, will impact everyone – from long-haul truckers, to white-collar workers, such as travel agents and insurance brokers, who can now be replaced with online services. However, they do say that workers can stay on the profitable side of automation with ongoing skill-building, making sure new skills are complementary to technology. Quite what this means for employee engagement remains to be seen, but there's no doubt that there will be a significant impact on the way we experience work.

(http://www.eng.ox.ac.uk/about/news/new-study-shows-nearly-half-of-us-jobs-at-risk-of-computerisation)

Views on the future of engagement from thought leaders

A few years ago I came across an article from David Zinger (2010), who runs the great resource that is the Employee Engagement Network. The article talked about his future predictions for employee engagement. I was really interested in David's predictions, so I asked him if he would provide an updated version for this chapter. His response is below.

Employee engagement predictions for 2020, version 2

By David Zinger

At the end of 2010 I made 11 predictions for the decade ahead in employee engagement. This piece will revisit those predictions and offer updates and revised predictions for the last five years of this decade.

I founded and host the Employee Engagement Network. It has grown from 2,100 members in 2010 to over 6,300 members today. I believe that I am both a student and an expert on employee engagement. I also believe that half of what I offer is right and half of what I offer is wrong, and I don't know the difference, as only time will tell based on our collective engagement actions:

- *20/20 Vision*: What do you see as the future of employee engagement over the next five years? How will this concept and approach to work change during this decade?

  It would be nice to have 20/20 vision but the future is murky at best. It is a risky thing to try to predict the future but I will suggest a few of the changes I believe will occur in the second half of this decade. Of course, I am biased and these are often predictions I want to see occur. I encourage you to determine and write your own predictions and revisit your predictions in five years when 2020 is upon us.

  Update: The employee engagement field is moving in all directions at once from the growth of the engagement network and the development of the UK's Engage for Success movement to the abandonment of programmes by some companies who believe engagement failed to deliver on its promise. At the same time we have 'nailed the evidence' and there is an even stronger business case for engagement. The field reminds me of the old statement, 'He got on his horse and rode off in all directions at once.'

- *Wearable technology and real-time measures will trump surveys*: Surveys are too anaemic to measure and communicate engagement. Long surveys or once-a-year surveys will become the dinosaurs of engagement measurement. Yes, measurement is important and necessary but doing a survey once a year just does not cut it. We will see real-time micro-surveys based on portable technology, GPS systems, etc.

Update: Surveys are still going strong but I believe they will decline in the second half of this decade. Wearable computer devices are rapidly ascending and many people are using them to monitor their own sleep and well-being. I believe these devices will become quite prolific and embedded into work and engagement by 2020. Our engagement measure may become more biological than attitudinal as heart rate measure and some of the other 100 interpersonal measures will trump survey tick boxes.

- *Data will become more open and more linked*: It will become important for data to become more transparent and open. I expect organizations will be less guarded, especially with their own employees. Employees should be the owners of the data they offer and be partners in assessing the results. To get a glimpse of the future of data (including employee engagement data) see the inventor of the world wide web Tim Berners-Lee's TED talk on the next web (2009).

  Update: We have a long way to go on this with many in our field invested in not sharing data so that they can control benchmarks and sell services to clients. I sometimes believe we could stop so much benchmarking concerns by just comparing our data to the standard statistical bell curve. I do hope employees will have much greater access to their own engagement levels and data and that real-time engagement dashboards will become a vital tool for both individuals and organizations.

- *Engagement will move beyond a fad*: I expect engagement will vastly mature beyond happy dances in workplaces and Christmas party 'feel-good' exercises to specific behavioural actions that are of benefit to employees, organizations and customers. We must ask ourselves – engagement in what and for what purpose? I believe the cynics would say employee engagement is a fad that will go away within a couple more years. I believe employee engagement is here to stay but will go through criticism, revision, refinement and change in the second half of this decade. We are also seeing the word 'engagement' attached to social media, student engagement, and many other phenomena.

  Update: Many people have jumped on the 'employee engagement' bandwagon and have stated what they do is engagement because they know it sells. Hopefully discerning companies and individuals will see beyond the self-serving labelling and ensure their work with engagement is integrated into all facets of how we work, manage and lead.

- *Enterprise 2.0 or social business software will accelerate engagement*: The use of social media within organizations and porous to external social media outside organizations will present new opportunities and challenges. The first task for many organizations will be to fully engage staff in this media and then to ensure these tools are used to enhance both engagement and results. Internal social media must be an engagement gain for the organization not an engagement drain.

  Update: Social media tools have grown in usage and importance in the first half of this decade and the trend will continue. Social media within an organization is an exceptional mechanism to foster and hear employee voice. Employee voice is a key enabler of employee engagement and social media offers both employees and organizations some brilliant tools to work with voice.

- *Engagement will become more real and authentic*: Employee engagement needs to be more robust, real, authentic and honest. Trust is a must or employee engagement will be a bust. We have ways to assess authenticity and people's social intelligence allows them to see through phony in about an 18th of a second.

  Update: I would like to be more optimistic about the growth of authentic and genuine interaction with high levels of trust. We have a long way to go on this so even a nudge or bump to a little more trust and authenticity would be welcome. We still rely on anonymous surveys because we don't trust employees to tell us about their work experience and employees worry if they are not anonymous they will be punished for their disengagement. I want to believe that engagement will become *a little more real and authentic*.

- *Engagement will detach from a narrow focus on the role of employee*: Employee engagement will need to detach the engagement part of employee engagement to more specific engagement. We will need to be more specific with such terms as 'work engagement', 'organizational engagement', 'community engagement', 'project engagement', etc. Employee engagement is too narrowly attached to a role and can easily create an us/them experience in organizations with managers/leaders seeing themselves as removed from employees. My preferred term would be work engagement but I am open to see how this changes.

Update: Engagement has caught the imagination of so many people and it is being paired with everything from sports to physicians and students. I see the second half of the decade as a time where we will start to work more strongly with the thread of engagement and weave it through all the various facets of work, organization and community.

- *We will witness stronger independent research on employee engagement*: This is vital and important. Hopefully Dilbert will not have just one cartoon lampooning engagement but Scott Adams will run a series over a week or two. Academics and universities can make great contributions to the field with their objective, scientific and independent research. Consulting companies have too much of a vested interest in specific results to place our faith in their research. We need more controlled studies with experimental groups. Although employee engagement is not a fad, there has been too much hype making it seem like a magic management panacea – rather than a key vital tool and approach to work. As a side note, I would love to see best companies or employers not identified by consulting companies with vested interests in selling services to the companies they identify as the best!

  Update: We do have more 'Dilbert' cartoons on employee engagement and John Junson from the Employee Engagement Network has created over 500 cartoons on engagement. I think it is a healthy sign that we can laugh at ourselves. I am now focusing more of my work on relevant experimental design of key engagement actions and behaviours to see if they really do make a difference. I trust that over the next five years I will work with real-world experimental and control groups manipulating progress and setbacks, strengths-based conversations, engaging performance management, meaningful conversations, etc.

- The search for the single 'Holy Grail' definition of employee engagement will be abandoned in favour of stronger behavioural and operational definitions of the term: let's drop the hope or search for one single definition of employee engagement. The MacLeod report (MacLeod and Clarke, 2009) found over 50 different definitions of engagement. Many writers seem to hunger for a common definition. I am not sure how important this is, and there are benefits to diverse definitions in the early years of this approach to work. I think we need more operational definitions of engagement so we know specifically how people are defining it rather than all of us defining it in the same way. For example, what is the specific score and questions that determine if an employee is placed in an engaged or disengaged category? How can one company say, 'We only have 20 per cent engagement around the globe and it is decreasing' while another consultancy claims, 'We have over 50 per cent engagement around the globe and it is increasing'? We don't all need to agree but we do need to understand fully how the term is being used. We still have not agreed on a common definition of love and love has been around a lot longer than employee engagement.

Update: I place most of my interest in behavioural engagement and want to focus more on what people do and achieve and how they treat each other rather than an attitude or satisfaction score. I hope we will focus less on the noun of 'engagement' and more on the verb of 'engage'.

- *Engagement will be woven into the fabric of management and tapestry of leadership*: This decade will witness both a broadening and a deepening of engagement. Engagement will become the new term used for management or leadership. Engagement and conversation will not be leadership or management skills, they will be leadership and management. Engagement is the logical successor to command and control. Henry Mintzberg (2009) made an excellent case for lessening our focus on leadership and suggested we should focus on 'communityship'.

  Update: Although many writers and theorists are talking about engagement from this perspective their thoughts have not permeated the day-to-day operations in organizations. I believe we are still heading in this direction but not as fast as I had imagined back in 2010. I am reminded of the statement, 'Everything takes longer than it does.'

- *Engagement levels will increase*: People are focusing on it, organizations are measuring it, managers are addressing it, unions are assessing it, and individuals are enacting it. This is not so much a prediction as it is my full intention and application to play a vital role in the increase of employee engagement worldwide for the benefit of all: employee, organization, managers/leaders (who are also employees), customers, and all other stakeholders who have a role in work including the families of employees.

Update: Perhaps I was too optimistic on this last prediction. We see some positive trends but also some negative trends. I am faithful that we can increase, enliven and enhance engagement but there is still much work to be done to ensure that work works for everyone.

- *Engage along with me, the best is yet to be, let's see not only where we end up in five more years – let's fully engage in our work to make it happen.*

  Update: Let's review this again in 2020, not to determine so much if we were right or wrong as to remember that those who are unaware of their history are often doomed to repeat it. Let's assess, improve and fully engage in the year 2020 and beyond.

David Zinger, MEd, is an employee engagement speaker, writer, educator, coach and consultant. David founded and moderates the 6,350-member Employee Engagement Network. David has written three books about work and engagement since 2010: *Zengage, Assorted Zingers*, and *People Artistry*. To learn more about David Zinger visit: **www.davidzinger.com**.

Employee engagement future trends: thoughts from People Insight

Employee engagement consultancy, People Insight **(www.peopleinsight. co.uk)** share their thoughts on future trends for employee engagement below.

1. Well-being-culture-engagement merge

A hot topic of 2017, well-being is a macro trend with a glimmer of improvement. Data collected from all the employees we surveyed in 2017 shows the score for 'My company does enough to support my health and well-being at work' is up 3 percentage points – when most other scores are flat.

Could we see more interventions like the French legislation that gives workers the right to disconnect (Beck, 2017)? Maybe not, but the general trend is positive as more and more health and well-being conversations are enabled. Josh Bersin highlights this development when he describes how 'during the last decade, as work-related stress and overwork have become endemic, a new generation of mindfulness, resilience, and well-being programs has emerged' (Deloitte, 2017a).

We've been working with many more organizations in 2017 who don't just want to look at engagement. The cultural context and the well-being agenda have become central to the employee experience, and survey programmes have evolved to reflect this.

2. So is it employee engagement... or employee experience?

Employee experience is becoming a buzzword... so does that mean we've moved on from employee engagement?

Absolutely not. Employee experience is a life cycle approach all about people getting a positive experience of the organization from joining to leaving. It's about the impression the things we do have on our people, and these impressions won't be kept to themselves. Glassdoor keeps us on our toes and employees aren't afraid to speak out. We all remember the PR surrounding that memo from a disgruntled Google employee that went viral back in August 2017 (Tiku, 2017).

If you are using a model like PEARL™ to measure employee engagement, you'll be getting a solid understanding of how employees feel about the organization, as it looks at:

- **Purpose:** How the individual feels about the organization's integrity and goals.

- **Enablement:** Their satisfaction with equipment, tech, the workspace, training and support.

- **Autonomy:** If the individual feels trusted and respected.

- **Reward**: Are they acknowledged and fulfilled, is there a culture of value and praise?

- **Leadership**: Is the experience of leaders positive – do they listen, support, and enable positive change?

Using these themes, specific tailored questions through the employee journey from onboarding to exit will help you understand and adjust your employees' experience accordingly.

The big organizations started taking this seriously back in 2016 – like when Airbnb's CHRO became Chief Employee Experience Officer. Since then we've seem more of these roles – a trend which will probably become more commonplace in 2018.

3. Future-proofing employees with a learning culture

So the bots are apparently here and 2018 onwards may see films like *I, Robot*, *Ex Machina* and *Her* become real life as AI replaces both routine tasks and more complex decision-making.

So how do we deal with these fundamental changes? Learning and adapting is how, especially bearing in mind the thought that 'the half-life of a learned skill is a mere five years. This means that much of what you learned 10 years ago is obsolete and half of what you learned 5 years ago is irrelevant' (Brown and Thomas, 2011).

Individually, we all need to be open to pursuing new skills, lest we be the forlorn coal miner of the 1980s, wondering where their livelihood went. Successful employees will be those who are proactive in learning. Like today's Gen Z: as university education soars in cost they find other ways to learn through tech, and have an insatiable appetite for learning. In fact, PwC's global survey showed a third of graduates valued learning as a benefit, compared to around a tenth who chose incentives (PwC, 2018).

For organizations, training, learning and adapting need to be seen as central strategic priorities in planning for the future. Fortunately, the availability of learning tools has exploded. There's a vast array of experience platforms, micro-learning platforms and even AI-based systems that recommend, find and deliver learning – and forward-thinking organizations are snapping these up. This is all about developing a learning culture. We need to encourage employees to see that embracing change is the norm. Indeed, according to Jonas Prising, the Chairman and CEO of Manpower Group, 'helping people upskill and adapt to a fast-changing world of work will be the defining challenge of our time' (Manpower Group, 2018).

4. Uncertain times require decision-making guts

The economic and political environment continues to be uncertain (they call it 'VUCA') and organizations will respond with more transformational change. It's a time of imperfect information and multiple scenarios, but nevertheless, leaders need to carry on making decisions.

In fact, the *Harvard Business Review* found that the most successful CEOs are decisive not ditherers. If a decision turns out to be wrong, they then take swift corrective action (Botelho *et al*, 2017). For instance, Jerry Bowe, the CEO of Vi-Jon, a private-brand goods manufacturer, describes how 'once I have 65% certainty around the answer, I have to make a call... I ask myself: First, what's the impact if I get it wrong? And second, how much will it hold other things up if I don't move on this?' (Botelho *et al*, 2017).

Of course, it's not just the CEO faced with ambiguity, we all are, and creating an organizational culture in which we make decisions, are allowed to fail and try again is key.

5. Emotional connection to work becomes critical

> *To keep our society moving forward, we have a generational challenge – to not only create new jobs, but create a renewed sense of purpose.*
> (Mark Zuckerberg, quoted in Pontefract, 2017)

It is not new to talk about the importance of purpose. Organizations the world over establish *what* their vision is, and *how* they plan to get there, but they are still struggling with what Simon Sinek calls the *why* (2009).

Our research shows that the sticking point is making the *emotional connection* for employees with the purpose. 'The purpose of my company makes me feel good about my work' is down 4 percentage points in 2017 (78 per cent to 74 per cent) whilst most other scores are flat.

Helping internal facing staff to see how end users feel about the organization's products or services is an effective technique to bring meaning to the day to day. At times of change, having a deeply rooted purpose to ground us can only help employees feel secure and certain about the organization they work in.

With more restructuring and ambiguity comes the threat of talent drain, good people leaving because the organization doesn't look like the one they joined. Companies that manage to maintain an *emotionally resonant culture* where people feel connected, help and reciprocate are more likely to engage and retain their talent and be more productive. This is what Dan Schawbel means when he says that a key workplace trend is that 'companies are being forced to focus more on corporate culture and values than pay in order to retain employees' (2017).

6. Beyond flexible working

More and more future employees want to know about any 'flexible working' policies early in the recruitment process. Flexible working is rightly here to stay – but needs managing:

1 Our best work isn't always done in isolation with *This Morning* on in the background in our PJs. The casual question, the overheard story and the snippet of news in the office provide vital pieces of micro data that help us do our job better as we pick up on tone, expectations, attitudes, priorities and ideas.

2 Loneliness is a real thing. We've got Skype, Workplace, Slack, e-mail, phone calls, text – you name it. Missing out on drinks after work, office banter (a 'social lubricant', *Financial Times*, 2017) and just human contact can have a negative effect on our emotions and our productivity.

   We need to make the effort to keep the *emotional connection* going, for example building five minutes of conversation into team conference calls and remembering to include those out of the office in social arrangements.

7. People, planet and profits

Another aspect to organization culture and values will be the growing importance of social responsibility.

The CONE Millennial Study shows that more than 80 per cent of teens to 25-year-olds want to work for an organization that contributes to society, and the 'triple bottom line' of people, planet and profits (Patel, 2017) has become hugely popular with tomorrow's recruits. Organizations will need to ask themselves:

People

- Is reward fair to our staff and our stakeholders?
- How can we support our employees to contribute to society?
- How do we minimize any negative impact of our business on people outside our organization?

Planet

- How can we reduce consumption or waste?
- How do we incentivize positive environmental practices?
- Can we source materials from sustainable operations?

Profit

- Can we share any profit with employees?
- Can we donate any profit?
- If we can't do the above, can we reduce wasteful spending?

8. Calling out inappropriate behaviour becomes a cultural norm

The explosion of allegations of sexual misconduct in the media in 2017 has given more people confidence to call out their own experiences. We all have to look at our actions and ensure we are doing our best to support equality and diversity in every aspect of work.

Employee satisfaction with equality and diversity is down. Across all our surveys, the score for the question 'My company ensures that all people are treated fairly and equally' fell 4 percentage points in 2017 (67 per cent to 63 per cent) while most other scores remained flat.

Whether it's because employees' expectations are higher, or because organizations are not prioritizing the issue is not clear at a macro level. There's a minefield to be explored, where one person's banter makes another uncomfortable. In the current environment it's worth revisiting, for example, ensuring employees are clear on what is and isn't acceptable behaviour in the workplace. Checking reporting procedures are appropriate and it's a cultural norm to use them. Perhaps most important is leading from the top, with senior figures role modelling respect and valuing differences.

Reviewing all our research above, it's clear that establishing a culture that embraces bold decision-making, diversity, well-being, emotional connectivity, social responsibility and learning will help navigate the years ahead. That's no mean feat!

Technological advances and the rising use of enterprise social media will surely have a significant impact on employee engagement over the coming months and years. In particular the face of the employee engagement survey is set to change. I asked Michael Silverman, of the industry experts and leaders within this area, to share his thoughts on the future of employee engagement research.

The future of employee research

By Michael Silverman, Crowdoscope

The field of employee research is shifting from giving feedback behind closed doors to providing feedback in an open forum. This crucial development is making organizations slowly acknowledge that static feedback mechanisms controlled by management are no longer in keeping with an increasingly social media savvy workforce. Developments in social and digital technologies are at the forefront of this, and while the widespread use of innovative technologies is prevalent in individuals' personal lives, their uptake inside organizations is only really now on the turn. These developments are offering some truly pioneering ease of enhancing collaboration and generating feedback. Capturing people's interactions through social technology and applying the latest text analytics offer new and rich sources of insight.

Developments in social technologies, increased frustration with traditional survey methods and a general movement towards mass transparency reflect society's growing preferences in the digital age. People are connected to the things they care about more than ever before due to the power of the internet. It has enabled the instant sharing of ideas, information and opinions across the globe. Given the relatively static nature of surveys, both the needs of organizations and employees for a real-time alternative are not being met. Social technologies allow the 'wisdom of the crowd' to be harnessed as it encourages multidirectional conversations between people and crowd-sourcing of solutions. The mass adoption of mobile computing goes hand in hand with such developments, ensuring we are always connected to our favourite online services. Lastly, we cannot ignore the power of data. Data is now being collected from all kinds of sources and if appropriately managed, it can reveal deep insights into what employees think, feel and do.

How will employee research change in the next 15 years?

In light of these changes, Silverman Research conducted a study using a collaborative, online tool to assess how the public view the changing face of employee opinion research – in particular how technology will change and shape the process of collecting employee opinion. Over 250 of the world's leading organizations contributed to the study, responding to the question: 'How will employee research change over the next 15 years?' Responses were peer-reviewed by participants with respect to levels of agreement and insightfulness. This makes it possible to crowd-source the suggestion that resonated most with the community as to what the future holds for employee research. The top three responses are as follows:

> *The difference will be amazing. Today, we create hypotheses and then go collect data. Tomorrow, we'll be doing the inverse. The constant, steady state accumulation of data will enable us to look at the data before we form our questions. That means that we'll be getting answers to questions we didn't know to ask. We will be unthinking a whole bunch of things we assume to be facts.*
>
> (John Sumser, Editor, HRExaminer.com)

> *As the demographic of our workforce changes and access to social media increases employee research will move away from the traditional annual employee survey to more frequent and interactive research. As people become more confident in using social media their confidence will grow in being open and honest around the way they feedback and comment on their employer...'*
>
> (Caroline MacDonald, Internal Communications Lead, Hewlett-Packard)

> *Employees' behaviour will be increasingly traceable and measurable as more information about their activity is electronically captured. Organizations will be better at studying these patterns of behaviour – in the same way that consumer behaviour is studied – so rather than asking people questions which are subject to their mood and interpretation, organizations will be using objective metrics.*
>
> (Roland Burton, Senior Communications Manager, Marks & Spencer)

In addition to crowd-sourcing the top suggestions to the discussion question, text analysis was carried out on the qualitative data to reveal the key topics that participants were discussing. Categorization of comments was done using a combination of automated theme detection and manual word categorization. The top 10 categories discussed in reference to the future of employee research are as follows:

1 *Analytics*: A more strategic approach to data and analysis. Using a broader range of data sources (workforce metrics, opinion data, unstructured text, performance data, psychometrics, social

networking/relational data, aggregation data) coupled with an increased capability to identify, segment, model and predict meaningful patterns within it.

2 *Surveys*: An evolution in the traditional survey methodology – from the typically long, generic, annual questionnaire to more frequent, focused, qualitative, real-time/interactive methods, using more sensitive approaches that can capture both meaningful information and more subtle shifts in attitudes/sentiment. Allowing employees to conduct polls themselves and using various question aggregators (eg crowd-sourcing the right questions to ask in the first place).

3 *Social media*: The widespread adoption of technologies that allow people to connect and interact will increasingly be used to collect and aggregate employee opinion. The increasing use of internal social networks will give rise to a proliferation of unstructured text data and associated text analysis.

4 *Collaboration*: The importance of promoting multi-directional communication and interaction (as opposed to traditional one-way and two-way communication) to establish a more collaborative approach to research that can tap into the collective intelligence of employees.

5 *Real-time*: Conducting employee research in an ongoing and automated fashion in order to gain real-time/current insights as opposed to focusing on the comparison of single response points, often a year or more apart.

6 *Devices*: An enhanced capability to use mobile technology for data collection/delivery and the increased prominence of devices such as wearable technology. This will open up feedback channels to non-office-based employees that have often been limited in their ability to participate in research.

7 *Qualitative*: A shift in focus from quantitative data and analysis to hybrid approaches encompassing unstructured text data and advanced text analysis to extract themes, emotion and sentiment. Moving away from the idea that qualitative data is too unwieldy to analyse properly towards a view that the best way to capture feedback from employees is to ask them for a written or spoken response.

8 *Leadership*: Senior leaders lacking awareness about advances in collaborative research technologies and being fearful of the potential

loss of control that comes with giving employees a say in an open forum. The importance of top-down-led changes in research and management playing a crucial role in instigating and leading change.

9 *Transparency*: An emphasis on the importance of openness and honesty between leadership and employees in order to promote trust and collaboration. A move from giving employees a say behind closed doors to giving employees a say in an open forum.

10 *Action*: Conducting research that produces tangible solutions as opposed to just diagnosing general problems. Committing to an approach wherein employee responses lead to changes in the organization rather than leaving the employees feeling that they are not being listened to. A move away from primitive engagement targets to targets based on subsequent action.

These themes highlight the huge technological advancements that will be seen in the workplace over the next 15 years – largely the proliferation of digital devices, such as smart phones, tablets, smart watches and other wearable technology which not only facilitate the collection of data, but also make them more readily and easily digestible. Advances in digital technologies also align closely with the theme of real-time information. Mobile devices afford increased real-time data capture. Moreover, they also provide a more rapid and engaging means of presenting data and insight.

Many participants also commented on the characteristic lack of action that typically accompanies traditional employee surveys. A clear prediction for the future of employee research is not only the improved identification of problem areas, but also a greater focus on the formulation of solutions and actions. The output of traditional employee surveys can often struggle in this area. It is difficult to action plan off the back of largely numeric reports that contain unclear conclusions. In this way, the creation of tangible and actionable outcomes for all levels of the organization was a recurring theme in this research: employee research in the future will be more about curing problems than purely identifying symptoms. An additional aspect to consider regarding action ability is that collecting employee feedback in an open, transparent and collaborative environment has enormous potential for participants to actually learn and share information during data collection. This can increase employees' readiness for change in that they are more aware of the issues at hand and are more likely to feel that their voices have been heard.

Summary

The main message to emerge from the study is that the field of employee research is likely to advance exponentially in the coming years. The interaction between enhanced functional specialisms, increasing technological capability and changing societal norms is fuelling fresh approaches to generating insight. We know that the materialization of employee research as a discipline, of course, far predates the digital age. As a consequence, it would appear that organizations are stuck in pre-digital era thinking with regards to getting feedback from their people.

The problem is that the field of employee research is wide, yet the vast majority of it is comprised of surveys. Apart from transitioning to the internet and some advances in analytical capabilities, the basic model of employee surveys has broadly stayed the same since its inception. Surveys can have various modifications and have seen limited developments in recent years. However, the study reveals that until surveys become more conversational with aggregation devolved to participants and until they are mixed with relational data – they are limited. This is the case no matter how frequently data is collected.

As previously mentioned, the relentless advance of social and digital technologies means that the evolution of employee research is progressing rapidly. The study highlights that the greatest difference is the shifting patterns of communication that social technologies have caused – from one-way and two-way, to multi-directional communication. Consequently, this is moving employee research on from giving employees a say behind closed doors to giving them a say in an open forum.

Within organizations, openness and transparency will be the vital business characteristics that will make all the difference in the coming years. However, for many leaders, this appears not to have sunk in yet. It seems that many leaders are yet to be convinced of the potential value that an authentic employee voice, through social media, can deliver. This is because the perils associated with an open approach and the benefits of more traditional closed systems are often overestimated.

Nevertheless, the study demonstrates that whilst these changes may not yet be reality, they certainly are at the forefront of practitioners' minds.

The full report and findings into the Future of Employee Research can be accessed here: **www.hrmagazine.co.uk/digital_assets/The_Future_of_ Employee_Research_Report.pdf**

Conclusion

In some ways employee engagement has come a long way in the past 15 years, and in other ways it has stood still. Advances in technology will certainly have an impact on employee engagement over the coming years, changing the way we measure and track how our employees are feeling. I would like to think that we will have moved past the definition debate, supporting organizations to answer this question in a way that works for them. I am hopeful that we will see more companies take a strengths-based approach to engagement, and take action to understand engagement at a personal level rather than using a one-size-fits-all approach.

REFERENCES

Achor, S (2011) *The Happiness Advantage: The seven principles of positive psychology that fuel success and performance at work*, Random House Group Publishing, London

Alfes, K, Truss, C, Soane, E, Rees, C and Gatenby, M (2010) *Creating an Engaged Workforce: Findings from the Kingston employee engagement consortium project*, CIPD, London

Alfes, K, Truss, C, Soane, E, Rees, C and Gatenby, M (2013) Linking perceived supervisor support, perceived HRM practices and individual performance: the mediating role of employee engagement, *Human Resource Management*, Vol 52, no 6, pp 839–59

Aon Hewitt (2012) Global Employee Engagement Database 2012 [online] http://www.aon.com/attachments/human-capital-consulting/2012_TrendsInGlobalEngagement_Final_v11.pdf [accessed 8 November 2013]

Aon Hewitt (2017) Global Trends in Employee Engagement [online] http://www.aon.com/attachments/thought-leadership/Trends_Global_Employee_Engagement_Final.pdf [accessed 8 November 2013]

Armstrong, A and Ashridge Business School (2013) Engagement through CEO Eyes, *Engage for Success* [online] http://www.ashridge.org.uk/Website/Content.nsf/FileLibrary/540766FAA92A977180257B87002D7042/$file/FAR_CRED_CEO_Engagement_Research_Report.pdf [accessed 12 May 2014]

Aston University, cited in D'Analeze, G, Dodge, T and Rayton, B (2012) The Evidence: Employee engagement taskforce, 'Nailing the evidence' workgroup, *Engage For Success* [online] http://www.engageforsuccess.org/ideas-tools/employee-engagement-the-evidence/#.U8eBJo1dXjY [accessed 8 November 2013]

Bakker, A B and Demerouti, E (2007) Job resources boost work engagement, particularly when job demands are high, *Journal of Educational Psychology*, **99**, pp 274–84

Barber, L, Hayday, S and Bevan, S (1999) From people to profits: The HR link in the service-profit chain, *Institute for Employment Studies Report 355* [online] http://www.employment-studies.co.uk/pubs/report.php?id=355 [accessed 8 November 2013]

Beck, K (2017) France's battle against an 'always-on' work culture, *BBC* [online] http://www.bbc.com/capital/story/20170507-frances-battle-against-always-on-work-culture

Berners-Lee, T (2009) The next web, *TEDtalks* [online] http://www.ted.com/talks/tim_berners_lee_on_the_next_web [accessed 12 May 2014]

Berrisford, S (2005) Using appreciative inquiry to drive change at the BBC, *Strategic Communication Management*, **9**, pp 22–25

Blackrock (2018) A sense of purpose [online] https://www.blackrock.com/corporate/investor-relations/larry-fink-ceo-letter

Bond, F W (2010) *How can job design improve worker well-being and workplace performance?* Institute for Employment Studies, Anniversary Conference

Botelho, E L, Powell, K R, Kincaid, S and Wang, D (2017) What sets successful CEOs apart, *Harvard Business Review* [online] https://hbr.org/2017/05/what-sets-successful-ceos-apart

Brown and Thomas (2011) *A New Culture of Learning: Cultivating the imagination for a world of constant change*, CreateSpace Independent Publishing Platform

Burton, J (2013) Strategic narrative: The original engagement anecdote, *Delta 7* [online] http://www.delta7.com/strategic-narrative/ [accessed 12 November 2013]

Campbell, J (2013) *The Hero's Journey: Joseph Campbell on his life and work*, 3rd edn, Phil Cousineau (ed) New World Library, Novato, California

Chartered Institute of Personnel Development (2010) *Absence Management: Annual survey report, 2010*, CIPD, London

Checkside (2012) Motivation Revamped: A summary of Daniel H Pink's new theory of what motivates us, *Checkside* [online] http://checkside.wordpress.com/2012/01/20/motivation-revamped-a-summary-of-daniel-h-pinks-new-theory-of-what-motivates-us/ [accessed 9 August 2014]

Christian, M S, Garza, A S and Slaughter, J E (2011) Work engagement: a qualitative review and test of its relation with task and contextual performance, *Personnel Psychology*, **64**, 89–136

CIPD (2011) Sustainable Organisation Performance: What really makes the difference? *Shaping the Future* [online] http://www.cipd.co.uk/binaries/5287stffinalreportweb.pdf [accessed 22 January 2014]

Collins, J and Porras, J (2005) *Built to Last: Successful habits of visionary companies*, Random House, London

Cooperrider, D L, Barrett, F and Srivastva, S (1995) Social construction and appreciative inquiry: A journey in organizational theory, in Hosking, D, Dachler, P and Gergen, K (eds) *Management and Organization: Relational alternatives to individualism*, Avebury, Aldershot

Corporate Leadership Council (2004) *Driving Performance and Retention Through Employee Engagement*, Corporate Executive Board, London

Covey, S R (1989) *The Seven Habits of Highly Effective People*, Free Press, New York

D'Analeze, G, Dodge, T and Rayton, B (2012) The Evidence: Employee engagement taskforce, 'Nailing the evidence' workgroup, *Engage For Success* [online] http://www.engageforsuccess.org/ideas-tools/employee-engagement-the-evidence/#.U8eBJo1dXjY [accessed 8 November 2013]

Deloitte (2017a) *HR Technology Disruptions for 2018: Productivity, design, and intelligence reign* [online] http://marketing.bersin.com/rs/976-LMP-699/images/HRTechDisruptions2018-Report-100517.pdf

Deloitte (2017b) Human Capital Trends, Deloitte

Demerouti, E, Bakker, A B, Nachreiner, F and Schaufeli, W B (2001) The job demands-resources model of burnout, *Journal of Applied Psychology*, **86**, pp 499–512

Easterbrook, G (2003) *The Progress Paradox: How life gets better while people feel worse*, Random House, London

Edelman (2017) Edelman Trust Barometer, *Edelman* [online] http://www.edelman.com/insights/intellectual-property/2014-edelman-trust-barometer/ [accessed 12 May 2014]

Engage for Success website [online] www.engageforsuccess.org [accessed 12 May 2013]

Financial Times (2017) When loneliness at work drives employees to quit their jobs [online] https://www.ft.com/content/a10a3d60-461e-11e7-8519-9f94ee97d996

Gallup (2006) Engagement Predicts Earnings Per Share, *Gallup* [online] http://www.gallup.com/strategicconsulting/157199/employee-engagement-earnings-per-share.aspx [accessed 8 November 2013]

Gallup (2017) State of the Global Workplace, Gallup

Gose, C (2013) Internal communications: the rise and fall of internal social networks, weblog post [online] http://blog.symon.com/blog/bid/215425/Internal-communications-the-rise-and-fall-of-internal-social-networks [accessed 1 March 2014]

Hakanen, J J, Perhoniemi, R and Toppinen-Tanner, S (2008) Positive gain spirals at work: From job resources to work engagement, personal initiative and work-unit innovativeness, *Journal of Vocational Behavior*, **73** (1), pp 78–91

Harter, J K, Schmidt, F L, Killham, E A and Agrawal, S (2012) *Q12® Meta-Analysis: The relationship between engagement at work and organizational outcomes*, Gallup Organization

Harvard Business Review (2011) Spotlight: The happiness factor, *Harvard Business Review*, January–February issue

Harvard Business Review (2016) The business case for purpose, *Harvard Business Review*

Hay Group (2012) Lighting the path to success, *HayGroup* [online] http://www.haygroup.com/fortune/downloads/2012-FORTUNE-Lighting-the-path-to-success.pdf [accessed 25 September 2013]

Herrero, L (2008) *Viral Change: The alternative to a slow, painful and unsuccessful management of change in organisations*, meetingminds, Buckinghamshire

Hope-Hailey, V, Searle, R and Dietz, G (2012) Where has all the trust gone? *Research Report*, CIPD, London

IPA and Tomorrow's Company (2012) Releasing voice for sustainable business success, *Engage for Success* [online] http://www.engageforsuccess.org/ideas-tools/

releasing-voice-for-sustainable-business-success/#.U8ju441dXjY [accessed 18 May 2014]

Kahn, W A (1990) Psychological conditions of personal engagement and disengagement at work, *Academy of Management Journal*, **33** (4), pp 692–724

KHPI (2009) Kenexa Research Institute White paper, *The Impact of Employee Engagement*, Kenexa Research Institute

Kotter, J (1996) *Leading Change*, Harvard Business School Press, Boston

Krueger, J and Killham, E (2007) The Innovation Equation, *Gallup Management Journal*, cited in MacLeod, D and Clarke, N (2009) *Engaging for Success: Enhancing performance through employee engagement*, Department for Business, Innovation and Skills, London [online] http://businessjournal.gallup.com/content/27145/innovation-equipment.aspx

Lewis, R, Donaldson-Feilder, E and Tharani, T (2012) *Managing for Sustainable Employee Engagement*, CIPD, London

Lieberman, D (2013) *Social: Why our brains are wired to connect*, Crown, New York

Macey, W H and Schneider, B (2008) The meaning of employee engagement, *Industrial and Organizational Psychology*, **1**, pp 3–30

MacLeod, D and Clarke, N (2009) *Engaging for Success: Enhancing performance through employee engagement*, Department for Business, Innovation and Skills, London [online] http://engageforsuccess.org

Manpower Group (2018) Human age 2.0: The skills revolution, *Manpower Group* [online] https://www.manpowergroup.com/workforce-insights/world-of-work/human-age2-the-skills-revolution

Mintzberg, H (2009) Rebuilding companies as communities, *Harvard Business Review*, July–August

Mogan, J (2017) *The Employee Experience Advantage, Wiley*, Hoboken

New Economics Foundation (2009) National Accounts of Well-being: bringing real wealth onto the balance sheet, *New Economics Foundation* [online] www.nationalaccountsofwellbeing.org [accessed 12 May 2014]

Office for National Statistics (2018) Measuring National Well-being dashboard (2018) ONS [online] https://www.ons.gov.uk/peoplepopulationandcommunity/wellbeing/articles/measuresofnationalwellbeingdashboard/2018-04-25

Oliver, J and Memmott, C (2012) *Growing Your Own Heroes: The common-sense way to improve business performance*, Oak Tree Press, Cork

Patel, D (2017) The millennial marketplace and the propagation of the triple bottom line, *Forbes* [online] https://www.forbes.com/sites/deeppatel/2017/07/28/the-millennial-marketplace-and-the-propagation-of-the-triple-bottom-line/#45f52ec9d04a

People Lab (2017a) Spotlight on Employee Engagement

People Lab (2017b) The vital role of trust in employee engagement, People Lab

Pink, D (2009) *Drive: The Surprising Truth About What Motivates Us*, Canongate, Edinburgh

Pontefract, D (2017) Tim Cook and Mark Zuckerberg want you to be purpose driven, *Forbes* [online] https://www.forbes.com/sites/danpontefract/2017/08/22/tim-cook-and-mark-zuckerberg-want-you-to-be-purpose-driven/#7a46bd1c1d6a

Pratt, M G and Ashforth, B E (2003) Fostering meaningfulness in working and at work, in Robinson, D, Perryman, S and Hayday, S (2004) *The Drivers of Employee Engagement*, IES, London

PwC (2018) Millennials at work: Reshaping the workplace in financial services, *PwC* [online] https://www.pwc.com/gx/en/industries/financial-services/publications/millennials-at-work-reshaping-the-workplace-in-financial-services.html

Robinson, D, Perryman, S and Hayday, S (2004) *The Drivers of Employee Engagement*, Institute of Employment Studies Report 408

Royal, M and Stark, M (2010) *Hitting the Ground Running: What the world's most admired companies do to (re)engage their employees*, The Hay Group, http://www.haygroup.com/downloads/ww/Hay_Group_FORTUNE_2010_presentation.pdf

Rucci, A J, Kirn, S P and Quinn, R T (1998) The employee-customer-profit chain at Sears, *Harvard Business Review*, **76** (1), pp 82–97

Scarlett, H (2014) Neuroscience and the four enablers: what helps our brains think and perform at their best? *Engage for Success* [online] http://www.engageforsuccess.org/wp-content/uploads/2014/03/Engage-for-success-neuroscience1.pdf [accessed 18 April 2014]

Schaufeli, W B and Bakker, A B (2004) Job demands, job resources, and their relationship with burnout and engagement: A multi-sample study, *Journal of Organizational Behavior*, **25**, pp 293–315

Schaufeli, W B, Bakker, A B and Salanova, M (2006) The measurement of work engagement with a short questionnaire: A cross-national study, *Educational and Psychological Measurement*, **66**, pp 701–15

Schawbel, D (2017) 10 Workplace trends you'll see in 2017, *Forbes* [online] https://www.forbes.com/sites/danschawbel/2016/11/01/workplace-trends-2017/2/#51face5f43e2

Sila, Ismail (2006) Examining the effects of contextual factors on TQM and performance through the lens of organizational theories: An empirical study, *Journal of Operations Management*, **25**, pp 83–109

Sinek, S (2009) How great leaders inspire action, *TEDtalks* [online] https://www.ted.com/talks/simon_sinek_how_great_leaders_inspire_action

Smith and Henderson and HR Zone, in association with Saba (2014) *The State of Employee Engagement: How the UK is approaching engagement and an action plan for change*, Smith and Henderson and HR Zone, http://www.hrzone.com/downloads/state-employee-engagement-uk/143322

Smythe, J (2007) *The CEO: Chief Engagement Officer: Turning hierarchy upside down to drive performance*, Gower, Aldershot

Tiku, N (2017) That Google manifesto really put executives in a bind, *Wired* [online] https://www.wired.com/story/google-manifesto-puts-executives-in-a-bind/

Tims, M, Bakker, A B and Xanthopoulou, D (2011) Do transformational leaders enhance their followers' daily work engagement? *Leadership Quarterly*, **22**, pp 121–31

Towers Watson (2012) Engagement at risk: Driving strong performance in a volatile global environment, Towers Watson Global Workforce Study [online] http://www.towerswatson.com/assets/pdf/2012-Towers-Watson-Global-Workforce-Study.pdf [accessed 8 November 2013]

Walumbwa, F O, Wang, P, Wang, H, Schaubroeck, J and Avolio, B J (2010) Psychological process linking authentic leadership to follower behaviours, *The Leadership Quarterly*, **21**, pp 901–14

Watson Wyatt (2009) Continuous engagement: The key to unlocking the value of your people during tough times, *Work Europe Survey 2008–2009*, https://executestrategy.net/materials/watsonwyatt.pdf

Wellins, R S, Bernthal, P and Phelps, M (2005) *Employee Engagement: The key to realising competitive advantage*, Development Dimensions International, https://www.ddiworld.com/DDIWorld/media/monographs/employeeengagement_mg_ddi.pdf?ext=.pdf

Whole Foods (2012) Annual report [online] https://www.wholefoodsmarket.com/sites/default/files/media/Global/Company%20Info/PDFs/2012-WFM_Annual_Report.pdf

Whole Foods (2018) Core values [online] http://www.wholefoodsmarket.com/mission-values/core-values

World Café (2008) [online] http://www.theworldcafe.com

Wrzesniewski, A and Dutton, J E (2001) Crafting a job: Revisioning employees as active crafters of their work, *Academy of Management Review*, **26**, pp 179–201

Xu, J and Cooper Thomas, H (2011) How can leaders achieve high employee engagement?, *Leadership and Organization Development Journal*, **32** (4), pp 399–416

Zinger, D (2010) Employee Engagement 2010 Dozen (Feb): The 2020 Vision [online] http://www.davidzinger.com/employee-engagement-the-zinger-2020-vision-5808/ [accessed 2 May 2014]

FURTHER READING

Amabile, T M and Kramer, S J (2011) The power of small wins, *Harvard Business Review*, **89** (5), May, pp 71–80

Cameron, K S, Dutton, J E and Quinn, R E (eds) *Positive Organizational Scholarship: Foundations of a new discipline*, Berrett-Koehler Publishers, San Francisco

Gifford, J, Finney, L, Hennessy, J and Varney, S (2010) *The Human Voice of Employee Engagement: Understanding what lies beneath the surveys*, Roffey Park Institute, Horsham

Gilbert, P and Foley, P (2012) 10 ways to improve engagement using employee surveys, *Workspan*, **55** (10) October, pp 60–64

Guest, D E and Conway, N (2004) *Employee Well-being and the Psychological Contract*, Research Report, Chartered Institute of Personnel and Development, London

Holbeche, L and Matthews, G (2012) *Engaged: Unleashing your organization's potential through employee engagement*, Jossey-Bass, San Francisco

MacLeod, D and Brady, C (2008) *The Extra Mile: How to engage your people to win*, Pearson Education, Harlow

McGee, R and Rennie, A (2011) *Employee Engagement: CIPD toolkit*, Chartered Institute of Personnel and Development, London

Murphy, N (2011) Employee engagement survey 2011: Increased awareness, but falling levels, *IRS Employment Review*, 28 November

Robinson, D, Perryman, S and Hayday, S (2004) *The Drivers of Employee Engagement*, Institute for Employment Studies, Brighton

Schaufeli, W B and Bakker, A B (2004) Job demands, job resources, and their relationship with burnout and engagement: A multi-sample study, *Journal of Organizational Behavior*, **25**, pp 293–315

Truss, C, Shantz, A and Soane, E (2013) Employee engagement, organisational performance and individual well-being: Developing the theory, exploring the evidence, *International Journal of Human Resource Management*, **24** (13–14) July, pp 2657–69

Zinger, D (2012) *The Ennoblement Imperative*: people artistry at work [online] http://www.davidzinger.com/people-artistry-the-book/ [accessed 2 May 2014]

INDEX

Note: page numbers in *italic* indicate figures or tables

More titles in this series

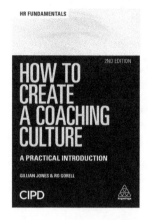

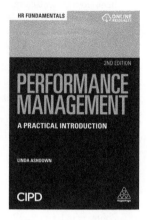

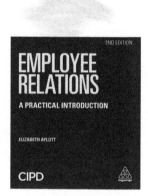

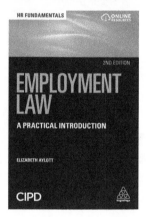

Employee Engagement is one of the titles in
Kogan Page's HR Fundamentals series,
which is endorsed by the CIPD.

Succint, practical guides for students
and people starting a career in HR.

Find out more at
www.koganpage.com/HRFundamentals

 @KPCoachHR

HR FUNDAMENTALS